". . . Designed to produce miracles. I love it! It teaches how to be loving, sensitive, and fully human . . . without anyone being victimized. I endorse this marvelous book enthusiastically!"

Wayne Dyer, Ph.D.
Your Erroneous Zones and *Gifts from Eykis*

"Your ideas, although eternal in principle, have never been made so practical and applicable. A fresh, new approach to being a parent! You have shown us all how to truly experience love for ourselves as well as for our children."

Rev. Peggy Bassett
Church of Religious Science

"Must reading! The Pauls focus on the crucial foundation of parents understanding themselves . . . opening the way to truly respect the child as a person, expressing love and promoting self-esteem."

John Vasconcellos
California legislator
Creator, California Task Force
on Self-Esteem

If You Really Loved Me...

Drs. Jordan & Margaret Paul
with Bonnie B. Hesse

CompCare Publishers
2415 Annapolis Lane
Minneapolis, Minnesota 55441

Published in the United States
by CompCare Publishers,
a division of Comprehensive Care Corporation

Paul, Jordan.
    If you really loved me—from conflict to closeness
for parents and children.

    1. Parent and child—United States.   2. Parenting—
United States.   3. Conflict management—United States.
4. Interpersonal communication—United States.   I. Paul,
Margaret.   II. Title.
HQ755.85.P38   1987   306.8'74   87-20934
ISBN 0-89638-108-0

Cover and interior design by Susan Rinek

Inquiries, orders, and catalog requests should be addressed to
CompCare Publishers
2415 Annapolis Lane
Minneapolis, Minnesota 55441
Call toll free 800/328-3330
(Minnesota residents 559-4800)

To our children

By being who you are, you give us the opportunity to learn how to become more loving people. When we don't see your light, it's our vision that needs clearing.

Contents

INTRODUCTION

When we first met, we knew a kind of happiness we had never known before. It was wonderful being in love! But the honeymoon euphoria of early courtship and marriage—which we assumed would last forever—didn't. In fact, it didn't last long at all. The first time we had a difference of opinion brought trouble and that was upsetting. We had conflict—and with conflict came fear and self-doubt. Then we discovered that these feelings got in the way of our love.

In the process, and it truly was a *process*, of working through the turmoil in our relationship, we wrote our first book, *Free to Love*. Little did we realize, at least in the beginning, just how appropriate that title was. At first, it seemed to mean simply that we were becoming open and free to love each other. We later understood a second, much more profound meaning—that *people, in general, have to free themselves—from fear, doubt and self-protective behavior—in order to be able to be loving toward each other.*

Our own struggle to establish a relationship—one allowing each of us to maintain our individual freedom and also allowing intimacy and commitment to increase between us—brought us to an essential question which became the title of our second book: *Do I Have to Give Up Me to Be Loved By You?* The resounding answer was "NO!"

After many years of living and working together, we had learned that *conflict* is the culprit which activates our fear responses, which creates our need to protect ourselves, and in so doing creates distance between us. However, now we had gained a new insight: within conflict is the crucible for change—but that change doesn't have to be negative; it can also be positive. Our culture has a deeply ingrained view that conflict is wrong, bad, and to be avoided—yet conflict is also an opportunity to learn and to grow.

Thus it is our *intention* that turns conflict into either a problem or into a learning and growing experience. When it is our intention to learn, rather than to protect ourselves, we move along the path toward emotional and spiritual growth, becoming more loving, which results in greater intimacy and better relationships with ourselves and with our mates.

"But how do you do this with children?" is a question we've been asked many times. And so now we come to the task of applying the principles we've learned from our relationship to the issues of parenting and families. This book shares what we're learning from our desire to create a family in which each person feels loved and is free to love—a family in which each person can express his or her uniqueness while we, as a group, maintain our family intimacy.

Although we've demonstrated through our work as therapists and through our seminars that our ideas can work in any family, we believe the truest test must come from our own experience.

We and our children—Eric, 21, Joshua, 19, and Sheryl, 16—have been involved in the process of integrating five very different personalities into an environment where each of us gets our needs met. As a result, our family has not always been tranquil, but it is also rarely dull. We find as our children pass through the stages of their lives, even the teenage years are wonderful times. We have conflicts and these are not always met with openness and excitement, but as we work through our difficulties, we realize more and more the importance of the process we are involved in—understanding ourselves and each other. It's our intention to learn from conflict that creates our Evolving Family.

How do you help children do better in school? What should you do when your child lies to you? How do you instill the right values in your children? These are important questions for parents—but our answer is always the same: We're only interested in helping you learn from your conflicts, and so become a more loving parent. As you become more loving, you'll find creative solutions to your specific problems that will work best for you. We will not offer solutions to various and specific problems, but offer instead a lifelong approach to one problem: the lack of love and joy and self-esteem and how to have more of the wonderful possibilities that life has to offer. In the process, you'll also learn a new meaning for the phrase "loving behavior."

If authority, power, judgment of right and wrong, and being in control of the children are labels which you attach to your ideal of parenting, then perhaps this book is not for you. In the Evolving Family, the goal is for behavior—both for parents and children—to come from desire rather than from fear, obligation, or guilt. Thus it becomes the parents' role to model and inspire behavior, not command, "Do as I say, not as I do."

In the Evolving Family, adults are not worth more than children. The price tag on each individual is the same. On the other hand, adults are more experienced than children. Adults have learned the consequences of touching fire, while children have not yet been burned. Thus the parents have a responsibility to pass on what they have learned.

Almost everything taught about child-raising focuses on helping the parent change the child's behavior. Approaches swing between passive and aggressive, gentle and firm, but all eventually lead to many difficulties. This book takes a very different approach; it focuses on you, the parent.

Very few people recognize the profound opportunity that relationships give us to learn about ourselves. The fairy tale of falling in love is that you magically live happily ever after. Truly living happily together, though, takes a willingness to be open and vulnerable, which people seldom maintain in their primary relationships.

Have you ever wondered why grandparents are more loving with their grandchildren than they were with their own children? Have you noticed yourself being more accepting of other people's children than of your own? Nothing touches us as deeply as our family relationships. The more important the relationship the more our fears and learned childhood reactions become activated. And we become unloving. We find it hardest to give love to those who need our love the most—our family.

This book is for those parents who value individual freedom, creative thinking, the full expression of feelings, parents' involvement with their children, and self-knowledge and self-esteem for both. More than anything, this is for parents who love and respect their children, have faith in their innate goodness, and respect for their abilities. If your hope is to make things run smoothly while spending a minimum of time involved with child-raising, this book isn't for you. If your goal is merely to find ways to get your children to do what you want them to, this book isn't for you. But if you already have the faith, or are open to the possibility, that learning about yourself and your children is the way for both of you to get what you need, then read on.

Jordan and Margaret Paul
West Los Angeles
June 1987

Part 1

From Conflict to Closeness
for Parents and Children

Western civilization's dictionary describes conflict as a struggle between opposing forces, a condition of opposition and discord, mutual antagonism of ideas and interests. The Eastern philosophy of conflict is illustrated by a Chinese character meaning both potential danger as well as an opportunity to change. Since conflict is a given in any personal relationship, the challenge is to learn and grow from these situations. Conflict can become the crucible for change.

·1·

If You Really Loved Me or If I Really Loved You?

A New Look at Loving

> *I now see that the major shift in human evolution is from behaving like an animal struggling to survive to behaving like an animal choosing to evolve. In fact, in order to survive, man has to evolve. And to evolve, we need a new kind of thinking and a new kind of behavior.*
>
> —Dr. Jonas Salk

Brian, age twelve, walked in the house from a tennis match. Exceptionally intelligent, handsome, and well-liked by his friends, Brian doesn't feel good about himself, which no one, including his mother, can understand.

"Hi, mom."

"Hi, hon. Did you win?"

"Nope. Matt beat me."

"You're kidding! How come you lost? You never lose to him."

"Well, I did today," he said, his voice beginning to quaver. "So what's the big deal? If you really loved me, you wouldn't care!" Brian ran to his room and slammed the door.

"You know I love you!" his frustrated mother shouted after him. "I'll never understand him," she said sadly.

Ron, age forty-five, father of three, paced the floor in front of one of his teenage sons who was sprawled in an easy chair.

"I have told you and told you to do your homework! No wonder your grades have gone down. When are you going to come to your senses?"

"You're clueless, dad. You haven't listened to me at all."

"I know you think you have all the answers—but you're wrong. If I didn't care about you—if I didn't love you—do you think I'd waste all this energy trying to get you to do what you're supposed to?"

"You are so close-minded I can't even believe it!" said the boy, rushing out of the house and into his car. "If you *really* loved me . . ." the son muttered under his breath, as he raced the motor and pulled out of the driveway.

Confused and angry, Ron said sadly, "Life is just not turning out the way I thought it would."

Parents who love their children, but children who don't feel loved—how can this be? Families who live and work together, who want more than anything to be happy together, but who spend most of their time in conflict, struggling against each other—why does this happen? Does family life have to be this way? Although it may seem so at times, the real answer is no! Families will always have problems and difficulties. Yes, there will be stress and pain, but there can be overriding joy and fun and loving feelings for both parents and children. How can this happen? The key lies first in taking a new look at the old phrase: *If you really loved me . . .*

Who Are Parents? What Are Children?

In the beginning, at least in the best possible situation, parents are people who are in love with each other, especially at the time a child is conceived. For the mother-

to-be, private thoughts likely include a sense of fulfillment. The father, on the other hand, probably feels a
sense of accomplishment.

These reveries carry within them remnants of
myths and beliefs which have been handed down for
generations, and usually include the notion that adults are
more important than children. Some parents believe that
because they are adults, they have more dignity and
worth than their children. When this belief gets the upper
hand, the children *feel* less important, and that doesn't
feel good.

Other parents, whether or not they realize it,
operate under the assumption that their children are more
valuable than they are. In these cases, the children assume
the status of royalty. This puts the parents in an awkward
position, however, because even though they have the
education and the experience, their children have the
power. Still other families vacillate between these two
extremes, which doesn't work either, because in times of
conflict parents and siblings jockey for position and
everyone feels uncomfortable until a temporary truce is
made.

Differing family and parenting styles will be discussed further as we go along, but for now let's go on to
the next question: What are children? As simplistic as it
sounds, they are just very young people. In other words,
they are human beings just like adults; they are separate
entities, not merely extensions of their fathers and mothers. They are not possessions or subjects. As human
beings, they are equal in value.

Children are born open and accepting, with a
natural ability to give and receive love. Also, they're very
much in touch with what they want and feel and have a
natural desire to grow and learn and love. As soon as
toddlers can talk, they'll announce in no uncertain terms
that they have their own identities:

"I am not being a baby—I'm being me!"
or
"You're not the boss of me—I'm the boss of me!"

Our understanding of human relationships has evolved greatly over the centuries, but the concept that children are equal is still difficult for many adults to accept for several reasons. First, people often believe that equality means that children are the same as adults. Of course, they are not. Adults are more educated, experienced, and have developed a sense of responsibility. By and large, adults have learned natural laws (such as if you touch fire, you get burned), civil laws (if you don't obey the speed limit, you get a ticket and must pay a fine), and social customs (if you eat with your fingers at the neighbors', you may not get invited back).

There's another reason adults resist the idea of children's equality: they confuse equality with freedom, thinking it means that children have unlimited freedom and therefore are entitled to behave in any way they choose—run wild in the movies, spend the parents' money at will, or go joyriding in the family car. That's not what equality means. After all, adults don't get to do those things either.

However, equality does mean that children are entitled to the same dignity and respect as adults. Their needs are just as important. Also—and this is very important—their feelings are just as valid. Further, many of these feelings, especially the feelings about themselves, persist long past childhood, perhaps staying with them all their lives. "I felt discounted because my father wanted a son," our client Joan related. Or "Being chubby as a boy made me feel like a second-class citizen," one young man admitted.

Many parents are unaware that they devalue their children's feelings, but the children know—or at least feel—the effects of their parents' beliefs. Take a look at the following dialogue:

> Child: I'm afraid of the dark.
> Mother: Don't be silly—there's nothing to be afraid of.

This mother, probably without realizing it, has told her child that his or her feelings are not important, that they are "silly." She is operating with the belief that an adult's feelings are more valid, more real, than a child's. A great many adults believe that their feelings are more important than those of children, but not many people realize they think this way, and even fewer understand how such a belief affects their behavior or that children feel diminished by it. In the case of the dialogue above, all they know is that the situation—being afraid of the dark—has not been resolved. Usually the child is blamed for that: "Don't act so ridiculous! There's nothing to be afraid of!"

To fully understand how significant or valid children's feelings are, adults would do well to reflect on their own childhoods. When you, the parent, were growing up, how important were your feelings? As a five-year-old when your cat died, a ten-year-old when you were afraid of the school bully, a twelve-year-old when your best friend moved away, a sixteen-year-old when you were in love—how real were these feelings to you? And how did you feel when your parents did not take you seriously or even told you to stop feeling your feelings: "Don't be such a baby!—He won't hurt you!" Or "Stop crying! You'll make a new friend." Or even "You just have a crush on him!" You probably were angry or sad and very likely you felt alienated and alone. Certainly you did not feel respected and loved. In fact, you may have said to yourself regarding your parents' behavior: "If they really loved me . . ."

Of course, parents really do want to be loving to their children, just as much as children want to feel loved. However, *when behavior toward a child is unloving, whether or not a parent feels love for that child, the child feels unloved.* The real question then becomes, "If I really loved you . . . how would I behave?" Understanding this fundamental truth and what it means in terms of a parent's behavior is the cornerstone for dealing successfully with conflict in the family. And successfully handling conflict in the family—whether it's with a two-year-old or a teenager—is the key to a family life that has evolved from being a survival unit to a relationship between people which fosters the growth of every family member and promises love and fun and joy for each one as individuals and as a group.

What Do You Really Want for Your Children? For Your Family?

An old Chinese proverb states, "If we do not change our direction, we are likely to end up where we are headed." The application for families is clear: parents need to take the time to reflect on goals for their families. No one would think of running a business without setting goals, but amazingly few parents take the time to do this for their families.

If you write down your thoughts, the results might surprise you. Money, vacations, a nice home—these are desirable things for the family. The list for your children might include "get good grades" or "be a good athlete." But in an exercise where you would be asked to prioritize these things along with some others such as "health," "self-esteem," and "caring for each other," the aforementioned—material goods, educational and athletic achievements—fall surprisingly far down the line. It is even more revealing to note that most of our parenting problems center around conflicts over low-priority goals. Furthermore, these conflicts are obstacles to achieving our highest priority goals. So what's the point? Families need to take stock or they're likely to end up where they are headed—achieving low-priority goals at the expense of the things they consider most important in life.

So what do you really want for your family? To feel close to each other, comfortable, and caring, to enjoy each other and have fun together—these are at least some of the priceless qualities which make life rich and meaningful.

Next, what do you really want for your children? In his wonderful book by the same title, Dr. Wayne Dyer creates an interesting list of goals for children. Some of these goals are: for children to value themselves, to be self-reliant, to be free from anxiety and stress, to fulfill their higher needs, and to feel a sense of purpose. This is an important list and contains the essences of thoughts expressed by most psychologists working with parents and families today.

For children to have self-esteem, value themselves, or feel good about themselves—whatever words you choose—is probably the essential item on almost everyone's list. One elementary school in Southern California surveyed its parent community to assess what the fathers and mothers saw as the students' needs in the school setting. In this area, there was a high concentration of wealth; also the parents were primarily professionals and/ or college graduates. Of the 430 students, 98 percent returned the survey. The results were frankly surprising. Over any kind of academic achievement, including learning to read, the parents rated self-esteem as the highest priority!

From self-esteem flow other important qualities—being happy, outgoing, and confident, able to give and receive love.

Being responsible is probably the second most valued goal. However, when you're discussing self-esteem and responsibility, it's a case of which comes first, the chicken or the egg? When people are responsible, they build and reinforce a positive image of themselves. In turn, when people have self-esteem, they tend to be responsible. The meaning of the word responsible has several elements: to be accountable for one's own behavior; to be capable of making decisions; to be trustworthy and reliable. Also involved in this definition is the assumption that responsible people, both parents and children, are internally motivated. They initiate action themselves, behaving not because they were nagged or commanded, or in some way coerced into doing whatever it is—visit grandmother, do homework, go to church, get along with siblings.

Families feeling close and caring, children enjoying life—these are wonderful, loving goals. And most parents believe that these things will happen naturally . . . in the beginning. But this blissful parenting state lasts about as long as the honeymoon did in the marriage. Trouble comes when the first conflict occurs. The child does something "wrong," the parent doesn't handle the situation "right," and all of a sudden parenting doesn't seem so easy anymore. Where is the ". . . and they lived happily ever after" part? Many parents would settle for a few peaceful moments. What went wrong?

A New Look at Old Ideas

When things don't go the way they want, most people just try harder, doing the same things they've been doing that haven't been working. The results are usually disastrous, whether in family relations, other personal relations, or even in business. Three things cause this repeating behavior: the persistent hope that trying harder will eventually mean success (this is often in the face of overwhelming evidence that says it won't); ignorance of any other way of going about getting what they want; and the fear of trying something new (the pain that is felt being preferred to pain that is feared).

Whether acting out of hope, ignorance, or fear, parents do know that when the old ways don't work, life can become unbearably painful. At that point they are usually willing to change. Others become willing to change when they recognize the difference between the way their family operates now and the way it could be—less stressful, happier, more satisfying. This book is for those who are ready to approach parenting from a totally new perspective, with a new kind of thinking and a new kind of behavior.

Most books about families merely suggest ways to get children to change. But suggesting ways to get children to change just gives support to the notion that children are fundamentally wrong. Some books are more humanistic and teach problem-solving techniques. These techniques often work to solve immediate situations, but when problems reflect deeply ingrained beliefs, fears, or power struggles, the solutions will be temporary at best. To create family harmony out of the conflicts that typically tear families apart, leaving the children with low self-esteem and parents with a sense of failure, requires a completely new approach to conflict and the meaning of parenthood.

The main purpose of this book is to illustrate a process by which conflict becomes the vehicle for both parents and children to evolve—that is, to change and to grow—emotionally, intellectually, and spiritually. This process primarily calls on the parent to be willing to learn from conflict. Since both attempting to control children and trying to find specific solutions to problems rarely lead to understanding and resolving the source of family difficulties, they are analogous to what Dr. Salk refers to in the epigram at the beginning of the chapter as "struggle to survive" mechanisms. On the other hand, when parents learn about themselves—and consequently about their children—from their own reactions to conflict, they open the gateway to growth.

What is suggested here is a radical departure from the traditional approach to parenting. The usual strategies suggest, in essence, what to do about the *children*. The emphasis shifts here to the *parents*. How can you, the parent, become aware of your own reactions to conflict? What fears and beliefs affect your behavior? How can you communicate or act out the love you feel for your children? In short, *what do you need to know as a parent, not to better manage your children, but to better love them?*

It would be presumptuous to suggest to anyone what he or she feels. It borders on the outrageous to suggest to most parents that they don't love their children. Of course they do! But often there is a dramatic difference between how a person feels and how a person acts. It is this differential we refer to when suggesting that parents need to better love their children. Bringing loving feelings into alignment with actions so that the result is loving behavior—so that the children feel loved, so that the family can be close, caring, and everything you hoped for when you became a parent—becomes the ultimate goal for parents on the path to creating the Evolving Family.

Loving Behavior—A Definition

What is loving behavior? Patting your child on the back? Serving your family a warm dinner? Either of these things could be considered loving behavior, but whether they are or not depends on the motive or intent behind the action. If the pat on the back comes because the son has reluctantly agreed to play football (his father's choice) instead of soccer (his own preference), then the pat was not expressing the father's love but rather his approval for the son's acquiescence. Serving the warm dinner is not an expression of love when the cook, most likely the mother, is exhausted from working all day, races home to cook the meal, and serves it to two teenagers who spent the afternoon watching television. That dinner fosters the adolescents' irresponsibility and is probably an expression of the mother's own guilt and her need to be needed, not love for her children.

Loving behavior is that behavior which fosters one's own and others' emotional and spiritual growth. A second and equally important part of the definition is that *loving behavior promotes personal responsibility.* For example, it *is* loving when the parent takes responsibility for what children are not capable of doing for themselves. A three-year-old cannot judge the dangers of traffic. A ten-year-old cannot earn enough money to pay for dental work. However, it is *not* loving to take responsibility for what children can do on their own; in fact it is debilitating and discouraging. Three-year-olds can dress themselves; ten-year-olds can take care of their own dental hygiene.

Like the lens of a camera brings the photographer's subject into focus, when behavior is looked at through the framework of this definition, it becomes clearer and clearer when behavior is loving and when it is not; or when another motive—the need to be in control, for example—is the moving force behind the behavior. The negative consequences of unloving behavior also become evident, particularly with a strong-willed, resistant child. With a compliant child, the negative effects may be the same but may not be evident at the time.

Let's take a brief look at a situation which typically causes a great deal of difficulty between parents and children—homework. Third-grader Kelly has failing grades in spelling. The teacher has phoned to let her father know. Kelly has above average intelligence, so there is some dynamic at work here other than whether or not Kelly *can* learn to spell. John, Kelly's father, feels a great deal of love for his daughter. How then might he act out this love, fostering Kelly's emotional and spiritual growth? Which of the following would be the most loving behavior?

1. *John could try to get Kelly to do her homework.* Typical means might be: explaining to Kelly the virtues of doing well in school; getting her a tutor; doing the homework with her; making a schedule for her to follow and enforcing it; restricting her free time; yelling, punishing, hitting, threatening, demanding.

All these attempts would be "for the child's own good" and therefore believed to be loving. But none of them nurture the emotional growth of either John or Kelly.

One assumption underlying John's demanding behavior might be that Kelly is not capable of making the right choice about doing her spelling. One belief might be that a father should always be in control of his children. Another factor might be John's embarrassment because his daughter is doing poorly in school.

2. *John could do nothing about Kelly's schoolwork.* Underlying this behavior may be John's fear that Kelly will be angry and resentful if he makes suggestions about her schoolwork. Or John may believe that if he gets angry with Kelly he'll be seen as a bad father.

3. *John could care enough to become involved with Kelly.* He could take the time to find out why she's not doing her spelling. Maybe there are some undiscov-

ered learning disabilities. Maybe she needs to have her eyes checked. On the other hand, perhaps Kelly is in a power struggle with her father. Perhaps she has complied with her father's demands in other areas but is resisting in an area where he cannot control her, knowing that he really can't force her to learn anything. Or perhaps she really wants his attention and has discovered one way to get it. John doesn't solve the problem for Kelly, but he does show caring by helping his child to look at herself and take responsibility for her situation; he is also open to learning about himself. Both grow emotionally and spiritually in this way.

In numbers one and two, John's fears and faulty beliefs about being a father are the main motivating factors guiding his behavior. However, in number three, John's primary concern is Kelly and her spelling difficulties.

Thinking about what would be a loving response in a particular situation is rare indeed. Instead, we usually just react. Virginia Satir, one of our most esteemed teachers, summarized to us how she views this idea: "Unloving behavior is reactive. Loving behavior is creative."

In a conflict with children, once parents discover what the problem is, they can decide then what the most loving behavior will be. If the difficulty involves some kind of reaction against the parents, then the parents need to look at themselves and their own behavior.

Loving behavior cannot occur merely by a decision to be more loving. Why? Because standing in the way for every person are some very powerful, deeply ingrained fears and false beliefs which block the love everyone is capable of giving. Overcoming these beliefs requires your dedication to a process of confronting these beliefs and changing them. The process, which will be discussed at length in later chapters, is an intellectual, emotional, philosophical, and spiritual journey, moving you closer and closer to acting out the loving nature that lies within you; in addition, the process helps your children learn to live more harmoniously with themselves and the world around them.

As a parent, you will be asked to look deep within yourself. You will need to look at many of your beliefs, especially those regarding adequacy, control, vulnerability, responsibility, anger, fear, and faith. You will be asked to believe in the power of love and to believe that children raised with love—the love that helps them grow emotionally and spiritually—will find a way of living and being in this world that is responsible and right for them. Furthermore, you will be asked to have faith in your children—faith in their own basic goodness, loving nature, capability, and responsibility. And probably this faith will be tested like never before.

To look at the situation pragmatically for a minute, there is no other realistic way to approach parenting. After all, children will grow up "in spite of their parents," as the cliché goes. And when their emotional and spiritual needs are met, children grow into self-respecting, respectful, successful, and happy adults. Conversely, when children are not trusted or respected, they grow up with self-doubt which blocks the fulfillment of their personal potential. If, for example, they are not accepted for who they are as children by the very people who are most important in their lives, they probably will not like themselves as adults.

Two important points must be made here. First, "loving behavior" is not simply another euphemism for permissiveness—far from it! While it is not loving to take the authoritarian approach of forcing a child to behave a certain way, it is equally unloving to do nothing with regard to a child's unloving behavior. Neither approach to parenting, authoritarian or permissive, fosters the emotional and spiritual growth of the child. Neither leaves the child feeling loved.

How important is feeling loved? Dr. Ross Campbell, child psychologist and author, makes the following statement:

> I challenge you to look at every statistic regarding children and adolescents in our nation today . . . academics, attitudes, respect for authority, emotional disturbance, motivation, drugs, crime, and so on. The situation is horrible. I maintain that the principal reason for our national dilemma with youth today is that our children do not feel genuinely loved, accepted, and cared for.

The second point is that blaming yourself or your own parents for unloving behavior *in the past* is never helpful. We all do the best we can, given the level of our self-limiting beliefs and fears. No one is wrong and no one is to blame. Past actions should not be judged in the light of your present knowledge. Only current behavior can be corrected. Interestingly though, as you begin to understand how you as a parent are motivated by your own fears and false beliefs, you may be better able to understand and forgive the actions that hurt you as a child, and perhaps continue to hurt you now as an adult. You can never change the parents you have, but you do have a choice about how to react to them. Also, when you see how your own success is being limited by the way you personally react when someone tries to control you, you will probably choose to deal with your children in a different way.

Conflict—A Problem or an Opportunity?

Most of us are very loving—as spouses or parents—until conflict occurs. A conflict is any situation which creates upsetting feelings—disappointment, sadness, hurt, fear, irritation, insecurity, or emotional pain. It's a difference of opinion or an unmet expectation, a clash of values, a difference in desires or needs. When you are upset by your children's thoughts, feelings, or behavior, that's a conflict. Conflicts occur in all relationships but are particularly troublesome in primary relationships (parent-child, parent-parent, mate-mate, siblings). *Difficulties happen not because of the conflict itself but because of the way you deal with the conflict.*

Western civilization's dictionary describes conflict as a struggle between opposing forces, a condition of opposition and discord, mutual antagonism of ideas and interests. The Eastern philosophy of conflict is illustrated by a Chinese character meaning both potential danger as well as an opportunity to change. Since conflict is a given in any personal relationship, the challenge is to learn and grow from these situations. Conflict can become the crucible for change.

As simple and sensible as learning from a conflict may sound, it almost never occurs. You may never have seen it modeled. When you were growing up and you did something that upset your parents, did they use that as an occasion to learn about themselves? Did they sit back and ponder questions like: Why am I getting so upset? What does this conflict have to teach me? What fears and values of mine are being tapped into? I wonder what important reasons my child has for behaving like he or she is? If you're like most people, all you'll remember is some sort of negative reaction like "No!" "Go to your room!" or "You're asking for a spanking!" Your parents made you wrong, trying to get you to change your behavior to conform to what they believed was right so that, even though the reasoning may have been below their awareness, they wouldn't feel upset any more. Chances are you do the same thing to your children.

Let's take a minute to make an important point. We're *not* saying here that children's behavior doesn't need guidance, or that parents should sit idly by and ignore something like a temper tantrum because "I can't do a thing with that child," or drug-taking because "kids will be kids"—or whatever rationalization they have for avoiding the issue. What we *are* saying is that children will not get guidance, or will get only negative learnings, unless their parents are willing to learn the dynamics of the relationship between them, beginning with taking responsibility for their own reactions to what is going on.

If you are parenting by authoritarian methods, you may think what you're doing is working. In that case, ask yourself if it's possible that there are any negative consequences. For example, it may be like the husband who punishes his wife when she doesn't make love with him. So the wife goes along with him, and then he says, "See—she loves me." The wife did go through the motions, but how long will she be willing to be motivated by fear? The same may be true for your children. You can achieve results by force when they're young, but when they're old enough or strong enough to realize there are other options than to obey, they have a strong tendency to go in the opposite direction from the one you point them in. After all, if someone tried to force you to do something, wouldn't you run away as far and as fast as you could?

Another way to cope with conflict is to become indifferent, to push your own feelings aside, giving in and going along with what your child wants. However, avoiding conflict doesn't get you anywhere either.

How do the typical interactions go when your child does something that upsets you?

- Do you express your feelings, with the hope that your child will then change?
- Do you ignore your child's feelings?
- Do you attempt to get your child to stop the behavior that's upsetting you with threats, lec-

tures, explanations, hitting, criticism, nagging, yelling? How does your child react?

- Does your child feel his or her needs, desires, and feelings are respected?
- Do you feel your needs, desires, and feelings are respected?
- Do you attempt to explore and understand your own fears and beliefs as well as your child's?
- Do you attempt to understand your part in creating the difficulties between you and your child?
- Do you understand the very important reasons your child has for thinking, feeling, or behaving the way he or she is?
- Are you and your children learning and growing from your conflicts and becoming more loving in the process?

If you cannot honestly answer yes to the last question, chances are that parenting feels like a burden to you, and like "Ron" at the beginning of this chapter, you may feel that life is not turning out the way you thought it would. There is good news in store for you—there is something stealing the good times from you that is within your power to change! The culprit that keeps each of us from giving and receiving more love is our automatic protective response when faced with conflict.

Conflict and Intent—The Keys

In the supermarket your four-year-old daughter creates a scene by crying loudly until you buy the toy she wants. On the baseball field, your sixth-grade son strikes out again and you overhear one of the fathers in the bleachers make a cutting remark. These are examples of conflicts—events that upset you. Put yourself in these parents' shoes. How do you feel? What are your beliefs? That no self-respecting parent allows a child to scream at the grocery store? That anyone whose offspring can't hit a baseball must be inadequate?

For most parents, fears and beliefs get touched off which, by force of habit, are interpreted as threatening to some aspect of their personhood, and thus they quickly, though often subconsciously, take action to protect themselves, usually by trying to get their children to change. Most often, the way this is done is by making the children feel guilty and wrong. However, parents don't have to react this way in conflict. This is what they have control over—their own reactions to the situation. Instead of protecting themselves, they can choose to learn from the conflict and to behave in a loving way toward the child.

All of the many varieties of responses to a conflict come from only two basic motives or intentions: 1) the *intent to learn*—an openness to learning from the conflict, which leads to *loving behavior* or 2) the *intent to protect*—defending against any potential pain that might come from the conflict, which leads to *unloving behavior*. Any response other than an openness to learning is a protection.

Each response produces very predictable consequences. Protective responses lead to power struggles, rebellion, irresponsible children, feeling uncared about and uncaring, and conflicts that never seem to get resolved. However, on the path of learning all family members grow emotionally and no one feels like a loser. Everyone wins. Parents as well as children feel better about themselves, and children as well as parents become more responsible.

The distinctive paths that follow from either the intent to protect or the intent to learn are illustrated on the chart "The Paths through Conflict" on the following page. The chart will be explained in greater detail in chapter 2.

THE PATHS THROUGH CONFLICT

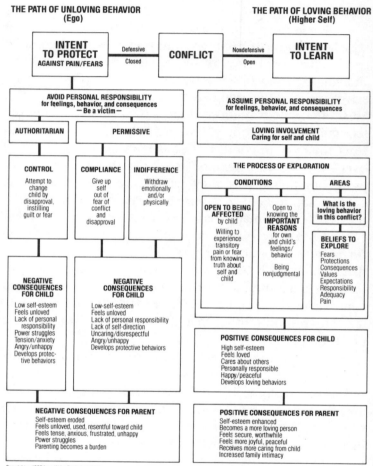

THE PATH OF UNLOVING BEHAVIOR
(Ego)

THE PATH OF LOVING BEHAVIOR
(Higher Self)

INTENT TO PROTECT AGAINST PAIN/FEARS	Defensive Closed	**CONFLICT**	Nondefensive Open	**INTENT TO LEARN**

AVOID PERSONAL RESPONSIBILITY
for feelings, behavior, and consequences
— Be a victim —

ASSUME PERSONAL RESPONSIBILITY
for feelings, behavior, and consequences

AUTHORITARIAN

PERMISSIVE

LOVING INVOLVEMENT
Caring for self and child

CONTROL
Attempt to change child by disapproval, instilling guilt or fear

COMPLIANCE
Give up self out of fear of conflict and disapproval

INDIFFERENCE
Withdraw emotionally and/or physically

THE PROCESS OF EXPLORATION

CONDITIONS

AREAS

OPEN TO BEING AFFECTED by child

Willing to experience transitory pain or fear from knowing truth about self and child

Open to knowing the **IMPORTANT REASONS** for own and child's feelings/ behavior

Being nonjudgmental

What is the loving behavior in this conflict?

BELIEFS TO EXPLORE
Fears
Protections
Consequences
Values
Expectations
Responsibility
Adequacy
Pain

NEGATIVE CONSEQUENCES FOR CHILD
Low self-esteem
Feels unloved
Lack of personal responsibility
Power struggles
Tension/anxiety
Angry/unhappy
Develops protective behaviors

NEGATIVE CONSEQUENCES FOR CHILD
Low-self-esteem
Feels unloved
Lack of personal responsibility
Lack of self-direction
Uncaring/disrespectful
Angry/unhappy
Develops protective behaviors

POSITIVE CONSEQUENCES FOR CHILD
High self-esteem
Feels loved
Cares about others
Personally responsible
Happy/peaceful
Develops loving behaviors

NEGATIVE CONSEQUENCES FOR PARENT
Self-esteem eroded
Feels unloved, used, resentful toward child
Feels tense, anxious, frustrated, unhappy
Power struggles
Parenting becomes a burden

POSITIVE CONSEQUENCES FOR PARENT
Self-esteem enhanced
Becomes a more loving person
Feels secure, worthwhile
Feels more joyful, peaceful
Receives more caring from child
Increased family intimacy

People are not wrong for protecting themselves. It is a very deeply ingrained reaction. Protections arise from our fears of being vulnerable and from ignorance of any other alternatives. The problem is that no one, not parents in their interactions with their children, or mates interacting with each other, can be open and closed at the same time. That is, you can't be open and loving while being closed and protected—it's just not possible. Then the question remains, what if you allow yourself to be open and vulnerable? Is it worth the risk?

Do I Have to Give Up Me to Be Loved by You?

The struggle around the question "Do I have to give up me to be loved by you?" begins in childhood and haunts us the rest of our lives. The question provokes nearly everyone, striking a universal note of fear that in order to be loved, we have to lose at least some measure of control over our lives. Needing both an independent identity *and* love and belonging puts us all in a difficult dilemma. We seem to be caught in a classic Catch-22, trapped by a choice between two giant, fundamental fears: loneliness vs. loss of control.

So on one level we behave like animals, letting survival mechanisms or protections operate automatically to keep us safe, while on a higher level our evolved brains pine away for closeness, angry and frustrated that our relationships with other human beings aren't satisfactory. What keeps us on the horns of this dilemma is a failure to understand simply that we have another choice. That other choice is to venture forward using a process of communication which we call *exploration*. Through exploration, we come to understand ourselves and others and the respectable, important reasons for thinking, feeling, and behaving as we do. When people are understood and accepted by themselves as well as by the other people in their lives, there is no need to remain protected. Attacks, attempts to change the other—the various methods of control which are assaults on the self—fall by the wayside. There is no need to be defensive, blaming, controlling, or to hide behind compliance or indifference when you are accepted by yourself and your loved ones and loved unconditionally.

To embark on this process of exploration requires a conscious decision to risk, that is, to lay down your arms—your protections—and let yourself and your loved ones know how you really feel. But the risk is not life-threatening—emotionally painful at times perhaps, but not truly dangerous, although our fearful reaction to conflict tells us it might be. This is one of the erroneous beliefs which gets touched off when conflict occurs.

When you are willing to be vulnerable or open, two very significant things happen which make the risk more than commensurate with the gain. First, when you are willing to be vulnerable, you are more lovable. Like magnets both repel and attract, when people are protecting themselves, the force they give off is the repelling force. When people are open, soft, and accessible, the force they exude is one that attracts.

Second, and this is a corollary of the first, when people admit their true feelings, they endear themselves to their partners. In other words, the fear that they won't be accepted for their true feelings, which is one of the reasons they remained protected, is unfounded. In fact, it works just the opposite—they are loved not less, but more. Here's an example from a conversation between Ann and Jack:

> Ann, angry because her husband Jack has not been supportive of her as she's been going through a difficult situation, begins to chip away at his armor, trying to get some reaction from him.

Ann (caustically): Why are you just sitting there saying nothing—I don't get it!

Jack sits in sober-faced silence.

Ann (angrily): I'm talking to you and you don't even have the courtesy to respond. Don't you care about what I've been going through?

Jack remains uncommunicative.

Ann (loudly, angrier): I can't believe you have nothing to say. What on earth is the matter with you?!

Jack finally speaks up (pensively): The truth is—I have so many problems of my own that I can't handle yours and mine both.

Ann, immediately soft and loving, goes to him, puts her arms around him and speaks softly: That's all I needed to know.

Studying the paths through conflict toward intimacy for couples is the subject of our previous book, *Do I Have To Give Up Me To Be Loved by You?* Couples who have embarked on the journey outlined in the book, and are growing more intimate and more loving than ever, have often asked us: "Won't these same principles work in family relationships?" As you know by now, the answer is a resounding YES! That's what this book is about.

In the next chapters the intent to protect and the intent to learn will be discussed in greater detail. However, just because you now know about the possibility of learning from a conflict doesn't mean that you'll always be able to go from conflict to loving behavior. Protections are so deep and strong that they come up instantaneously; so before you know it, your protections have activated your children's protections and you're in a protective circle.

Rather than expecting to move easily into a whole new way of interacting, a much more realistic expectation is that you will continue to protect, your children will too, and you will continue your protected dance with all of its negative consequences. But now, with the awareness of learning and loving behavior, you can, at some point when the immediate emotions stirred up by the conflict have subsided, go back to the conflict and learn from it. That's what people typically just don't do. The more usual pattern is to let the passage of time cover over some of the negative consequences until another conflict occurs.

Reacting protectively to a conflict is not so terrible if you eventually learn from it. You can do that by waiting until you're in a calmer, more rational state of mind and then exploring and learning about what happened. What did you do and why? How did your children react? What happened between you? What kept you from responding differently? What can you now learn about your protections? What can you learn about the issue of the conflict? What would have been a loving response? What fears and beliefs blocked responding in a loving way?

At times we, the authors, have difficulty going directly from conflict into learning and loving behavior. One evening our son Eric, who was then sixteen, didn't come home at the time we expected. It was a school night. He had gone out at 7:30 and we expected him to be home by 10:30. At 11:00 we began to be concerned. This was not like him. He had always come home early on school nights or called to explain why he would be late.

As we lay in the dark worrying over his safety, we tried to tell each other he was all right. He must have had some good reason, we said, for not calling to check in. But as the hours ticked off, our anxiety level increased. By midnight we had reached the point of wondering who we should call. Hospitals? The police? His friend's parents? Finally at 12:30, unable to stand it any longer, we called the friend's house. We were told that the boys had, in fact, been out together and Eric was on his way home.

Our anxiety level subsided and we further calmed ourselves by reviewing our theory about learning from this conflict, knowing that we would soon explore and learn about the good reasons for his behavior.

Hearing the door close, we called Eric into our room, all ready to ask him calmly what had happened. Somehow that wasn't what came out of our mouths. It was more like a muffled explosion. "Where the hell were you? Don't you know it's late? Why didn't you call? Don't you know that we've been lying here all night worried sick?"

Eric exploded back at us, "Why are you guys so uptight? We got to the theater late so we waited until the next show. I tried to call you but the line was busy. Anyway, I told you that there's no school tomorrow and that I might be late tonight."

"You never said anything about being late. Why are you defensive?"

"Because you're attacking me. I can't talk to you when all you do is make me wrong." (Here's where we knew that teaching him our theory was a mistake—he was throwing *our* theory back in our faces. How infuriating!)

"Eric, you're impossible. Just get out of here and go to bed."

We were alone again in the dark. "I feel awful." "So do I." "We really blew it, didn't we?" "Yep." We began to explore why we got so angry and blaming. We talked about our belief that we needed to be angry to teach him a lesson. We discussed how anger had been the cover-up for our worried feelings. Finally we drifted off to sleep.

The next morning we went to Eric's room and shared our unhappiness about our part in creating the awful interaction the night before. When we first approached him, he was wary and defensive. But as we talked and he realized we weren't going to attack him, he began to melt, and eventually we were all able to hug and cry and repair the damage from the night before. The details of the event became unimportant as we learned together and experienced once again what happens when we treat each other in protective ways.

The more you as parents learn about your protections and work toward resolving the beliefs and fears that produce them, the less protection you need and the more often you can move from conflict directly into learning and loving behavior. Even when you get protected, however, the length of time you spend in your protected interactions will get less and less. Where we used to spend days or even weeks being protected, now it's usually only hours or minutes before we realize that we've gotten protected and we're willing to open to learning.

This is probably not the first book you've picked up on parenting. It may, however, be the first book you've encountered that doesn't give much advice on how to deal with specific problems. For many of you this approach will cause some discomfort since we're all so used to looking to others for answers. But there are no easy, pat answers for parenting. Each child is unique. Each parent is unique. What worked for one child may not be appropriate for another. What one parent has been able to do may be impossible for you.

Rather than advice or solutions for your problems, we offer a process that will lead you to make personal choices that are right for you and for your children.

As with any process, you will find yourself at times frustrated and unsure, and at other times, ecstatic and confident. As you learn to depend more on your own inner knowing and less on "experts," it will get easier. If you're fortunate enough to have a mate who is willing to be in this process with you, you will have an invaluable helper and the process will be another way to create intimacy and love between you. Such a helper is not mandatory, but he or she can certainly add an important dimension to your learning.

We don't expect spectacular changes and, in fact, are suspicious of quick "miracle cures." Instead, we look for family life to get slowly better as you acquire deeper understanding, more confidence, and greater self-respect.

·2·

The Paths through Conflict
A Step-by-Step Illustration

> *. . . Parenthood is a kind of death. It is the death of those parts of ourselves . . . we identify with, no matter how obsolete. We're afraid of the death of our individuality, when it's really our selfishness that dies . . . We're afraid of the death of our childlikeness, when it's really our childishness that dies . . . We're afraid of the death of who we are, when it's really who we're not that dies. A major initiation of parenthood is this letting go of our false self, so that our real self can shine forth.*
> —Joyce and Barry Vissel
> *Models of Love*

The ability to parent is something like skill at making love. Both are highly regarded "talents" with an aura of mystery around them and highly unrealistic role-modeling in the movies and on TV. Being macho for men and sexy for women on one hand, or being "good" fathers and mothers, on the other, are seen as public expressions of the state of our entire private beings. These are labels which are part of the definition of our selves. So prowess, or lack of it, in either area touches off fundamental fears of adequacy and worth. And as with all issues this deep, failure—real or imagined—to perform up to standard can bring extreme emotional pain.

Since both of these roles—mate and parent—are so important to our sense of self-worth, we feel the need to have some proof of our ability to perform, something visible that validates what we hope other people think is true. It's very threatening to our self-esteem to be saddled with what looks like evidence of failure. For instance, as teenagers, when we couldn't get a date for the prom, it hurt. As adults and parents, when our children get into trouble, it embarrasses *us,* maybe even more than our kids.

In the area of sex, both women and men can take steps to try to prove their attractiveness and then at least they can look the part. Compared to "proof" of good parenting, it's easy. For when it comes to parenting there is another kind of difficulty—the children. My self-image, goes the private logic, is dependent on that extension of myself—my child. But is my adequacy dependent on that toddler who just pulled down his pants and watered the plants in the preschool yard? Does my own self-respect rest on that adolescent with orange hair who goes everywhere with a ghetto blaster stuck to her ear? Even the Bible says, "By their fruits ye shall know them." Does this mean my high schooler's failing grades prove to all the world how stupid *I* am? What, in fact, does all this mean? It's very upsetting.

For most parents it means that they are scared silly and don't know what to do when there is conflict with their children. Consequently, they do what they've learned to do—they protect themselves from fear and pain. In so doing, they set off a predictable progression of negative actions and reactions which inevitably compounds the problem and brings greater pain. Why? Because their protective behaviors frightened the children and then they, too, protect themselves. This mode of behavior and the ensuing chain of events is called the Path of Unloving Behavior, as described on the chart. Why would someone choose this course? (Since the choice is usually subconscious it may be difficult to recognize it as a choice, though the fact that it is subconscious is also a choice. We have the option to choose consciousness.) As it was pointed out in the first chapter, probably because he or she is not aware of another way, or perhaps is afraid to try a new way, preferring the pain felt to the pain feared.

When people are willing to risk, willing to experience emotional pain, willing to learn and be open and loving, another very different chain reaction is ignited, which is labeled The Path of Loving Behavior on the chart, and which leads to the ultimate goal for the family.

Let's take a look at the chart, step by step. Those of you who are familiar with the "Paths through Conflict" chart in *Do I Have to Give Up Me to Be Loved by You?* will recognize similarities, for there are only two paths to take in any kind of conflict, whether it's between mates, parents and children, or even employers and employees. However, there are critical differences as well. For one thing, there is the unique sensitivity around the issue of children as a reflection of the parent's identity or self. Secondly, there is a unique force behind the need to get *through* conflict in the relationship with your kids, because you can't get *out!* You can divorce your spouse and you can quit your job, but your kids are yours forever.

The Paths through Conflict – A Step-by-Step Illustration

```
CONFLICT
```

Problems between a parent and child begin with a conflict such as:

> Differing desires or needs:
> The parent wants the child to go to sleep at 8:00.
> The child wants to stay up until 10:00.

> Differences of opinion, a values conflict:
> The parent believes in tidy bedrooms.
> The child believes in managing his/her own space.

> Unmet expectations:
> The parent expects the child to do well in school.
> The child expects the parent to get off his/her back.

Underlying these conflicts is the following parental belief:
> "If you really loved me, you would do things my way."

The child doesn't feel loved because he or she knows that:
> "If you really loved me, you would accept and value me as I am. You would try to understand me rather than change me."

> A conflict is present in any situation that creates upsetting feelings:

disappointment	disgust
sadness	disdain
hurt	anger
fear	anxiety
irritation	pain
insecurity	

Conflict will occur in *all* relationships.

THE PATH OF UNLOVING BEHAVIOR
(Ego)

THE PATH OF LOVING BEHAVIOR
(Higher Self)

All of the many varieties of responses to a conflict stem from only two intents:
> to protect
>   or
> to learn

The intent underlying the responses predicts and determines the subsequent interaction between the parent and child.

It's not the conflict itself, but what we do in the face of conflict that leads either to difficulties and distance or to caring, comfort, cooperation, and responsibility.

The intent to protect comes from our fears and the false beliefs that create these fears. These fears and beliefs and resulting behaviors constitute our ego. The ego is the part of us we created when we were very young to try to protect ourselves from the fear of being abandoned and from the pain of rejection. It is our false self, an illusion which we hope will gain us love and approval, or at least allow us to avoid pain and disapproval.

THE PATH OF UNLOVING BEHAVIOR
(Ego)

We protect when we are upset. We are protecting against having to experience some pain we fear.

As parents, we become upset when our children do or say something we think they shouldn't. What we judge to be our children's faults and flaws are seen as reflections of our own adequacy and worth.

The protective responses we use, learned in our own childhoods, are seemingly automatic, instantaneous, and for the most part, subconscious.

We become defensive: closed, angry and blaming, uninvolved or withdrawn.

Our behavior is *unloving*. (Our behavior does not nurture emotional/spiritual growth.)

When our primary intent is to protect ourselves, our behavior toward our children is unloving. Thus, even when we feel love for our children, if our behavior is unloving, our children do not feel loved.

THE PATH OF UNLOVING BEHAVIOR
(Ego)

Protections let us avoid personal responsibility for our own feelings, behavior, and any resulting consequences. As parents, we shift the responsibility for our feelings to our children, believing that we are victims of their choices. They are "wrong" and we are "right."

At this point we have stopped being open to learning about ourselves and our children.

The primary intent of a protective response is not *against the child,* but *for oneself.*

All of us have very good reasons for wanting to protect ourselves. But when we act to protect ourselves, paradoxically we create more pain in place of the pain we seek to avoid.

THE PATH OF UNLOVING BEHAVIOR
(Ego)

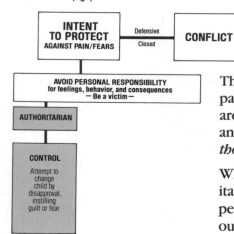

There are two categories of parenting behaviors which are primarily self-protective and therefore unloving: *authoritarian* and *permissive*.

When we are being authoritarian parents, we avoid personal responsibility for our feelings by making our children "wrong."

We want to control our children, trying to get them to give up their own desires, needs, and individuality to fit our expectations and demands.

To do this, we use some form of punishment or disapproval to create guilt or fear:

anger (overt or silent)
threats
demands
criticism
lectures, explanations
sarcasm, ridicule
physical abuse

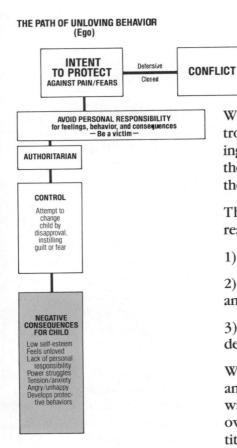

THE PATH OF UNLOVING BEHAVIOR
(Ego)

INTENT
TO PROTECT
AGAINST PAIN/FEARS

Defensive
Closed

CONFLICT

AVOID PERSONAL RESPONSIBILITY
for feelings, behavior, and consequences
— Be a victim —

AUTHORITARIAN

CONTROL

Attempt to
change
child by
disapproval,
instilling
guilt or fear

NEGATIVE
CONSEQUENCES
FOR CHILD

Low self-esteem
Feels unloved
Lack of personal
responsibility
Power struggles
Tension/anxiety
Angry/unhappy
Develops protec-
tive behaviors

When parents try to control children, they are asking the children to give up themselves to become what the parents want.

There are three possible reactions to this demand:

1) compliance

2) resistance or noncompliance/indifference

3) presumed compliance/ deferred resistance

When children are resistant, they fight back, not wanting to give up their own identities. Often identity boundaries are stiffened to the point of rebellion, as the children learn to cope by adopting their own protective devices.

When children are truly compliant, they give themselves up to please the parent, but in so doing lose their sense of self.

Some children pretend to go along with their parents' demands to change, to meet their expectations, and so on, but act in antisocial or self-destructive ways outside the home, away from the parents. Or they may just bide their time until they can go out on their own.

THE PATH OF UNLOVING BEHAVIOR
(Ego)

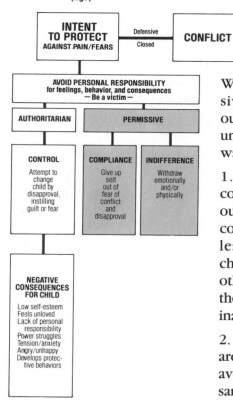

When we are being permissive parents, we protect ourselves, and therefore act unlovingly, in two general ways.

1. *Compliance:* We are compliant when we give ourselves up to avoid the conflict which we fear will lead to rejection by our children and disapproval of others who might perceive the conflict as evidence of inadequacy.

2. *Indifference:* When we are being indifferent, we avoid conflict out of the same fear by simply withdrawing emotionally and physically. Various ways to do this are work, television, drugs or alcohol, sports or hobbies, volunteerism, illness, depression.

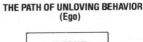

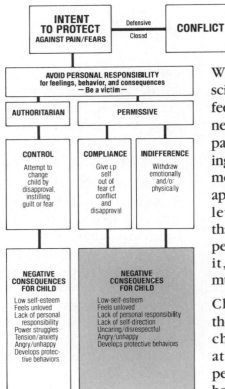

Whether children are consciously aware of it or their feelings are below awareness, they sense that the parents' behavior is unloving. The behavior—giving money for example—may appear loving, but at some level the children know that it is not. They take it personally and internalize it, believing something must be wrong with them.

Children attempt to get their parents' behavior to change by demanding attention, crying, disrespectful language, negative behaviors in school, breaking the law.

Children learn from the parents' behavior, not the parents' inner feelings. Thus they care for self first, and others only when expedient. They do not show love for others or respect for their parents.

Often these children feel anger and often act out in anger. They want their parents to love them. Also, how can they feel lovable and worthy themselves if their parents don't love them?

THE PATH OF UNLOVING BEHAVIOR
(Ego)

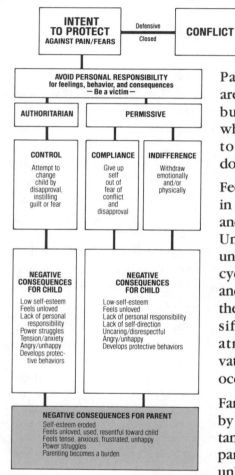

Parents sense that things are not as they should be, but do not understand why. As a result, attempts to solve problems are doomed to failure.

Feelings are either acted out in anger or are suppressed, and detachment increases. Unloving behavior begets unloving behavior, and so a cycle of protective actions and reactions is created and the negative feelings intensify. Often the family atmosphere is so aggravated that marital problems occur.

Family life is characterized by fighting and pain or distance and deadness. Both parents and children feel unloved and unloving.

Self-esteem is eroded for both parents and children. Parents' general confusion is illustrated by typical questions such as:

Where did I go wrong?
Life isn't turning out the way I thought it would.

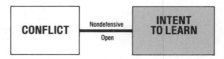

THE PATH OF LOVING BEHAVIOR
(Higher Self)

The only responses to a conflict that are not protective come from an intent to learn from the conflict.

When we protect ourselves we are defensive and closed. The opposite of defensive and closed is nondefensive and open and loving. In this posture, we are able to learn from others in our family, to review our myths and mental pictures of how families "should" be and adjust to the reality of how our families are.

We are also vulnerable and seem to be in a position of risk. However, what we are risking is one of the areas of confusion for most people. We do not risk death and destruction as an animal does when it ventures from its safe cover. We risk only the emotional pain that may come from relationships with others. In reality, there is no real risk, since our own sense of lovability and integrity is enhanced by our loving behavior.

When our intent is to learn, we are open, soft, curious, warm, available.

The intent to learn can be felt and heard, especially in tone of voice. Therefore, when we act with the intent to learn, our behavior is loving.

Learning about ourselves leads to discovering and getting in touch with our Higher Self—the loving, open Self that each of us was born with. The Higher Self is our true or authentic Self, as opposed to the falsely constructed self, the ego.

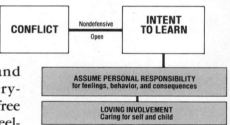

When we are open and wanting to learn, everything changes. We are free to act out our loving feelings so that others can feel that we love them. So, instead of a relationship of antagonism, "you against me," or "you are wrong because you're a child and I am right because I'm an adult," the spirit is one of acceptance: "You are important and worthy. Therefore you must have some very good reasons for your behavior."

We give up blaming others and assume personal responsibility for our own feelings, our behavior, and any resulting consequences.

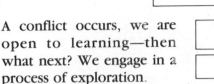

THE PATH OF LOVING BEHAVIOR
(Higher Self)

CONFLICT	Nondefensive Open	INTENT TO LEARN

ASSUME PERSONAL RESPONSIBILITY
for feelings, behavior, and consequences

LOVING INVOLVEMENT
Caring for self and child

THE PROCESS OF EXPLORATION

A conflict occurs, we are open to learning—then what next? We engage in a process of exploration.

We want to understand ourselves and our children on a deeper level and to help them understand themselves more deeply.

We ask questions like:

Why am I so upset?
What are my fears? Unmet expectations?
What is the purpose of my anger?
What part am I playing in creating this present problem?
What are the consequences of the way I respond?
What is the loving response in this situation?
What are the beliefs that are in the way of my responding with love instead of protections?

We ask our children the same questions we asked ourselves:

What are your fears? Expectations?
Why are you angry? hurt? disappointed?

The focus of the exploration is not a search for solutions to our problems, but rather discovering our false, self-limiting beliefs. We search for the new understandings which give respect and dignity to behavior, and we discover what the loving behavior would be.

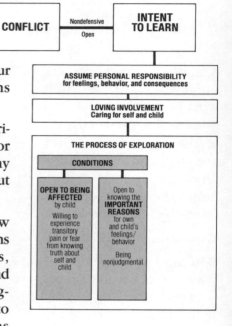

THE PATH OF LOVING BEHAVIOR
(Higher Self)

| CONFLICT | Nondefensive
Open | INTENT
TO LEARN |

ASSUME PERSONAL RESPONSIBILITY
for feelings, behavior, and consequences

LOVING INVOLVEMENT
Caring for self and child

THE PROCESS OF EXPLORATION

CONDITIONS

| OPEN TO BEING AFFECTED
by child | Open to knowing the IMPORTANT REASONS
for own and child's feelings/behavior |
| Willing to experience transitory pain or fear from knowing truth about self and child | Being nonjudgmental |

For an exploration to occur the following conditions must be met:

1) A willingness to experience transitory pain and/or fear that may accompany knowing the truth about ourselves and another.

2) A willingness to know the very important reasons motivating our feelings, thoughts, and behavior and to accept them nonjudgmentally. A willingness to table our cultural myths concerning "right" and "wrong" and to just want to understand.

When we believe there are very important reasons for behavior, we stop accusing our children of being wrong, and the door is opened to understanding and acceptance (not necessarily of the children's actions themselves, but of the reasons behind them).

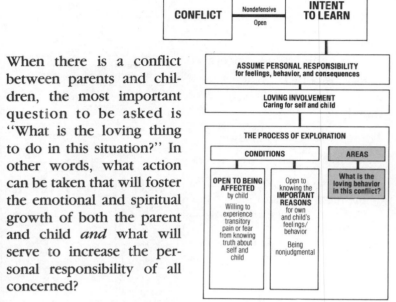

THE PATH OF LOVING BEHAVIOR
(Higher Self)

When there is a conflict between parents and children, the most important question to be asked is "What is the loving thing to do in this situation?" In other words, what action can be taken that will foster the emotional and spiritual growth of both the parent and child *and* what will serve to increase the personal responsibility of all concerned?

When we ask ourselves what would be the loving thing to do, the answer comes from within, from our Higher Selves which knows the truth for each of us.

Loving behavior will vary, but it will always be consistent with feeling whole and will enhance the self-esteem of both parent and child. It is a creative, caring, nonjudgmental response, as opposed to an automatic, learned, and reactive response.

Whether a behavior is loving or unloving is determined solely by intent.

The intent to learn is always loving.

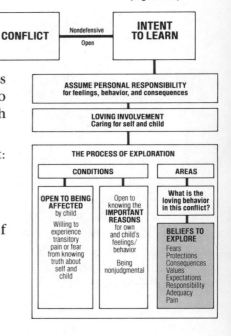

THE PATH OF LOVING BEHAVIOR
(Higher Self)

In the exploration process family members will also explore the beliefs which they hold.

These include beliefs about:
adequacy
pain
fear
protections
the consequences of protections
values, right and wrong
expectations
personal responsibility
love
God and spirituality
human nature

It is important to explore each of these areas to fully understand both the issue of the conflict and our protective intent.

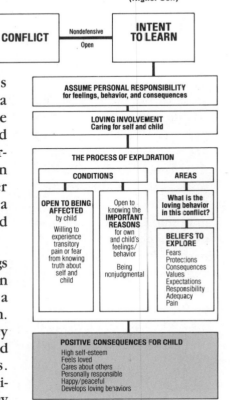

THE PATH OF LOVING BEHAVIOR
(Higher Self)

When a person feels accepted, whether it's a child or an adult, he or she feels worthwhile and loved. Thus when the parent accepts the child as an individual person rather than the fulfillment of a parent's image, the child feels loved.

Many other positive things happen as a result. Children who feel loved have a strong sense of self-esteem. They act responsibly. They care about their parents and other family members. They have a generally positive outlook on life. They know and accept who they are.

The exploration process leads to mutually satisfying resolutions to conflicts and personal freedom and growth combined with increasingly loving relationships. For parents, frustration and confusion are at a minimum. There is a sense of inner peace and balance, with a feeling that "all is well." Family life is characterized by joy, learning, evolving intimacy, caring for and from children, and increased self-esteem for everyone.

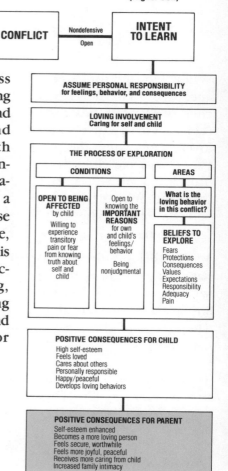

THE PATH OF LOVING BEHAVIOR
(Higher Self)

| CONFLICT | Nondefensive Open | INTENT TO LEARN |

ASSUME PERSONAL RESPONSIBILITY
for feelings, behavior, and consequences

LOVING INVOLVEMENT
Caring for self and child

THE PROCESS OF EXPLORATION

CONDITIONS

OPEN TO BEING AFFECTED by child
Willing to experience transitory pain or fear from knowing truth about self and child

Open to knowing the **IMPORTANT REASONS** for own and child's feelings/behavior
Being nonjudgmental

AREAS

What is the loving behavior in this conflict?

BELIEFS TO EXPLORE
Fears
Protections
Consequences
Values
Expectations
Responsibility
Adequacy
Pain

POSITIVE CONSEQUENCES FOR CHILD
High self-esteem
Feels loved
Cares about others
Personally responsible
Happy/peaceful
Develops loving behaviors

POSITIVE CONSEQUENCES FOR PARENT
Self-esteem enhanced
Becomes a more loving person
Feels secure, worthwhile
Feels more joyful, peaceful
Receives more caring from child
Increased family intimacy

On the previous pages, the paths through conflict have been discussed as they naturally progress, one step leading to another. However, it is important to look at the overall picture, for some crucial understandings then become clear.

Most of us would like to play it safe and act protectively—after all, who wants to feel pain and fear? Yet we want the results of having been open. As you can see from the following chart, we cannot begin with an intent to protect and go directly to the benefits of an intent to learn. Try as we might, we simply cannot be closed and have the advantages of being open.

Likewise, we cannot act in unloving ways and expect to reap the rewards of being loving.

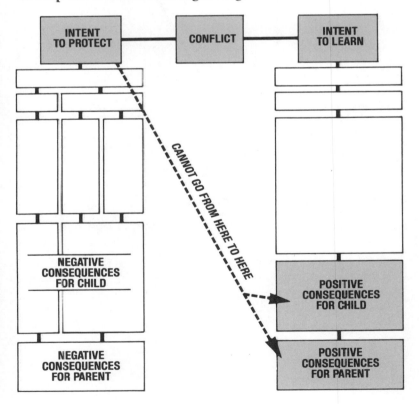

Intent is the motive or energy that directs our behavior. As a result, meaningful behavior changes occur only when intent changes. And, further, consequences will change only when intent changes.

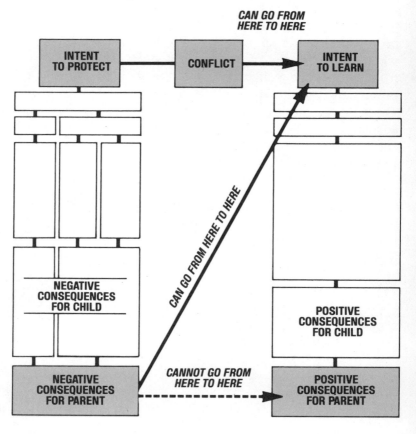

Family Constellations

It is no news to anyone that within every family there are different personality types and that the different personalities interact in different ways with each other. Also, there are obviously many factors which influence each person, birth order being one of them. It is tempting to generalize about these factors—for example, that the first-born child is most often the resistant-controlling child, while the second or middle child tends to be the compliant-resistant child. However, while some general rules prove true for most cases, still there are a significant number of exceptions. So, while labels describing the various responses (resistant, compliant, authoritarian, permissive) are handy for discussion purposes, they really are counterproductive when used to describe a person. When that happens, the labels tend to become fixed like name tags, limiting and influencing the way we think about each other and even the way the labeled person thinks about himself or herself.

The important thing about this discussion is that there is value in being aware of the energy vectors that exist within your own family. First, when you identify your own intent, you can makes choices about your own behavior. *Without awareness there is no choice.* Second, when you understand your children's various reactions to your behavior, you can learn more about yourself. You can know when you are being loving or unloving, and based on that, you can predict the responses to your actions.

To give a specific, simple example, let's say you demand that your eight-year-old son clean his room. This would be authoritarian behavior on your part, based on your belief that rooms should be clean, and that this is the way to teach responsibility. Now what is going to happen? If your son is resistant, you can predict with real certainty that you will have a struggle on your hands. He may spend hours dawdling, playing with toys, eventually falling asleep on the floor. In doing so, he may even win out in this test of wills. His behavior is easily translated: "I don't want to do this. See if you can make me." He may then win and you lose. Or you may rouse him and nag him into finishing. That means you win and he loses. In either case, neither of you feels good about what happened.

If your child is compliant, he will go ahead and clean his room, but unless he too wanted a clean room at the moment you made your ultimatum, "Clean your room or else!"—he will not feel good about doing it. He will feel his own power and worth undermined. He will not feel good about your making the demand, and he will not feel good about himself because he gave himself up— he gave in; he was weak or overpowered. He will not feel loved and will not feel worthy, which will certainly not help him feel personally responsible. A very high price for a clean room.

These are just samples of two of the many action-reaction patterns which can occur as a result of the typical parental behaviors and subsequent children's responses. Obviously, there are many more possible combinations of interactions, not only because there are different person-ality types, but also because each person vacillates in his or her position—from authoritarian to permissive, for example—-when conflict arises.

Note, however, that *the parent is the one who determines the path—protection or learning—of the interaction chain of events.* The parent is the originator of the direction, because even if his or her choice is indifference, the feelings generated by that non-action spark the response from the child.

Some parents are not interested in questioning their intent. Others approach the issue tentatively and with caution. After all, what will happen if they admit they are protected? How could they possibly admit to being unloving? Is their only choice to give up themselves and lose control? Still others are learning and are aware, but have great difficulty redirecting their energy from the intent to protect to the intent to learn.

Each of these reasons is an indication of the deep roots and strength of protections. How do you protect and why do you remain so protected? These issues will be discussed in the next chapters.

Part 2

If You Really Loved Me

The process described in this book is designed to help you become less fearful, protected, and more loving. As this transformation gradually occurs, you will come to understand how the words "If you really loved me" are used in manipulative attempts to get others to meet your needs so that you don't have to feel pain. You will be free to be the loving person you are capable of being when your focus shifts to the principal question: "If I really loved you."

·3·

When I'm Upset, You're Wrong!

Learning about Protections

> *. . . Parents unconsciously use and mis-use their children. Do well. Make me proud. Don't aggravate me. The unspo-ken deal is this: If you will bury the parts I don't like, then I will love you. The unspoken choice is this: Lose yourself or lose me.*
>
> —Judith Viorst
> *Necessary Losses*

One Sunday evening in the winter of 1971 Archie and Edith Bunker burst forth with their off-key singing duet, "Those Were the Days," introducing the landmark tele-vision program, *All in the Family*. The laughter coming from living rooms across America was loud and charged with the energy of release. Real family life had finally come out of the closet. What a relief! Finally someone was being honest about the real kinds of interactions between fathers and kids, mothers and kids, and between fathers and mothers over what to do about the kids. In real families, there's shouting and name-calling. There are heated, hurtful arguments. There are blatant attempts to control each other and, just as often, there's giving up and giving in. All this confusion and conflict between people who seem to love each other—all within the family.

Archie and Edith sang about the good old days because life wasn't so confusing for them then. In those days, Father did know best—after all, he brought home the bacon. And Mother did look cute in her apron giving advice while she cut vegetables at the kitchen sink. The children listened politely and obediently. At least this was the collective image of family life back then.

But what worked then doesn't work now. Women have literally marched to freedom and personal power and have won a myriad of mothering options. The kids have been liberated by the mass media. They see other kids resisting and rebelling. They also see a number of different ways to run a family. Men's roles have changed more slowly, although now they are gaining some acceptable new definitions for themselves.

Of course, Archie Bunker didn't change. Instead, he looked at the confusion and conflict and did his best to protect himself. He blamed the "meathead" son-in-law for most of his misery. But somehow that really didn't help. So, Archie would slouch in his red chair on center stage, bitter and miserable, a poignant picture of an almost totally protected person. And Archie never understood the irony that was obvious to the audience—it was his own behavior that was the primary cause for his own unhappiness.

What Do Protections Do for You?

Once you have learned about protections—those behaviors each of us uses as a defensive shield—you'll probably never view human behavior the same way again. It's like flipping on the light in a dark room—now you can see what's really going on!

For the most part, protections are not planned, but are subconscious and come up seemingly automatically when you encounter conflict. The purpose of protections is two-fold: 1) to protect you from feeling emotional pain, whether it's fear, sadness, insecurity, disappointment, or whatever; and 2) to make others responsible for your happiness and unhappiness, thereby protecting you from recognizing your own responsibility. It seems easier that way. Then the others—mates or children—have to change to fit your expectations. And you don't have to look within yourself to find the fears and beliefs that are the real source of your unhappiness.

However, as we could see with Archie Bunker, even though protections are supposed to keep you safe and happy, in reality they have the opposite effect. They actually generate most of the pain and unhappiness in your life. Why? Because protective behavior not only makes us feel bad about ourselves, but it almost always creates a negative response. In other words, a defensive behavior creates a defensive response. You yell at your kids—they yell back. You blame your son, and he reacts defensively. You criticize your daughter, and she cries, runs into her room, and slams the door. It's a simple, predictable chain reaction.

Most people don't connect their protections with the misery these behaviors produce. But when this connection is understood, it's profoundly affecting. You'll probably never want to make the choice to protect again. But that doesn't mean you never will. Protections are tough to stamp out. Their roots are deep and you're only human. However, the first step in reducing protections and the unhappiness they cause is to recognize how you protect.

Becoming Aware of Protections

Protections are so much a part of your personality that you probably are not aware of them. One of the biggest obstacles to awareness is your judgments concerning right and wrong. If you believe that it's wrong to protect, i.e., to blame, criticize, withdraw, comply, lie, etc., then it will be difficult for you to admit that you do these things. People fear being wrong because they believe that being wrong means they are unlovable and unworthy and that they will therefore be rejected. For most people, the fear of being wrong is so great that it totally blocks any openness to learning about themselves. They are afraid to look inward for fear of discovering something they judge to be wrong.

In order to learn about your protections you need to temporarily suspend your judgments about right and wrong. Protections are not wrong. People protect for very good reasons. They protect when they get scared and either know no other way of handling their fear or are too afraid to be vulnerable.

Everyone reacts protectively in conflict most of the time. Whether you are menacing or civil, calm or hysterical, compliant or indifferent, you are protecting when you ignore children or attempt to make them change their behavior. *Wanting* children to change is not the problem; attempts to *make* them change create the difficulties.

Trying to make children change implies that there is something wrong with them for behaving as they do. When you really believe there are compelling reasons for behavior, you won't try to change it by making that behavior wrong. If your child had trouble with his vision, would you try to get him to see better by yelling at him or praising him—making it an issue of right against wrong? Meaningful change cannot come about until the compelling reasons are no longer present. That kind of change, however, comes from the explorations and understanding that accompany an intention to learn.

Even though protections are often manipulative and hurt your children, your spouse, or yourself, the *primary intent* is not to hurt others, but to *protect* yourself. When your primary motive or intent is to protect yourself, you are closed and defensive. On a deep level you love your child, but this love is eclipsed by surface feelings like fear, anger, or irritation, and your behavior isn't loving at all.

Here's an example which may help clarify the difference:

Tyler, seventeen, wears old jeans with holes in them. Nan, his mother, relates that she loves her son very much and is very proud of his good looks. But here's the interaction between them.

> Nan (intensely): Tyler, please wear the new jeans I bought you.
>
> Tyler (resistant): No, I like these.
>
> Nan (voice rising): But you look terrible.
>
> Tyler (stubbornly holding on to his own viewpoint): I like the way I look and I'm old enough to decide about my own clothes.
>
> Nan (judgmental tone): Only bums wear clothes like that.
>
> Tyler (sullenly): Then I guess I'm a bum.
>
> Nan (frustrated and angry): Now you're being rude and sarcastic.
>
> Tyler (voice rising): Yeah, well I don't like being yelled at.
>
> Nan (very loudly): If you weren't so difficult, I wouldn't have to get angry!

Nan's behavior is a very common, clear example of protected, unloving behavior. She wants Tyler to change and meet her expectations. Note that Nan is not wrong for how she feels—she has every right to think her son looks better with different clothes. But her approach to Tyler accomplished nothing positive and certainly did not foster her own or her son's emotional growth. Her judgment is that wearing torn jeans is wrong, that it is the sign of some sort of bad person. Her belief is probably that parents should control how their children look. Her fears may be, therefore, that people will judge Tyler as a bad person and will judge her as a bad, uncaring, or out-of-control parent if she cannot make him dress differently. It boils down to the fear that both Tyler and she have lost value because he wears old, torn jeans.

If Nan had taken the time to examine this belief, she might have changed her whole approach to the situation. As it was, however, she acted out of the fear caused by the belief and the resulting unmet expectation. She used the common, protected behaviors—criticism ("you look terrible") and ridicule ("only bums wear clothes like that") and anger (yelling, tone of voice). Finally, she made Tyler wrong and responsible for her feelings ("If you weren't so difficult, I wouldn't have to get angry").

Nan did accomplish something, but it was all negative. Tyler did not agree to wear the new jeans. He became angry and resistant, and probably more determined than ever to wear his old jeans. He felt estranged from his mother because she didn't like him the way he was and she didn't understand his reasons for liking old jeans. As a matter of fact, she didn't even ask. Finally, Tyler didn't feel loved—he felt ridiculed, criticized, yelled at, and wrong.

The irony is that most people like Nan, after an interaction like this one, are confused. "Why doesn't he do what I want him to?" "Doesn't he understand that I'm only interested in his welfare?" "Doesn't he know how much I love him?" Our response is "How could he know that you love him?" When you react from fear, your behavior isn't loving. Your child only knows what he or she hears, sees, and feels. Your child learns from what you say and do, not from what you think and what you believe you feel.

Let's let Nan have another try at a conversation with Tyler.

> Nan (softly): Tyler, I love you but I don't like old torn jeans.
>
> Tyler: But I like these jeans.
>
> Nan: Why do you like them? (Her intention is not to get her way, but to understand.)
>
> Tyler: They're comfortable. They feel lived-in. All the kids like old jeans.
>
> Nan: Yeah, I can see where they would be comfortable. But it scares me that people will think you're a hippie or a bum or something.
>
> Tyler: Well, I don't care what people think. My friends wouldn't think that anyway.
>
> Nan: But my friends would.
>
> Tyler: I don't think you should worry about it so much.
>
> Nan: Yeah, that's probably true. I guess it's my problem to deal with isn't it? (Nan might now explore, either alone, with her son, or with someone else, her fear of other people's judgment.) Well, I guess I can live with torn jeans.
>
> Tyler: That's the spirit, mom.
>
> Nan: I do love you, Tyler.
>
> Tyler: I know, mom. I love you too.

This conversation could have gone further, if Nan had chosen to examine her own beliefs and fears with Tyler. But the main point is very obvious: this time Nan stayed open and loving. She expressed her own honest opinions and fears, yet she also tried to understand without trying to force, blame, or give up responsibility for her own feelings. The result was dramatically different. Tyler also remained open. He held his own ground but was not resistant, rebellious, or angry. The jeans stayed in both interactions, but when Nan was closed and unloving, Tyler reacted to that behavior and then felt unloved. When Nan was open and loving, Tyler felt loved and offered love in return. The way is open for him to change his mind or for her to change her beliefs through the learning process. Even if the situation which caused the conflict never changes, they will live with it much differently.

It's not a novel idea that if you act angry, you're most likely to get anger in return. When you say to someone in your family, "You idiot! What did you do that for?" you don't really expect him or her to respond lovingly, "I'm sorry, dear, that I was so foolish." But it is a new concept to understand how that behavior is protecting you in reaction to conflict. And to take it one step further—the most important step—it is a profound realization when you understand how and why that protected behavior is unloving. Once you understand this, in all likelihood you will feel a real urgency to shift your intent from closed to open, protected to learning, unloving to loving.

Old habits are hard to break, especially when you don't really realize what you are doing. So it's important to spend some time identifying the typical unloving, protected behaviors to help you hold the mirror up to your own actions.

Adults protect themselves in conflicts with their children either by becoming authoritative or permissive, that is, either by attempting to make children change their behavior or by ignoring the kids' behavior and its effects. However, seldom is a parent totally authoritarian or always permissive. Often they vacillate back and forth between the two approaches. Permissive allows; authoritarian restricts. Permissive gives in; authoritarian attempts to get the child to give in. Somebody wins and somebody loses. You may be permissive until the child's behavior becomes intolerable and then you become authoritarian. Or you may be authoritarian until your child refuses to meet your demands and then you become permissive.

In both authoritarian and permissive approaches, supportive involvement and the loving behavior that fosters the child's growth and personal responsibility are missing. Since these are the key ingredients to feeling important and cared about, the child's self-esteem and self-worth are seriously eroded by either approach.

Authoritarian Protections

Authoritarian responses are any attempts to make children change their behavior by creating fear or guilt, making children wrong, punishing them (as opposed to establishing limits concerning health, safety, and the establishment of personal rights and allowing logical consequences), or even praising them when the motive is to manipulate their behavior. These are the ways parents try to control, possess, dominate, and intimidate their children into complying with their demands.

Along with these methods go the ideas that children need to be tamed, that they do not have inherent good sense, that they will run amuck without parental control. (Note here that there is a difference between *guidance* and control.) Further, it is implied children are not capable of making good decisions about what to eat, what to wear—even who to love. ("What! You don't love grandma? How can you say such a terrible thing! I don't care if she doesn't smell good—everyone loves the people in their family.") When parents do not believe their children are capable, they feel they have the right and, in fact, the duty to determine what's best for the children and to stay firmly in control of them.

This set of beliefs generates a lot of anxiety and fear in the adults themselves. The parents become responsible in their own minds for forcing the children into a certain mold. They have preconceived ideas of how a child should be, which for the most part are the standards they saw their own parents model. The next logical step in this line of thinking is that parents are responsible for their children's performance—how well they do, how motivated they are, how highly they achieve.

The bottom line is that the parents have little, if any, faith in their children's innate goodness or good sense. ("My child won't know what to do unless I tell him.") When parents operate from this basis, the message to the children is very discouraging. It says simply, "You are not good enough until I make you better." Hence, for the children, self-esteem, self-worth, and personal responsibility are seriously eroded. When the parents function most of the time in the authoritative mode, the children experience a tough, insecure, and often puzzlingly sad childhood.

Erin, a beautiful, bright child, was unexplainably melancholy and withdrawn except for a strong emotional attachment to her best friend Beth to whom she clung jealously. Erin's mother declared she had done everything she knew how to do for her daughter—bought her good clothes, decorated her room, scheduled her piano and ballet so she'd have plenty of time to do homework. But as Erin began to cling more and more frantically to her best friend, the mother finally sought the advice of a therapist. When the therapist asked Erin about her feelings, she responded simply, "My mother loves stiff. Beth loves cozy." Even at an early age, Erin had the intellectual understanding that her mother loved her, but Erin simply could not feel it. Her mother's love was hidden behind authoritarian protections. Her best friend's love was available and unconditional.

The danger for the children of authoritarian parents only escalates when they get older. They either learn to rely on authority figures without questioning or they rebel against authority for the sake of establishing independence. And neither the followers nor the rebels know what they themselves want.

Are you an authoritarian parent? Is your behavior indicative of these beliefs? Let's look at some of the typical protected, unloving behaviors which result from authoritarian beliefs. Let's also keep in mind why these behaviors are unloving by definition: they do not nurture emotional and spiritual growth of either parents or children, nor do they foster personal responsibility. Further, there is no attempt on the parents' part to learn about themselves or their children. The parents are closed, set, and, if challenged, defensive.

Overt Blaming Anger

Hitting, shoving, slapping, spanking, yelling, scolding, speaking harshly, speaking with irritation or annoyance, complaining and accusing are all acts of anger which try to make children change their behavior. The hope is to frighten children into shaping up. Parents believe that anger will get them what they want. This just isn't true. Anger may get the children to comply as long as they are afraid of the parents. However, as Dr. Frank Main says in *Perfect Parenting & Other Myths:*

> We conveniently forget how incensed and rebellious we were (or are) in the face of autocratic models. We often perpetuate the fiction that we can kick our children in the pants, only to discover that our "child" is now 6'3", 235 pounds, and big enough to eat hay. Then we spend the last two years of the kid's high school career white-knuckled and breathless, wondering how things got out of control. When adults pursue the useless goal of dictator, they will experience the

same end as all despots, no matter how benevolent—
dethronement.

Not only are hitting and yelling abusive to children, these blaming, angry responses do not encourage your children to become personally responsible or to behave out of caring for you and themselves.

Even before we (Jordan and Margie) had children, we had always felt that there was no justifiable reason to abuse another. So not hitting (or spanking) another person, especially someone small and defenseless, was fairly easy for us to follow through on. But we hadn't really thought about the effects of yelling. When we got mad, we yelled. It was little Josh who caused us to rethink our ideas.

MARGIE:

One day when Josh was about two and a half years old, I was yelling at him for something, when he looked up at me and said with big tears rolling down his cheeks, "Mommy, when you yell at me like that, I feel like I'm gonna die!" I burst into tears, dropped to my knees and embraced this delicate little person who was feeling so awful. I had never before experienced my yelling having such a devastating effect on anyone.

Jordan and I began a long series of talks about the effects of yelling, both on our children and on ourselves. We discussed whether an emotional violation was any less harmful than a physical one. We asked ourselves what gave us the right to take out our frustrations on other people and how we felt when others yelled at us. I realized that although I had never let Jordan see my pain, whenever he yelled I felt awful. Either I yelled back or clammed up.

Jordan recalled his feelings about being yelled at both from his childhood and his relationship with me. He realized the difficulty of letting anyone, especially a woman, know he could be hurt. Then he had to confront his beliefs about it being wrong for a man to be so sensitive. He also looked at his fear of letting anyone be important enough to hurt him like that.

We can't say that after these explorations we never yelled again, but like everything else, we're working on it and it keeps getting better.

Joseph Chilton Pierce in *Exploring the Cosmic Egg* has this to say about yelling or any other form of verbal abuse:

> Deep within we know that our words wound far more insidiously than anything else, and leave no outward mark. The "battered child syndrome" of current interest is a physical manifestation . . . but the psychological equivalent is more prevalent. It just isn't immediately detectable. The psychologically battered child is observable only in the irrational behavior of each next generation.

Because children learn from modeling their parents' behavior, when you hit and yell out your hurt, fear, and frustration, you teach your children that it's okay to hit people smaller than you, yell at others, blame others when you are frightened, hurt, or frustrated. You are showing them the way you deal with your frustrations. Our children do what we do. Confronting your beliefs, behavior, and feelings about yelling and hitting opens a Pandora's box. Finding a way to express your anger and frustration without hurting your children (or anyone else) presents any parent with one of life's greatest challenges.

Parents often justify their anger by saying, "I can't help it," but acting angry is *always* a choice. After all, almost everybody can control acting out their anger with people bigger, stronger, or more powerful than they are—their bosses, for example. But defenseless children are easy targets for built-up rage and frustration that may not even have anything to do with them.

MARGIE:

I often have parents in my office who say, "I know I shouldn't hit my kids but something comes over me and I just lose control." What I say to them is that they choose to lose control because responding to their children without anger is not a high priority. But what if someone had a gun to your head and said, "The next time you get angry at your child, the next time you yell at, spank, slap, or criticize your child, I will blow your head off." Then not getting angry would have a high priority and you would *choose* not to get angry. I use this example to illustrate that we *always have a choice.*

Another belief that attempts to justify blaming anger is that it is a natural emotion. Babies express frustration and rage—but the difference is that they do not *blame* others for causing these feelings. As we were growing up, however, expressing our natural and vulnerable feelings often brought disapproval and rejection, so we learned to cover them up. Blaming anger is a secondary emotion which makes others wrong in an attempt to change their behavior, and at the same time protects us from feeling our vulnerable and painful feelings.

Anger is not protective and manipulative when the *intent* in getting angry is to discharge blaming feelings so that you can get to the vulnerable feelings, and learn from them. When anger is expressed with an intent to open and learn you do not need to express it directly to your children. You do need to get it out, which you can do alone or with the help of a friend, a spouse, or a therapist. But when you express it directly to your child, then your *intent* is to protect by trying to control your child.

Silent Anger

Covert expressions of anger are just as menacing as the outward variety. In fact, the disapproving and discounting message of covert anger, for many children, is more disturbing than being yelled at or hit. There are times when some connection, even painful contact, is preferable to no connection at all.

While the anger may be silent, that is, not outwardly expressed, it can observed in body language—arms may be folded, fists or jaws clenched, lips pressed together, eyes narrowed, head shaking, toes tapping. There is a strong negative energy and brusque manner that can be felt even if you're not looking at the person, or even if you're in a different room. If looks could kill, the person at the other end of silent anger would die. The message delivered nonverbally is "You have upset me. You have done something wrong and this is your punishment. I will remain cold toward you until you (a) change (b) make amends (c) promise never to do this again (d) all of the above. In addition, I want you to know that this is what you will get every time you transgress. So watch out."

The fear produced in a child by the silent treatment is very disturbing. Parents' love and approval is of utmost importance to children, and when parents disconnect and shut them out they feel so alone and afraid.

Sharing Hurt Feelings

Although it may not seem like it at first, sharing your hurt feelings can be, and often is, an attempt to manipulate your children's behavior. The virtues of expressing feelings have been extolled for so long that we hardly question it any more. But expressing your feelings can be blaming or nonblaming, depending on your *intent.* Blaming feelings are attempts to make your child stop the behavior that's upsetting you. For example, "You hurt my feelings" has an underlying message: "You're wrong and responsible for my feelings." Nonblaming feelings are soft, vulnerable, and are combined with an openness to learn about yourself and your child. If your intent in telling your feelings is to protect yourself ("You hurt my feelings") then you will likely get a protected, defensive response in return ("Oh, Mom, get off my back"). Your children will be protecting themselves from being controlled by you. If your intent is to learn, the interaction will be very different.

Criticism

Criticism, whether shrill or subtle, always implies that the other person is wrong. Criticism may be something like raised eyebrows, "tsk-tsking," sighing, shrugging shoulders, or shaking your head disapprovingly. Or it could be a direct verbal attack: "What on earth is wrong with you?" "How could you be so stupid?" Sarcasm and ridicule, often under the guise of humor, are frequent forms of criticism. Sarcasm and ridicule wound deeply, though the critic often denies a hostile motive. "I was only kidding—can't you take a joke?" "You're too sensitive. Don't you know when someone's joking?" Attacks on one's personhood are never funny to the person being attacked. Even when children have learned to laugh when they are the butt of a "joke," their feelings are hurt every time. Human beings are very sensitive and feelingful and it hurts to be put down.

Criticizing becomes a way of life in many families. On the surface it seems logical to us to criticize our children to improve their behavior—and sometimes it does improve, but then we're mystified by their offensive tone of voice in response, and the myriad of behaviors that often seem unrelated but are a result of the child's self-doubt.

Explanations and Lectures

Explanations and lectures are often hard to see as attempts to control because they are usually delivered with cool, rational logic in a reasonably calm tone of voice. The difference again is in the intent. If you are imparting new information that is requested or is vital to the health and safety of the child, such as not to talk to strangers, how to change a tire, etc., you are fulfilling an important responsibility as parents—to foster your children's ability to take care of themselves. This is loving behavior on your part.

However, if you are trying to persuade your children to see the error of their ways, to convince them of your opinions, to like what you like, to see things the "right" way, then your behavior is not loving; it is protective. Why? Because your *primary* concern is for yourself, not for them. It's coming from your fear. Maybe you're taking responsibility for your children because you're afraid they won't do it themselves. Giving information which your child has the freedom to reject is not controlling. However, when the intent is to manipulate then it becomes controlling.

The hope contained in explanations, along with nagging, preaching, badgering, and pestering, is to get a child to change. But what if you're right about what you're trying to get them to do or not do? It may be better for them to take piano lessons, not to take drugs, to do well in school, take a bath or a shower, brush their teeth, eat well, and so on. In cases like this, it's as important as ever to be open and loving, since attempts to control will backfire on you.

Threats

Threats come in a wide variety of shapes and sizes. As with any kind of protection, you only use the things that work, so you would never threaten a person who is financially independent with withholding money. You could, however, use this with a child. Anything that children want and need can be used to control them.

Whether delivered calmly or angrily, a threat is a threat is a threat. Here are some common examples:

- Physical violence—"If you don't get over here, I'm gonna whack you." "Shut up or I'll really give it to you." "Stop crying or I'll give you something to cry about."
- Becoming ill—"Don't get me upset, my heart can't take it." "I'm getting a headache (stomachache, ulcers, etc.) from all of this." "Darling, be a good boy and go talk to your father. Your not talking to him is killing him."
- Mental illness—"You're making me crazy." "I can't handle this anymore. I'm going to have a nervous breakdown."
- Suicide—"I feel like killing myself when you say those things to me." "I can't go on living like this."
- Emotional withdrawal—"If you don't stop, I'm not going to have anything to do with you." "I'm not going to talk to you until you stop that."
- Physical withdrawal or abandonment— "I'm going to leave this house if this

continues." "I'm not going to be around if
you continue that behavior." "Keep that
up and I'm going to send you to an
orphanage."

- Financial withholding—"If your grades
don't improve, you're not getting your
allowance for a month." "I'm not going to
support you unless you shape up."
- Exposure—"Wait until your friends (father,
teacher, mother) hear about this."
- Invoking a higher authority—"God will
punish you for that." "I'm going to tell
your father when he gets home and he'll
take care of you."

Setups for Control

Setups are the behaviors that precede attempts to control—expectations, manipulative questions, being nice,
and praise.

Expectations are how we believe our children
should behave if they really care—"If you loved me you
would . . ." Expectations, the opposite of "If I really
loved you," are certainly unloving. Expectations are
setups when you expect a particular response, then
disapprove of your child when you don't get it. Expectations are not setups when you're open to learning about
yourself when your expectations are not met (that is,
learning about why you have the expectations you do;
how and why you protect when your expectations are
not met; the very good reasons your child has for not
meeting your expectations).

A manipulative question is a demand or accusation
clothed as a question. It is often a question whose answer
is already known and judged to be wrong. After Judy
received a call from Mark's school saying he had been

absent that day, she seethed as she waited for him to come home. When Mark arrived she asked him, "How was school today?" When he answered, "Fine," she blew. He was now doubly accused of cutting school and lying. But Mark knew that if he had been honest, his mother would have been furious anyway. Judy did not really want to know and deal with the truth; she only wanted to make Mark wrong with the hope that he would stop cutting school.

Asking a question to which only one answer is acceptable is also a trap. Judy next asked Mark if he wanted to talk about what he had done. He said no and she blew up again. Since she didn't want to understand why he didn't want to talk with her, only one answer was acceptable. The question was manipulative and unloving.

Even praise, when given in an attempt to change a child's behavior, is manipulative. For months we had been trying to get eight-year-old Josh to wash his hair more often. After an infrequent wash Margie tried this one, "Your hair looks really good right now." Josh immediately and angrily responded with, "Do you mean my hair doesn't look good at other times?" Margie didn't understand why he got so angry until she realized that attached to her statement was an attempt to get Josh to change his behavior, and that was what he sensed and responded to.

Punishment

Punishment usually involves carrying out a threat. Spanking rather than threatening to spank. Taking away a privilege rather than threatening to take it away.

When you punish a child, nobody learns anything of value. Punishment does not teach children respect for their parents—what children do learn is to hate, resent, and repress.

When we (Jordan and Margie) are giving a seminar, it's about this time that red flags start to go up all over the room. Parents start waving their hands like schoolkids. "What on earth are you guys saying—that taking away privileges is some sort of crime against the kid?" "Good grief, the kid gets a ticket for drunk driving and you're saying we shouldn't take the car away?"

Well, wait a minute! That's not what we're saying. Not at all. What we *are* saying is this: There will be times when your children get into trouble at school, with the law or whatever or you will be upset by their breaking the rules that have been set for the family. The most effective, productive way to offer the guidance that is needed, and that is your responsibility to provide as a parent, is to use loving behavior instead of unloving behavior. That's all. But that's a lot. It means that you think of what's best for your child in the particular situation instead of reacting automatically to protect yourself. It means stopping to think so you can set aside your protections and be open to learning about what's going on with your son or daughter. It means being willing to risk the pain of learning things you may not want to know. It means sharing the emotions your child is going through and respecting those feelings as being as important as yours.

What we are saying is that for each upset, difficulty, or problem that comes along (and believe us, with three children of our own, we know there are many!) there is a myriad of specific solutions from which you may ultimately choose. But there is only one approach which encourages the best possible outcome—and that is to lay down your protections and consider what will nurture growth and responsibility—both for you and your children. In other words, choose loving behaviors.

This idea is really crucial and it's one of the main points of the book. We mentioned earlier that you wouldn't be finding specific solutions in this book. Coming up with solutions is sometimes appropriate, but it is often an attempt to put a band-aid on a problem so that you don't have to deal with it and learn from it. And we certainly have no intention of telling you what rules should be set for your family. We are simply proposing that *the most positive, most powerful approach that we know of is to shift our consciousness and our intent from "How can I protect myself from my painful feelings" to "How best can I be loving for others' sake as well as my own?"*

When you stop to think about it, most interactions are manipulative and unloving attempts to get others to change. There are many other strategies we could add to the list above—comparisons, complaints, humor, bribes, lies, and so on. Even praise and being nice can be subtle forms of control. If you have any trouble identifying the methods you use, ask your children to tell you.

How Do I Try to Control My Children?

The following is a checklist of some of the most common ways parents try to control their children. You may want to add other ways you try to control in your relationships.

—hitting/spanking	—complaining
—yelling	—convincing
—criticism	—being judgmental
—shaking head	—talking child out of
—irritation	feelings
—accusing	—analyzing
—sarcasm	—interrogating
—illness	—being indispensable
—lying/withholding truth	—being self-righteous

—false flattery or compliments
—giving gifts with strings attached
—taking responsibility for others
—pouting
—silent treatment
—anger
—explaining
—lecturing, moralizing
—blaming
—disapproving sighs, looks
—"tsk, tsk"
—blaming tears
—"poor me" tears
—put-downs
—telling feelings
—superior attitude
—temper tantrums
—angry withdrawal
—arguing
—bribing

Threats of:

—financial withdrawal
—emotional withdrawal
—exposure to others
—suicide
—leaving, abandonment
—illness
—violence

BELIEFS TO QUESTION: Authoritarian

- I can eventually get my children to do what I want them to do.
- The only way I'll get my children to do what I want is to make them.
- When I know I'm right, it is loving to control my children.
- My attempts to control my children will eventually earn their love and appreciation.
- My attempts to control my children can be camouflaged so that they don't know they are being manipulated.
- My anger is something that just happens. I have no control over it.
- Controlling children teaches them personal responsibility.

- Being angry is a loving thing to do if it is for the children's own good.
- There are times when hitting or yelling is necessary to get children to behave.
- I should never let children see that I am hurt or frightened.
- Parents are always right.
- There are no good reasons for children to be disrespectful.

You will find additional beliefs to question in the Appendix.

Permissive Protections

The key difference between the authoritarian and permissive positions is how you deal with your feelings in conflict. The authoritarian tries to get the child to change, so the adult doesn't have to feel the pain and fear of being upset. The permissive parents "stuff" their feelings, give up themselves, and go along with the child. Neither position comes from a belief in equality. The authoritarian believes the adult is more important. Whereas the authoritarian parents ask, in essence, for the children to give themselves up for the comfort and safety of the adult, the permissive parent does just the opposite.

The permissive adults are protecting themselves, just as are the authoritarians. However, most of the authoritarians' fears are based on the belief that if they don't stay in control, the children will do something wrong and therefore upset the parents. But the permissive parents operate from the basic fear that *they* will do something wrong. They feel guilty for being inadequate and, as a result, disregard their own needs and feelings when there is conflict with their kids. Permissive parents are afraid of putting limits on their children. ("All right, all right. I'll get you the candy. Just don't cry.")

Authoritarian parents don't listen to their children. Permissive parents don't listen to themselves. The latter also miss the children's cries for structure and organization. Children are overwhelmed when they are given the freedom to run over others' rights, or they are given no adequate role-modeling concerning how to take responsibility for their own lives.

The children of authoritarian parents don't develop personal responsibility because they're always being told what to do. But neither do the children of permissive parents, because they get no feedback on their behavior. They are allowed freedom at the parents' expense or the expense of others. This means that parents go along with something they don't believe in, becoming indifferent, or distant, withdrawing emotionally and physically.

Let's look at some of the ways permissive parents deal with conflict.

Compliance

Under the category of *compliance* are those things we do out of fear, obligation, or guilt. We became the "good boy or girl" that our parents expected us to be, and that we now expect ourselves to be. We give ourselves up to go along with what children want, either because we fear their anger or withdrawal, or we want to avoid our own guilt or fear. As Dr. Fitzhugh Dodson says in *How to Discipline with Love,* "The permissive parent may feel, 'Since I feel guilty and I'm not sure I'm doing right by you, I will try to make up for it by devoting myself to you. That way I can atone for any mistakes I am making in raising you.' The parent may fear that 'If I don't do what my child wants, he won't love me.' "

Here's a simple example of compliance: Charles, a lanky twelve-year-old, has been sprawled in front of the TV all Saturday morning. Getting hungry, he demands, "Mom, make me some lunch," then turns his attention back to the show he's watching. Reluctant to face the whining and complaining if she doesn't make lunch and fearful that Charles won't get the proper nutrition if she doesn't, Mom does as she's told. Along with these feelings, she's angry with her son for being lazy and rude and angry with herself for allowing it. Her behavior—making lunch upon demand—was unloving; it didn't foster her or Charles' emotional growth or personal responsibility.

Behaving out of desire is the opposite of compliance. Doing something out of desire is what love is. The more we behave out of desire, rather than fear, obligation, and guilt, the better we feel about ourselves and our children.

What Are the Ways I Comply?

The following checklist is designed to help you identify ways that you are compliant either because you want to avoid your children's anger or because you feel guilty.

- —I say something is okay with me when it's really not okay.
- —I go along with whatever my children want me to do.
- —I give up what I want to do.
- —I don't stand up for myself.
- —I don't make waves.
- —I do things to please my children and get confused about what I want.
- —I take the easy way out.
- —I rescue my children while ignoring my own needs.
- —I give in for now, thinking I won't have to next time.
- —I tell myself that what I want isn't important.

—I tell myself it's not worth the battle.

—I tell myself I don't deserve it.

You will find more ways to comply in the Appendix.

Indifference

Indifference is not the silent withdrawn anger which is a mechanism of control. Instead, it is, or gives the appearance of being, a withdrawal of any emotion; the parents don't—or try not to—care. These parents bury their pain and don't seem to be affected by their children's behavior. They make no attempts to change their children's behavior, but rather busy themselves in some kind of activity. Clearly, the children do not feel loved.

Parents can withdraw emotionally and numb their feelings by watching TV, reading, drinking alcohol, taking drugs, eating excessively, talking on the phone, sleeping, being preoccupied, meditating, doing housework, or by becoming ill. Parents can withdraw physically into work, sports, friends, parties, school activities, volunteer work, taking classes, or shopping.

Does this mean that all of the above activities are examples of unloving behavior? Of course not. It depends on intent. If the activity is a way of avoiding a potentially painful situation, then it is protective and unloving. Sometimes these avoidance behaviors are among the most difficult to be honest with yourself about.

Learning about our behavior—how we react to conflict, how we protect ourselves—and the consequences of that behavior can help us in all our relationships, especially the primary ones. If we find ourselves withdrawing from our children, for example, we may well question how we react in our relationship with our mates. Our reactions in conflict affect our entire lives, so the learning has a great spill-over value.

How Do I Withdraw?

Here is another checklist to help you identify possible ways you withdraw. Again, you may know other ways to add to the list.

I shut down or ignore my children in one or more of the following ways:

—work	—TV	—gambling
—drugs	—alcohol	—reading
—hobbies	—friends	—sports
—food	—sleep	—illness
—meditation	—spending	—fantasizing
—spacing out	money	—ruminating

BELIEFS TO QUESTION: Permissive

- Going along with what my children want will insure that they love me.
- I can avoid problems if I give myself up.
- Giving myself up doesn't lower my self-esteem.
- Love requires doing things that you really don't want to do.
- A good way to resolve conflicts is to give in.
- I have to comply or lose my children's love. I can't be myself and be loved by them.
- Good parents comply in order to make their children happy.
- Complying is more loving than any of the other protections.
- I can shut down my feelings and still have a loving relationship with my children.

BELIEFS TO QUESTION: Protections in General

- Our protections will eventually get us what we want.
- Our protections work to avoid pain.
- It's possible to be protected and still be loving.
- It's possible to be protected and open to learning at the same time.
- It's possible to be protected and to feel happy, loved, adequate.
- Being unprotected leaves me too vulnerable.
- If I'm open and loving, people will take advantage of me.
- Being soft and open is being weak. People will think less of me.
- Being protected feels good.
- Being protected is really taking care of myself.

Protections vs. Loving Behavior

Fortunately for families, few authoritarian parents are so completely overbearing and controlling that they cannot be bent by a despondent child. And most permissive parents are not so withdrawn that they cannot be moved by their children in times of crisis.

The summer before Todd started high school, he was tense and often angry. His parents put it down to his being a teenager, but family life was not pleasant. Todd was hard to be around and his attitude colored all the family's time together. His younger brothers were often targets of physical outbursts which were really painful because Todd was big and strong, ahead of his peers. The football coach had called to welcome Todd, who had always been on every school team. His dad had played college football and so had his grandfather. The coach, his parents, and grandparents were looking forward to Todd's high school career.

One midsummer evening, Todd came into his parents' room and sat on the end of the bed. He said nothing for a long time, so his mother spoke first.

> Mom: Well, sweetheart, are you excited about going to high school?
>
> Todd: No, I don't want to go.
>
> Mom: Why not? There's so much to look forward to with football and everything.
>
> Todd (adamantly): But I don't want to play football!
>
> Mom and Dad in unison: What?!

At this point Todd began to cry, deep sobs shaking his shoulders, as both parents watched in stunned silence.

This is a true story with its own real ending, but for illustration, let's look at one possible way the conversation might have gone from that point if the parents had chosen to stay protected, hiding their feelings behind authoritarian protections.

> (Authoritarian)
>
> Dad (urgently): Don't be ridiculous! Every red-blooded American kid wants to play football. It'll make a man out of you.
>
> Mom (wheedling): Look, honey, this is nothing to cry about. That's just silly. You're too old to cry. You'll like it once you get started. Stop being such a worrywart.

In this scenario, both parents attempted to avoid facing their upsetting feelings and disappointment by trying to force their son into doing what they wanted him to. They used criticism and ridicule. They assumed they had more important information about the situation than he did. They denied the importance of his feelings and didn't even ask why he didn't want to play. The important questions to ask at this point are: How does Todd feel after their conversation? How does he feel about his parents and what is his attitude toward sports likely to be?

Here's another possible ending with the parents acting out permissive protections.

(Permissive)

Dad (withdrawn, unemotional): Oh well, whatever. It's your life.

Mom (tears in her eyes): It doesn't matter to me. Football isn't important anyway. It's late—you'd better go on to bed.

In this case, both parents withdrew from the boy, gave up their own feelings, and attempted to show that his behavior didn't affect them or that the issue was no longer important. Again, the question to ask is: How does Todd feel now? Does he feel loved and respected? Does he feel better about the situation and himself? Close to his parents? Was there any learning involved?

Both the authoritarian and permissive responses were unloving behaviors. Certainly Todd did not feel loved; also, there was no growth for the parents or child.

Fortunately, this true story had a different ending. Let's pick up where we left off.

Todd sat with his shoulders shaking, sobbing quietly.

Mom (tears in her eyes at the sight of her son's pain): Are you too old for a hug?

Todd leaned over against her. Dad reached out and patted his hair.

Dad (softly): I thought you wanted to play football.

Todd: I just didn't want to disappoint you. I know how everybody's been counting on it—even you, Mom.

Mom: I guess that's true. But it's also true that I never wanted you to be unhappy.

Dad: I'm confused though—is there some special reason you don't want to play?

Todd: Well, to tell the truth, I just don't like it. I've always liked all the other sports better and I can't see playing a game I don't really like.

Dad: I wish I'd known sooner so I could have gotten used to the idea, but . . .

Todd: But what . . . ?

Dad: But if you're that unhappy, well, I love you a lot more than I love football.

Todd: What about you, Mom?

Mom: Well, I admit I was looking forward to your football too. But I'd never choose for you to be this miserable. You make your own choices and let me handle my own feelings about football.

Todd (smiling with an obvious sense of relief): Are you guys sure?

Mom and Dad: We're sure.

Actually, at the time of this incident these parents hadn't yet been introduced to the idea of protected behaviors. However, Todd's pain was such overwhelming evidence of his need that they were compelled to put their own protections aside and react to their overriding love for their son. They were honest about their own feelings, but were supportive, open, and loving.

Todd's reaction would have been very different if his parents had stayed closed to him. What happens when parents remain protected? The consequences of protections will be discussed in the next chapter.

·4·

Life Isn't Turning Out the Way
I Thought It Would

The Consequences of Protections

*Pain is the ransom you have gladly paid
not to be free.*

A Course in Miracles

Cheeks flushed from fresh air, twelve-year-old Doug burst
into the family room, grabbed some popcorn, and
plopped down on the couch next to his father Jim to
watch a basketball game.

"Where have you been?" Jim asked.

"Outside playing."

"I told you to do your homework."

"I will in a minute."

" 'In a minute' isn't good enough. I told you to do
it now and that's what I meant!"

"I can handle my own homework, Dad."

"No, you can't. If you could, you would have
finished it already like I told you to." (Silence for a
moment.) "Can't you eat that popcorn with your mouth
shut? Look, you've dropped some on the carpet too.
What's the matter with you, anyway?"

Expressionless and without comment, Doug got up,
put the popcorn on the sink, and started to leave the
room. "Wait a minute," said his Dad, "aren't you going
to watch the game? I, uh . . . really like having you
around."

"Oh yeah? Well, you sure have a funny way of showing it!" Doug said, and he left quietly, closing the door.

Jim had completely different expectations for this interaction than what actually happened. He had deep loving feelings for his son and didn't realize that his protective behaviors came across as unloving. But Jim's behavior was what his son experienced and what his son felt. Behavior plus the words and tone of voice that go with it are all that anybody can respond to in a relationship.

What were the consequences of Jim's behavior in this case? Doug vacillated between actions of compliance and resistance and feelings of indifference and resentment. Jim felt powerless, dissatisfied, unhappy, and confused. All of this is typical of the consequences of protective, unloving behavior—behavior that has its origins in faulty beliefs and fear.

The questions of importance here are not whether Doug should do his homework or keep popcorn off the carpet. The questions are: Is Jim's behavior successful in making these happen? Are Jim's sarcasm, and judgmental comments helping Doug become more responsible? Is Doug growing from this experience? Does Doug feel loved? Does Jim feel good about taking the apparent position of power over his son? And just what do these protective behaviors, initiated by the parents and responded to by the children—what do these unloving behaviors produce? That is the most important question.

Parents want children to be respectful and caring about them and others. When you treat children with respect they will be respectful. When you don't respect their feelings, wants, desires, interests, thoughts, and needs, they certainly will not learn to respect yours or others'. If you believe they should respect you just because you're older or because you're the parent, then you will probably attempt to teach them to respect you with punishment, lectures, threats, insults, criticism, and so forth. But you cannot teach your children to respect you by behaving disrespectfully towards them. They may learn to *act* respectfully out of fear or guilt but that will last only as long as they fear you or feel guilty. Genuine respect flows from feeling understood, cared about, and respected.

There is no one way that every child will respond, given a particular way of being treated. Some adults survive horrendous childhoods and grow up functioning very well; others become incapacitated. But on a deep psychological level every child is affected. The truth is that whenever you disrespect your children by hitting, yelling, humiliating or ignoring, you are teaching them to avoid you, fear you, and/or hate you. The scars from childhood, even when not shown outwardly, show up most often in the ability or inability to give and receive love.

Power

All our behavior patterns start with the issue of power. It's a big word, power, and it inspires feelings of longing or fear. "I want power" or "I'm afraid I don't have it" are two common expressions of these feelings. The issue of power goes very deep, as deep as the level of survival itself. People want power not just over themselves and their own choices, but power over not being hurt or controlled by another person—that's where the fear comes in. It's the power over not being abandoned, rejected, or dominated by another person. In other words, what we all want is not just the power to go to sleep when we want to or do homework when we want to, but the power to protect our own integrity, our own wholeness.

But what really happens is this: as children we don't have the power to do just what we want to do for ourselves, so we want to have power over other people to make them do what we want. This way we can gain the sense of getting what we need. We also want to protect ourselves against others' having power over us. We wouldn't get into these patterns if we didn't come up against people who not only tell us what to do, but threaten to abandon us, to pull their love away.

When we're young, the issue is one of real physical survival, instead of just emotional survival. Very young children can't survive without their parents, so in the earliest stages it's a dilemma of "How much can I pull away from my parents without losing their love—and my life?" Later on, the child, whether a toddler or a teenager or somewhere in between, wants power over the parents so their love can't be pulled away. Also, they want power over their own individuality.

Interestingly, animals don't have this problem. Lacking rational thought, they have no need to protect the psychological integrity of the self, and therefore no need to try to control other animals (except in defense of physical attack). It's trying to control others that trips up us humans (I want power over others) or it is complying with another's control demand (I'm afraid of being me because I might lose your love. I'll give in so you don't reject me).

When we, as adults or children, attempt to control others in order to get power, or when we give in and comply for fear of losing love, we are protecting ourselves in either case. Our behaviors are defensive. And everyone controls, resists, or complies at different times. Nobody is all one way. Even children who appear compliant will resist in some way.

Alex, a sixteen-year-old high school junior, wanted to take five classes, but was told by the school counselor that he had to take six classes because that was school policy. Knowing full well that he would have more than enough units to graduate, Alex agreed to take the sixth class, but then he confided at home that he would fail it on purpose. Alex was resistant, finding a way to maintain his sense of control. Resistance is not doing what someone wants you to do, by refusing, finding a way around it, doing it badly, not on time, too slowly, etc. Another way to resist is to comply in one area, but to resist in another.

People are not born protective; each of us is born loving and open with the intention to learn, but we lose sight of it in our instinctual need to survive, and become separate and independent. This is critical to our development. The first word a baby learns to use to assert independence is No! He or she learns that before Yes. Freedom to say Yes comes more easily from the freedom to say No.

If parents, teachers, and older siblings were perfect, little kids wouldn't need to learn to protect. If everyone could love and support the child completely and let go of attempts to control at the same time, the child wouldn't need to develop the kind of protective behaviors that protect against loss of self and loss of love.

Power Struggles: The Consequences of Authoritarian Responses

The dilemma posed in the question "Do I have to give up me to be loved by you?" is essentially an issue of power and is played out each time you attempt to control your child. (Please remember that *control* does not mean that you cannot or should not guide your children or teach, inform, or keep them safe.) The way a child reacts depends on the personality of both the child and the parent. Some children give themselves up completely to highly controlling parents, while others passively resist or defiantly rebel. Some children give themselves up even when their parents are not extremely controlling. (There are factors beyond our current understanding which determine the personality of a child before birth.)

Almost all children will resist in some area. The basic premise is that by resisting, they won't be totally swallowed up by the parents. It may seem to the parents that their children are arguing over a simple, silly point, and they often express amazement at the intensity of the children's reactions. Little do they know that for the child, integrity is at stake.

Steve, age fourteen, was reminded that he would be required to go to an upcoming holiday party which the whole family had attended for several years. He reacted with a temper tantrum, stamping, tears, finally yelling, "You can't make me!"

Completely taken aback by his unusual reaction because other years he'd gone willingly, his mother thought, "Something else is going on here." Not sure what it was, but taking a guess, she said calmly to her son, "I have an idea. How about this—I won't force you to go and then you can choose to go or not to go." Steve's emotional outburst stopped immediately. "Okay," he said calmly, "I guess I'll go." When he was given the power to choose, he had no more need to fight.

Almost anything you want from your children can become fuel for a power struggle: cleaning their rooms, being polite, being neat and clean, getting themselves dressed, reading the books you'd like them to, listening to the kind of music you like, coming in on time, etc.

We (Jordan and Margie) began learning about power struggles from our first child, Eric. Eric had a strongly developed personality from birth and was not destined to be an easy-going, docile child. Being new parents, we weren't trained to recognize the obvious signs that could have helped us understand Eric and ourselves better. We plunged into our new job believing things would just work out. Margie retired from her teaching position, excited to raise our son. A dream she had had from childhood was finally a reality. What a shock it was when the dream started to turn into a nightmare.

Feeling responsible for Eric's upbringing, Margie launched into a training program, teaching Eric reading, schedules, and anything else a child needed to learn. There was only one problem—Eric didn't like to be taught. He wanted to learn on his own. He wanted to do things his way.

They started to battle—Eric not wanting to be controlled, and Margie determined not to give in. Jordan would often return home from teaching school to find Margie exhausted on the couch having just "won" a battle with Eric. Eric began to pull away from Margie more and more. He didn't want her to be affectionate with him. She was devastated, and we began to have long talks about what was going on between them.

Nothing in our backgrounds or reading had helped us understand the issue of a child's need for independence and how to effectively handle the conflicts that would occur on a daily basis As we began to try to understand Eric's point of view, as well as Margie's fears and beliefs and the consequences of her attempts to control him, Margie was able to ease up and allow Eric to be himself more. Eric, at age two and a half, helped us when at one point in his favorite story, *Green Eggs and Ham* by Dr. Seuss, he repeated the words of his favorite character. "Mommy," he said, "you let me be."

Subsequently we learned that what has been done can be undone. It took a long time for the scars of those battles to heal as Eric remained angry and distant from

Margie. But patience, love, and understanding led to a better and better relationship, which today has an affection and warmth that never would have been possible had the power struggles continued.

A power struggle is like a tug-of-war with each participant at either end of the rope, neither side wanting to give in, to lose. Power struggles can only exist when both people participate. When one side drops the rope, the battle ends. In power struggles one person often sees the other as wrong and only wants to get that person to change without taking responsibility for his or her own end of the struggle. For example, let's say that I throw out a line with a hook on the end. You grab onto the hook and we get stuck in a terrible struggle. I'm pulling and you're resisting. After a while, you angrily yell at me, "You know, if you hadn't thrown out this line we wouldn't be having this problem!" And you would be right. But if I said to you, "I could throw out this line all day long and if you didn't grab onto it, we wouldn't be in this dilemma either," I would also be right.

It takes two people to create a power struggle. Accusations and attempts to get another to change only bring about defensiveness. Your intention to learn about your part in the difficulty (why you throw out the hook and why you won't let go once you're caught) creates an entirely different interaction and eventually leads to some meaningful changes. Your intention to learn about your part of the difficulty (why you grab onto the hook and why you won't let go once you're stuck) is also possible and creates a deepening of our relationship. Since the bottom line of the struggle is losing one's integrity, the sense of mortal combat that pervades the interaction is understandable.

The basic difference in the parent-child relationship and the adult-adult relationship is that children, especially at a young age, can't take the power because they're dependent on the parent. The adult is never dependent in that way. Parents can choose to take that power or give it away. However, if they give it away, they can take it back at any time. If the parent wants and keeps the power, the child can't take it because the child needs the parent.

Behavior often makes no sense at all until seen as a power struggle, as in the above incident with Steve and his mother. A similar struggle occurred between Jordan and Josh. One very muggy summer's evening Jordan told Josh, then two years old, to take off his heavy flannel pajama top so he would sleep more comfortably. Josh said no. Jordan calmly and logically explained to him that on such a warm night he would be more comfortable without his top. Josh could not be budged. Jordan got a little irritated with this resistance and told Josh in no uncertain terms to take off the top. Josh steadfastly refused. Jordan, armed with the adult knowledge that anyone in his right mind would agree with his suggestion, got really angry at Josh's stupidity, but the little guy just lay down in his crib and cried. Jordan, knowing that Josh wouldn't bend to his will, and unwilling to physically force the issue, left Josh's room beaten, shaking his head in disbelief.

Years later when discussing power struggles, the incident was recalled and we realized that Josh had taken a position and that his own integrity was the issue of that interaction. He had chosen to assert his will. He would rather be uncomfortable than controlled. Seen only in the light of rational logic regarding comfort, Josh's behavior made no sense at all, but seen in the light of a power struggle and the issue of integrity, his behavior was perfectly rational and understandable.

One way to know you're in a power struggle is when a seemingly simple request, often one that would be in the child's best interest, is repeatedly not complied with or refused. Requests to make a bed, clean a room, take out the trash, feed an animal, help carry in the groceries are often met with passive or overt resistance. Another sign of a power struggle is when you hear that your child has performed one of those same tasks quite willingly at someone else's home.

When in a power struggle, to change one's behavior is to give in, so "come hell or high water" your child is not going to do your bidding. Even when the request is something a child might want to do or is in his or her best interest, he or she won't if it feels like losing. When not in a power struggle, the child is free to do what you want out of caring for you, or out of a real desire to do it.

JORDAN AND MARGIE:
A friend was amazed one day when we asked Eric, then fourteen years old, to clean up his room because we were having guests and he gave a cheery okay and went about the task. Our friend said, "How come you don't get any resistance from him? If I asked my son to do that, he would have grumbled and I would have had to remind him over and over to get the job done." "For one thing," Margie said, "Eric knows that he has the right to say no and I won't bug him or punish him. He's just like me. I learned a long time ago that it's very hard for me to feel like saying yes unless I have the freedom to say no without someone getting angry with me. If Eric had said no, we would have spent some time understanding each other's needs so that this problem could have been resolved. I rarely get a no, however, because we're not in a power struggle."

The strength of a power struggle becomes apparent when dramatic behavior changes occur once a power struggle is broken. Behavior that was impossible to attain while in a power struggle becomes easy. Miraculous behavior changes—being on time, neatness, studying, being responsible for oneself—often occur when a power struggle no longer exists.

MARGIE:

Janet and her ten-year-old daughter Joanna came to see me for therapy because Joanna was continuing to wet her bed. As I talked with them, it became apparent that Joanna was angry and tense much of the time because Janet was consistently on her back to do her homework and clean her room. Joanna did keep her room fairly clean, but refused to do her homework and was doing poorly in school.

I explored with Janet the very good reason she had for wanting control over her daughter in these areas. She told me that she was afraid that if she didn't keep after Joanna, she would do even worse in school and that her room would be a pigsty. We explored Janet's fears of what people would think of her, a teacher and mother, if her daughter did badly in school and if they saw her daughter's messy room. After deep exploration and understanding her fears, Janet felt less afraid and, although she realized it wouldn't be easy, agreed to let go of all attempts to control Joanna to see what would happen.

When they came in four weeks later, Joanna was a different child. She seemed relaxed and happy. The bedwetting was rapidly improving, and lo and behold, she was doing her homework on her own! Not only that, but she was enjoying the good feelings she was getting from doing well, thereby becoming self-motivated. It was now becoming important to her to do well in school, which wasn't happening when she needed to resist being under her mother's control.

Her room, however, truly was a pigsty. But, she stated firmly, "I like it that way." Janet, pleased with the improvement in bedwetting and homework, had decided she could live with Joanna's messy room if the door was kept closed.

Months later, Janet called to tell me that Joanna had finally gotten sick of the mess and had started to clean her room on her own.

The request that initiates a power struggle is often reasonable, and your child's refusal may make no sense to you. You may then try to explain logically why you feel as you do and why you want what you want. Your child's continued resistance may then bring out your heavy artillery—threats, yelling, hitting . . . but nothing works. You become increasingly frustrated, hurt, and angry. What's your option? Keep trying? Give up? Unfortunately, neither will work. You can't give up wanting what you want and to keep trying entrenches your child into deeper resistance. The solution comes when your INTENT changes, moving from your protective intent into being open to learning.

Breaking power struggles is difficult because they are often subtle and reactions have become automatic: you want, they resist, you push harder. There is only one way that change comes about without creating a power struggle—to continue to want what you want, but when you don't get it, to explore why not and why what you want is so important to you. This exploration process will be described in later chapters.

When Children Resist

Resisting attempts to be controlled by a parent or other adult in authority, a child becomes locked in the power struggle. The resistance may be an overt or passive rebellion, or both, first one and then another. Often a resistant pattern emerges that dominates the child's personality. Passively resistant people rarely make decisions for themselves, but when others make decisions or want something from them, they resist. Highly resistant personalities have a difficult time becoming successful at anything, since their resistance occurs with anyone who is an authority figure—teacher, boss, doctor, or whoever.

Common family patterns find firstborn children to be more overt in their resistance and second children to be more passive resisters. The passive resister often agrees to do things, but somehow never gets around to it. Whether passive or aggressive, however, when adults or children resist, they often lose touch with what they want, focusing only on what the other person wants. They resist in order not to be controlled, but never ask "What do I really want?" When children do the opposite of what someone wants, especially when it's something they really would like to do, they become controlled by their own attempts *not* to be controlled. An example can be seen in those groups of young people who choose to dress in a certain way to be different from what is currently popular with the "mainstream" kids. However, their dress code is stricter and more limited than that of the general population.

Children resist when they fear losing themselves and being controlled, mostly by their parents. Children find many ways to resist their parents' control. Often they will choose an area where they will take a stand, saying with their behavior, "Here you cannot control me. Here you can't make me give in." For example, children learn early that they alone have control over their bowels. Some refuse to become toilet-trained, while others will train themselves with no help. There's nothing a parent can do about it other than *let go of control,* which is the message of the behavior. Another common area where children resist is with food. Obesity and anorexia are often symptoms of resistance. The child is saying, "You can't make me eat," or "You can't make me stop eating."

Any behavior the parent can't physically control can become the place where a child takes a stand. You can't force a child to sleep, eat, go to the bathroom, do homework, learn in school, and so on. Children of controlling parents who feel the need to avoid feelings of helplessness will find some way to resist, generally in an area that is important to the parent.

Ultimately, the resistance will transfer to others— teachers, employers, friends, and later, mates. When children lack high self-esteem, their resistant behavior may become self-destructive. Overeating, undereating, not going to sleep when tired, doing poorly in school, taking drugs or drinking, and being unsuccessful in jobs are common results of resistant/rebellious patterns.

Very often it is our children's protective behavior that we try to change with our own protective behavior. Yet all we succeed in doing is creating a vicious cycle where we continue to model the behavior that we are trying to get the child to change.

When Children Comply

Children who basically give in to attempts to being controlled lose themselves and become weak, compliant adults. These are often the children who are applauded for their fine behavior. These "good little girls and boys" often become the adults who have lost touch with their intuition, their inner sense of knowing what's right for them. While parents are often delighted with their "good" little boy or girl, being good is often the way a child learns to protect against being rejected and in pain. The "good" child is often numb inside, out of contact with what he or she feels. Overly good children usually have shut down their own pain to avoid upsetting their parents. They are so frightened of their parents' reactions to conflict, and of being rejected as a result, that they act as if everything is just fine. They are the children who grow up not having a sense of their own identity, not knowing what they need or want, having to look to another to tell them what to think or do. To some extent that's each of us, but in the extreme, these are the kind of children who may become slavishly attached to gurus, whether spiritual, religious, or military, to whom they can turn over their lives in the hope of finding the right way to be. As one young man said who joined a commune, "Now I don't have to think. They give me all the answers."

Whether the children are resistant or compliant, developing their own sense of right and wrong will be difficult if they're always told what to do. As Alice Miller says in *For Your Own Good:*

> Since authoritarian parents are always right, there is no need for their children to rack their brains in each case to determine whether what is demanded of them is right or not. And how is this to be judged? Where are the standards supposed to come from if someone has always been told what was right and what was wrong and if he never had an opportunity to become familiar with his own feelings and if, beyond that, attempts at criticism were unacceptable to the parents and thus were too threatening for the child? If an adult has not developed a mind of his own, then he will find himself at the mercy of the authoritarian for better or worse, just as an infant finds itself at the mercy of its parents. Saying no to those more powerful will always seem too threatening to him.

Resistant/rebellious and compliant children suffer from a lack of self-confidence. The message they continually get from the attempts to control their behavior is "You're not okay." They don't feel loved or respected.

Their needs and feelings are not truly considered because the primary motive that has guided family interactions has been to satisfy the parents' needs and feelings. This may seem harsh, but when you're upset and you try to coerce your children to stop what they're doing, you're not concerned with their feelings or the compelling reasons they have for behaving as they are. Your primary motive is to get rid of your upsetting feelings. And on the other hand, when your children are behaving badly and you ignore them by reading the paper, your intent is the same—to protect yourself from the conflict. In either case the children feel uncared for.

When children feel uncared for, they will almost always eventually feel uncaring toward others. They may *act* in caring ways out of fear, guilt, or obligation, or because they've learned that it makes them feel good to behave in caring ways toward others, but they usually don't really *feel* caring toward those who have not cared—or acted in a caring way—about their thoughts and feelings.

As these children grow to adulthood, many feel guilty because they don't feel loving toward their parents, especially as their parents get older. It's unrealistic to expect children to feel loving and caring toward their parents when they haven't been treated with love, respect, and care. Unfortunately, it becomes poignantly confusing to the elder parents. "I took good care of Johnny for twenty years and this is the thanks I get." "I lived my life for Mary and now she hardly ever even calls me." Emotional blackmail—"I'll be nice to you so you'll love me when I'm old"—is not the point here. Here's the real issue: If your intent is to be loving to both yourself and your children rather than protect yourself, as much as is possible, the outcome will be an ongoing loving relationship for both of you, parents and children of all ages.

Consequences for the Controlling Parent

When things go the way you want them to, being an authoritarian or controlling parent may seem like a wonderful idea. Unfortunately, it's something like trying to keep a lid on a pot full of water that's getting hotter and starting to boil. The consequences of the power struggles created by a control/resistance cycle are awful. When children are overtly resistant, their anger comes out in shouting, sarcasm, defiance, and a generally disrespectful mouth. Children learn from their parents (as well as from their peers and TV) how to control. Temper tantrums, withdrawal, sarcasm, threats, criticism—kids have learned them all by the time they're five years old. Parents and children get into terrible, emotionally wounding verbal battles. As a child gets older, even physical battles may occur. The angry tension and hurt leave all parties resentful and feeling justified in seeking revenge. Going back to the Archie Bunker family, we can recall some vivid scenes of shouting matches, fist-shaking, door-slamming, and in Edith's case, withdrawal. The characters' lines were funny, but the painful feelings were loud and clear.

When children are more passive in their resistance, the environment is peaceful on the surface but an uncomfortable air of tension pervades the household. Although passively resistant children seem agreeable to their parents' wishes, they may never fulfill their promises or may do things behind their parents' backs that are usually worse than what the parents were upset about in the first place. For example, the sweet little girl who gets pregnant ("We didn't even know she was going out with boys"); the straight-A "perfect" young man who is found out to be the school drug dealer ("But I never took any of those drugs—it was strictly business"); the quiet, average kid who is one of the many regular customers of the young entrepreneur in the previous example ("He did seem to get a little quiet in the last couple of years. In fact, he doesn't talk to us at all. But we thought it was just a phase he was going through"); the all-American sports hero who is cheating to get through his academic classes ("Big deal, I'm going to sign a professional contract and make more money than all those lousy teachers put together"). Teenage suicide is the deadly extreme.

Being in control is a terrible burden for parents, since they must always be on guard, worried that their child won't be safe or do the "right" thing unless they're around. Taking more responsibility than is necessary, the authoritarian/controlling parents become saddled with children who do not take responsibility for their own lives. Dr. Ross Campbell, in *How to Really Love Your Child,* writes, "What do you think enables a happy, well-adjusted teenager to control his behavior? His conscience. If you want to prevent your child from developing a normal responsive conscience which will enable him to *control himself,* build your relationship with him on a punitive basis."

Authoritarian parents often wind up feeling unloving toward their children when their children's rebellious behavior leads them into negative patterns. The parents often blame their children's friends, the society, school system, or just about anyone else but themselves. Nevertheless, we *all* are accountable as parents, by our choice to bring these new lives into being. So we must answer questions like the following: "What was my part in the development of this child's poor self-esteem so that he wasn't able to withstand peer pressures and went against what would have made him feel good about himself?" "What was my part in creating an environment where my children felt they couldn't come and share with me their fears, difficulties, and actions?" "Were my children rebelling against my attempts to control them?"

Parents need to understand that attempts to control children's behavior are disrespectful, since such attempts discount the very important reasons that children, just like adults, have for their behavior. When we attempt to control our children, they do not feel understood and cared for, even when we think we are doing it in their best interests. The more we control, the more problems we create.

It's impossible to completely avoid trying to control your children. However, the fewer attempts (reserved for really important issues, primarily health and safety), the greater the chances your children will listen and comply without injuring their self-esteem or your relationship.

Consequences of Permissive Responses

Consequences for the Child

We have all witnessed many examples of children who are allowed to "freely express themselves." The labels used to describe these children are "spoiled," "self-centered," "selfish," "brats." Basically, no one wants to be around them. These children have not learned to respect the rights of others because their parents were doormats and didn't allow the children to see how their behavior affected them. Or perhaps the parents assumed the role of victim and used their own hurt feelings as attempts to manipulate the children. Then the kids learned to disregard their parents' feelings, understanding on their own level that the display of feelings was an attempt to control them.

Children who are treated permissively—that is, whose parents have chosen to avoid conflict and confrontation as a way of protecting themselves—feel no responsibility for the effect their behavior has on others. They feel no responsibility in the family, and as long as their parents give in to their needs, they take no responsibility for fulfilling their own needs.

The sad reality is that even though many times permissive parents believe they are giving love, the child feels unloved and unimportant. To feel important, children need to know that their behavior affects their parents, that their behavior matters to them.

Consequences for the Permissive Parent

Some permissive parents choose to meet conflict by giving themselves up and complying with their children's demands and desires. Eventually these compliant parents almost always feel resentful and used by their children. Children who run over the rights of others become tyrants. Kids are amazingly perceptive and quickly learn the surest ways to tap into their parents' fear and guilt. Because so many parents are afraid of doing the wrong thing, children can often control their parents through guilt. Parents feel like slaves to their own children. Children who don't take much responsibility for their lives make their parents responsible and parents who accept that responsibility feel overburdened.

Parents of self-centered children feel unloved because their children don't care about their parents' needs. Why don't they care? *Because these children have not learned how to be loving. They haven't learned to balance what they need with the wants and needs of others.*

When a parent's compliance is accompanied by a hidden agenda, and it very often is, then it is a manipulation. Let's say that a twelve-year-old stands over his mother, asleep in bed on Saturday morning, and says loudly, "I'm hungry, Mom. Get up!" If Mom complies and gets up, even though she still wants to sleep, then her expectation, although it may be subconscious, is "I'm going to give in to your desires and I expect you to appreciate and love me for this and to give in to mine." When this expectation is not met, and it often isn't, since manipulations of any kind are usually met with resistance, the parent feels betrayed.

The anxiety of compliant/permissive parents increases as their children get more and more out of control. They feel helpless to do anything about it. At this point, the parents most often move in one direction or another, either becoming more authoritarian or more indifferent.

Permissive parents who become indifferent numb themselves so they won't feel their deep fear and sadness. The negative consequences of not feeling are that life becomes routine, meaningless, boring, without love. You pass through this life without really living it—cutting your losses, but minimizing any gains. You believe you have your life under control as long as there are no major problems.

If catastrophe doesn't occur, indifferent people go to their graves in passive anonymity—life has passed them by. But few people escape so easily (if that can be considered easy). Since we ultimately have control only over what we do and *not* over others and life in general, we are almost certain to be hit by some catastrophe. Indifferent parents are often jolted into reality by finding out that their child has been arrested for drug use, has run away from home, is failing in school, or doesn't want anything to do with them.

By the time an indifferent person wakes up, it's often too late to repair the damage done by a lifetime of denial and uninvolvement. There's a great deal of sadness in all the consequences of protections, but people with more active forms of protections have a much greater chance of confronting the negative consequences of their protections than the unaware, pathetic, indifferent person.

The Biggest Negative Consequence of All

The worst thing that comes from our protections is that we feel awful about ourselves. That may seem like too strong a statement, but that's only because we've lost touch with really feeling good.

Recall times when you've felt your best. Chances are you'll recall times when you felt free, expansive, open—perhaps on a vacation, falling in love, walking on the beach at sunset, creating something special, making love, helping someone in need. We feel best when we're in the present moment, free from anxiety, not needing to make something happen, not attached to some outcome.

Now recall how you feel when you're protected—angry, blaming, self-righteous, victimized, compliant, shut down.

Sometimes it feels awful to be protected, sometimes it feels okay, but it never feels great. When protected, we never feel good about ourselves, proud of ourselves, dignified, wholesome, lovable, or worthwhile.

People feel best about themselves when they stay balanced, not reacting but coming from their centers, from their Higher Selves. When you get tense, give yourselves up, or shut down, you lose your balance. Being centered is like being an expert skiier, flowing down a hill, moving past each obstacle with grace and balance. Those who are not expert skiiers know what happens when you tense up on a steep slope. You get off center; nothing works right and it doesn't feel good.

The best feelings occur when, no matter what's going on around us, we maintain our openness, our softness, our sense of self, our sense of personal power. When we maintain our center we are peaceful, soft and strong. We don't need to control others, nor do we give ourselves up. That's real strength—inner strength. We feel like our own hero.

Thus the weightiest negative consequence of our protections is loss of our own self-esteem.

The Protected Family

Protections devastate the family unit. All the dreams of a happy, fulfilling family lie smoldering in the remains of protected, unloving interactions. When people don't feel safe with each other, the atmosphere is tense and guarded. It is impossible to express yourself freely, to have spontaneous times of fun and play. Intimacy, which also requires feeling cared about, is equally absent.

Because power struggles prevent the resolution of conflicts, irritations or battles continue to occur over the same issues. The family may splinter as the children grow older, or remain together in the form of a family, but there is little joy in being together.

When the INTENT to learn is absent, no one grows emotionally or spiritually from the family interactions. Neither parents who react to conflict with controlling or permissive responses, nor children who react by resisting/ rebelling, controlling or complying, learn anything of value about themselves. The family, potentially our greatest source of love, learning, and growth, becomes the force children have to get away from to feel good about themselves and to develop their unique potential and personalities.

Protections: Negative Consequences for the Parents

The following is a list of some of the negative consequences of protections. Check those that apply to you.

—Power struggles
—Feeling a lack of caring about your children
—Your children not caring about you
—Your children often being angry or irritable with you
—Often feeling angry or irritable with your child

—Your child is often resistant, defiant, rebellious
—Frequent hassles over things like chores, homework, cleanliness
—Feeling helpless to deal with your children
—Emotional distance between you and your children
—Feeling inadequate as a parent
—Feeling unloved, unworthy, low self-esteem
—Feeling tension, fear, anxiety, frustration, anger, or guilt
—Feeling depression, deadness, apathy, sadness, boredom
—Feeling manipulated, rejected

Protections: Negative Consequences for the Children

The following is a partial list of the negative consequences for children when parents remain protected.

—Power struggles
—Feeling controlled by your parents
—Feeling the weight of obligations to your parents
—Feeling emotionally shut down or dead around your parents
—Unable to talk to your parents
—Feeling rejected by your parents
—Feeling inadequate in your parents' eyes
—Feeling angry or irritated with your parents
—Feeling misunderstood by your parents
—Feeling unloving toward your parents
—Feeling unloved by your parents
—Being alone, feeling isolated
—Feeling low self-esteem, inadequate, unlovable

—Repeating similar patterns in other relationships
—Doing poorly in school
—Feeling fearful, lacking confidence
—Being self-abusive or abusive with other people/things

What's Done Can Be Undone

As we worked on this chapter, we found ourselves getting more and more concerned that you, the reader, might feel overwhelmed and hopeless. The constant beat of the message has certainly been negative. When you have looked at how much of your behavior has been unloving because you have been acting out your protections, it can be truly depressing. What you had labeled "for their own good" can now be understood as "what I wanted," for the most part. But here's the good news: removing our heads from the sand and confronting the negative consequences of our protective, unloving behaviors can motivate us to work toward changing these negative patterns. With the new and deeper understanding of the dynamics of the relationship between you and your children, all these symptoms can be resolved. Things that have come to be accepted as normal in family relations—teenage rebellion, kids who don't talk to their parents, children who don't feel understood and feel unloved, kids who don't enjoy being with their parents—do not have to happen.

As parents, you are certainly not totally responsible for the way your children turn out. Children are greatly affected by their interactions with siblings, peers, teachers, television, outside family members and other authority figures. And, of course, there is the factor of one's inborn nature and the choices each child makes which affect everything as well. But in most cases, parents are the primary influence in the children's development since their love and approval are so crucial to the children's self-esteem, and since they are the primary models.

Because of these things, and because you hand down so many of your protections to your children, which they in turn take with them into their primary adult relationships, resolving your own protectiveness is of the utmost importance. You have the power to redirect your family interactions from the path of protective, unloving behaviors to the path of open and loving behavior. Changing your intent changes the consequences of the interactions both within your existing family and in future families. But you must start within yourselves. How to do this? A good first step is to look at the fears and faulty beliefs that get in the way of your own natural ability to be the loving parent you hope to be.

·5·

What Am I So Afraid Of?

Exploring Fears and the Beliefs behind Them

Fear has a thousand voices.
A thousand reasons why,
A thousand ways to bind us,
But fear always lies.
> –Robbie Gass
> "Trust in Love"

The opposite of love is not hate—it is fear. It's fear that keeps people from being open and loving, because when afraid they close up to protect themselves. Many would deny they have these fears; many are simply unaware. Yet those fears *are* there, lying buried, unacknowledged, subconscious. And in addition, these fears, or the shadow of them projected into our consciousnesses, dominate our lives.

In *Walking on Air,* a television play by the brilliant, imaginative Ray Bradbury, a young boy wants to go on a space flight with the astronauts. There are two major obstacles in his way. One is that he is in a wheelchair. The other is his parents' fear. The science teacher who has been encouraging the idea receives clearance from NASA and calls together the boy and his parents. At the turning point of the play, the boy's mother speaks: "I used to be full of fear—fear that he couldn't get around every corner. But finally I discovered that he made it around most of those corners fine without me. Our son can go.'' Her husband nods his approval. As the play ends, the tearful but joyous parents watch their son perform maneuvers outside the spaceship, for, of course, he needs no wheelchair when he can walk on air.

This story is a beautiful example of the way we believe the process works, confronting and learning about fears, and then choosing loving behavior.

Perhaps one of the special gifts handicapped children can give is an opportunity for parents to see their own fears plainly, confront and learn about them, and understand their own upsetting feelings. You cannot fail to recognize a child on crutches, but when a child has an emotional weakness—or when you are part of creating that very weakness or when you retard a child's growth due to your own fear—that's much harder to see.

In many areas of our lives we operate from a basis of fear. Sometimes our fears have to do with ourselves— our adequacy, lovability, fear of failure, of being wrong, of being out of control, fear of pain. Sometimes our fears have to do with our kids—their capabilities, achievement, fear of being rejected by them, fear for their safety. For two very important reasons this book emphasizes what parents need to learn about themselves. First, most of us don't know we have those fears or how much they affect us as parents. Second, very often it is our own fears—the fears for ourselves, not the fears about our children—that create the biggest obstacle to our loving behavior.

Where Does Fear Come From?

Although we all have instinctual fears for our physical safety, no one is born with emotional fears—not us, not our children. Each of us is born without values or beliefs; we acted spontaneously, guided by our emotions and desires. But when our natural responses were criticized or in some other way devalued, we became afraid of being wrong, disapproved of, rejected, and ultimately, abandoned. Because of this fear, we did two things—we protected ourselves and we developed a belief system about ourselves, about who we were and what we could and could not do so that we would be acceptable to those whose love we so desperately needed.

There are many kinds of beliefs about how the world works and what holds the universe together, but when it comes to beliefs about ourselves, each of us operates from one of two fundamental, underlying beliefs: I am good (lovable, worthy) *or* I am not good (not lovable, worthy). All other beliefs are colored in some way by these beliefs.

Unfortunately, most people do not believe they are good, or good enough, which leads to a huge amount of pain and fear. If your child is not doing well in school, it taps into the fear that somehow it's because you're not good enough. When you feel good about yourself, you don't take things personally. You assume that the other person is having difficulty and you reach out to help. Whether you feel hurt or caring comes from your own belief system. When you believe you are not good enough, you may need to be controlling or compliant to compensate for your resulting fear of rejection.

The basic belief that you are not good, however, is false. It is not accurate and it is self-limiting. The belief was created by you as a young child when you concluded that your experience of disconnection and rejection was your fault—that it occurred because there was something wrong with you. And this belief, in turn, is the cause of most of your fears as an adult. All of your fears (except some of those which relate to physical survival) come from false, self-limiting beliefs.

In order to get past the fear and test the beliefs, we have to be aware and admit that we are, in fact, afraid—

afraid of losing love and of losing ourselves, afraid of conflict and pain, of being unlovable, wrong, inadequate, foolish, or weak. To acknowledge these things is very difficult. Consequently, most of us prefer to remain ignorant of our pain and fears because we think it's wrong and weak to be afraid. Try it out for yourself right now. How does it feel to say out loud, "I am afraid." It is not easy to allow ourselves to be that vulnerable. So we stay stuck in one or more of the following ways:

• We don't want to know that we believe staying protected from fear is more important than anything else in the world—more important than being loving, being close to our families, more important than feeling free and happy.

• We don't want to know that our fear of being unlovable or inadequate is so great that we can't risk being truly open to learning about ourselves.

• We don't want to know that we are fully in charge of our own choices and responsible for their consequences.

This kind of denial cuts across most of the problems we have in our lives—with relationships of all kinds, such as with our own parents, our children, our mates; with addictive behaviors such as alcoholism and drug abuse; and with other kinds of compulsive-obsessive disorders, such as problems with work, eating, or sexuality.

Existential writers have termed this kind of denial "bad faith." As William Ofman writes in *Affirmation and Reality,* "Bad faith . . . is a lie to oneself: it is from me, from myself, that I intend to hide the truth."

Looking at the Beliefs behind Our Fears

Anytime we have fear, (again, except the fear that relates to physical harm), we're operating from a false, self-limiting belief. Any time we're feeling pain or unhappiness in our lives, depressed hurt, scared, or stuck, it means that we're operating from a self-limiting belief that is triggering those feelings.

The dynamic between a self-limiting belief about ourselves and fear works like this: When you have a belief that something should happen and it doesn't, you become afraid. Let's look at a belief and see how the progressive thinking goes.

> Self-limiting belief: It's the parents' job to make sure children do well in school. Therefore my daughter should get good grades.
> Action: My daughter gets a D in science.
> Protective reaction: I get angry with her.
> Fear underlying the reaction: People will think I am stupid, or weak and cannot control my child.

Here is another example:

> Self-limiting belief: Children should always respect their parents.
> Action: My son yells and swears at me.
> Protective reaction: I shut down and go have a drink.
> Fear underlying the reaction: If people see how my son treats me, they will consider me inadequate and reject me.

In the above examples, anger and shutting down and drinking are protective reactions, covering up the primary emotion fear—fear of not being in control, of being judged as a bad parent because of your daughter's grade or your son's yelling, fear that you are not good enough. If you were, none of this would be happening.

If you remain protected, you will continue to react with anger, criticism, silence, etc. You won't have the opportunity to test the accuracy of your belief. You will be stuck, controlled by your own fear, and will continue the unloving behavior toward your child.

The good news is that even if you're afraid, you can choose not to let the fear control you, but you must be willing to risk emotional pain. If you can stay open in the face of fear, and explore the reasons your daughter got a poor grade or why your son is angry with you, you will learn about each other and have the opportunity to test the accuracy of the belief which heretofore has caused you pain. Eventually then, you can change your beliefs. More about this later.

As another example of a self-limiting belief, parents may be afraid that if they set limits for themselves, their children won't love them. In this, they're operating from the belief that they (the parents) are not lovable, that they have to comply in order to be loved. This is clearly one of the carry-over fears that came from their own childhood feelings about their adequacy and worth.

Most of the self-limiting beliefs we have are residuals from our own childhood. There are many sources— our parents, grandparents, television, religion, and our own minds, our own perceptions of messages and events around us. We made the best choices we knew how to as children, but maybe we didn't have enough information, or were too young to draw other conclusions. Nonetheless, we established a belief system which we think is real and operate from it as if it's true. For example, if your parents told you that you were selfish, you may have decided based on that judgment that you were not a good person and that belief may persist unchallenged throughout your life. It may or may not have been an accurate statement. But you could have chosen to evaluate that belief ("Am I really selfish?"), then either negate the judgment or amend your behavior. There's no way to know why we choose the beliefs we do. Certain factors can be isolated—birth order, alcoholic parents, economic circumstances of the family, etc., but two siblings given the same set of circumstances will often make radically different choices about what to believe, both about themselves and life in general. However, once we decide on a belief, once we've made that choice, then everything follows from that and we get locked into acting on the belief as if it were true.

MARGIE:

I had the belief that my parents couldn't handle the truth about who I was. It may not have been an accurate belief, but that's what I decided. Once I decided that they couldn't handle who I was (they would be miserable and die or go crazy or whatever) and that I would get rejected if I was the real me, then I had to become compliant and had to take responsibility for their feelings. I decided I had to keep the real me from them because they might not like me. So I didn't tell them all my secret stuff, and my mother would say, "Why don't you ever tell me all the stuff other girls tell their mothers?" But I still didn't tell her.

Looking back, if I had decided differently— that I could handle their not liking me, or believed they were stronger than I thought, then I might have confronted them in ways that would have created much more growth for them and me. But the way I chose to be, I just didn't challenge them. There's no way of knowing what would have happened if I had decided on a different belief. So I chose what I chose and then had to deal with the consequences of that. The point is to look at the belief and say, "Is that accurate?" I might have been wrong about my parents.

The fears and self-limiting beliefs we carry forward from our childhood guide our adult behavior, so, as we have seen, when we become parents, we continue to operate with those beliefs. We may believe that the only way kids will love their parents is if the parents let them have their own way. Or that if the parents don't make their own happiness secondary to the children's, they're just being selfish. Other possible beliefs are that children are basically wild and need to be tamed and that parents should have control over their children, should motivate them, should be responsible for their achievement, and so on and on and on.

All of these beliefs, and just about any others you can imagine about yourself and other people in your world, have their roots in some very deep, fundamental false beliefs which lie at the base of the rest of our belief systems.

> I am a victim.
> —I am powerless over how I feel.
> —Others make me happy/unhappy.

> The world is a hostile place.
> —People are basically evil.
> —People are just out for themselves.

> There is something wrong with me.
> —I am unlovable.
> —I am limited, inadequate.
> —I am insignificant, unimportant.

> I can't handle pain.
> —The pain will be unending.
> —I will die or go crazy if I'm in pain.

> Anger gets me what I want.

> There is not enough to go around.

These beliefs and countless others that are essentially extensions of these generate our fears of rejection and loss. Other negative feelings are also triggered, guilt being at the head of the list:

—guilt	—depression	—hatred
—greed	—ambivalence	—deadness
—doubt	—confusion	—anxiety
—grief	—despair	—jealousy
—helplessness	—resentment	—hurt/pain
—anger	—fragility	—shame
—rage	—loneliness	—incompetence
—boredom	—irritation	—powerlessness
—blame	—frustration	—revenge
—indifference	—hopelessness	—regret/remorse

These are mighty fears and heavy, haunting feelings. No wonder we try so hard to protect ourselves. We spend a great deal of energy trying to do just that, directly or indirectly, with a variety of unloving behaviors. All of our protective behaviors are geared to protect us from these feelings, and yet ironically they end up creating them.

As you get a clearer understanding of the cause and effect relationship between your self-limiting beliefs and your negative feelings and behaviors, you can see how crucial it is to confront the beliefs that are causing you pain rather than to hide the truth from yourself.

The more you let go of the self-limiting beliefs, the less fear you'll feel, the less protective you'll need to be, and therefore the more loving you can be. Consequently, working through the beliefs that create your fears is crucial not just for yourself; it is probably the most important thing you, as a loving, involved parent, can do for your children.

When your child does something that embarrasses, hurts, or disappoints you, your fears are touched off in this upsetting situation like a match to flame. But instead of blaming the children, lashing out and making them wrong, or retreating in passive indifference as you might have done, you now have the opportunity to learn and to change. Taking advantage of this situation requires your willingness to risk emotional pain, and to look into the deepest parts of yourself and confront those beliefs and resulting fears that you have been avoiding your whole life.

Realizing the depth of your fears may make the task seem overwhelming, but remember that meaningful, long-lasting changes take place slowly, over a lifetime. The process described in this book is designed to help you become less fearful, protected, and more loving. As this transformation gradually occurs, you will come to understand how the words, "If you really loved me," are used in manipulative attempts to get others to meet your needs so that you don't have to feel fear or pain. You will be free to be the loving person you are capable of being. Amazingly, your focus will shift to the principal question: "If I really loved you."

As you read this chapter, just notice your fears and become aware of how they affect your life. Try to be patient and respect the difficulty of this task as you progress. Know that you can work on your fears as much or as little as you like and that the more your journey will be accompanied by love and acceptance, especially for the primary people in your life, the greater will be the healing.

Fears about Being Wrong, Inadequate, and Unlovable

We all enter parenthood with many doubts and fears about our adequacy and lovability. When you add to this the fact that you think of children as extensions of yourself (because almost all of us do), their behavior taps into many of your fears. When your children fail, are impolite, have problems, are confused, sad, upset, or frightened, you suffer both as a parent and as a person. When your sons or daughters are cut from the school team, not invited to a party, or rejected by a friend, fears of your own inadequacy can get set in motion. The more you fear others' disapproval, the more emphasis you may put on getting your children to change their behavior, hide their differences, and "fit in." The more you fear disapproval, the more you may attempt to control your children. Or, the more you fear disapproval, the more you may give yourself up or become indifferent to your children in an effort to protect against their disapproval and/or domination.

This same cycle is repeated in other ways. The more you were dominated and controlled as a child, the more you may fear domination, and the more you need to dominate to protect from your fear. The more you were emotionally or physically abused as a child, the more you may fear that old helpless feeling and so abuse your own children as you attempt to protect against your own painful feelings of helplessness and humiliation.

Much of the fear we experience comes from our basic lack of faith. The less we trust in the basic goodness, the essential rightness of the human being, the ability of every human being to know the truth and to live in harmony with our loving human nature, the more we feel the need and the right to control our children. The fear of not being in control is that if you don't make your children behave, they won't. You can learn about your beliefs by checking out what you fear may happen if you don't impose controls on your child and why you believe that way. Do you believe that your children would: Be dirty? Mess up in school? Be disrespectful? Get hurt or killed? Be a delinquent? Lie? Be violent? Take drugs? Be unpopular? Be antisocial? Be defiant? (Add your own if we've missed them.)

The flip side of the fear of not being in control is the fear of being controlled—if you're not in control, you'll be controlled. You may be afraid that out of fear, obligation, or guilt, you'll give in and do things you really don't want to. You may fear being used, taken advantage of, burdened, unloved, abused by your children.

Do you feel respected and loved by your children? The more inner security and self-worth *you* feel, the less you need to "make" your child love and respect you or perform for you so that you can get your good feelings vicariously through them. Unfortunately, the basic lack of self-worth from which most adults suffer leads to the attempts to control their children's behavior. The more you know deep in your heart that you're okay, the less you need to prove it or attempt to manipulate your children into loving you. A sense of okayness gives you the assurance that your children will know that you are lovable and will naturally respond with respect when they receive respect and love from you. The less secure you feel, the more frightened you are of being rejected, the greater is your need to make your children love and respect you by controlling them and holding them to you.

The lack of affirmation suffered as children leaves us all with big empty holes—needs for love, respect, and affirmation. We often unwittingly make our children responsible for filling these holes. A role-reversal occurs where the child becomes the parent to the parent, generally with disastrous consequences for the child. Dr. Ross Campbell, in *How To Really Love Your Child,* states: "Role-reversal is the primary relationship in the frightening phenomenon of child abuse. An abusing parent feels his child must take care of the parent's emotional needs, that the parent has a right to be comforted and nourished by his child. When the child fails in this, the parent feels a right to punish him."

It is the parents' job to do the nurturing. Children certainly can help and nurture at times—even very young children can comfort an upset parent, but this is not the child's job, and should not be expected of the child.

Another major fear from which most of us suffer is being wrong. If we are wrong, goes our logic, we are by definition unlovable. When we fear being wrong, we always need to try to be right. *The protection against being wrong is one of the major blocks to being open to learning.* Almost everyone fears looking foolish. For example, everyone has at least once refrained from asking questions out of fear that someone would say, "You mean you don': know that?" Being foolish, humiliated, losing respect and position are extremely threatening if we basically fee: insecure about our own worth. So when we fear being wrong, foolish, weak, etc., we spend a lot of energy trying always to be right.

Checking the Accuracy of Your Beliefs

What are your beliefs about what is adequate and lovable?

- Do you believe that there is something inherently wrong or bad about you or your children?
- Do you believe your adequacy is defined by others' approval and disapproval?
- Do you believe your adequacy is tied to how much money you make?
- Do you believe you always have to be right about everything to be adequate or lovable, and that if you are wrong you will be disapproved of or rejected?
- Do you believe you are too sensitive or too weak and therefore inadequate?
- Do you believe you are basically powerful or basically helpless and powerless?

- Do you believe your adequacy or lovability is tied to how much education you've had or how intelligent you are?
- Do you believe your adequacy is connected to how articulate you are or how well you express your feelings?
- Do you believe your adequacy or lovability is tied to how you look? How tall or short you are? How fat or thin you are?

Knowing you are adequate and lovable is a feeling that grows within you as you free yourself from self-limiting beliefs that perpetuate your doubts and fears. Questioning your beliefs allows you to discard the ones that are false, but that you're holding onto out of ignorance or fear, and to strengthen the ones that encourage your emotional and spiritual evolution.

Where Did These Beliefs Come From?

When you want to discover how you got your beliefs, take a moment to look into your childhood and remember how you were treated.

- Were your thoughts and feelings valued and respected?
- Were you given attention and affection for just being you?
- Were you treated as an equal?
- Did your parents share with you their own thoughts and feelings about their difficulties and joys?
- Did you see your parents loving and respecting each other?
- Were your parents interested in and open to understanding your fears and pain?
- Did your parents enjoy spending time with you?

- Did you know you were important to your parents?
- Were your thoughts and feelings disapproved of, ignored, ridiculed, discounted?
- Did your parents make you wrong for your thoughts and feelings or try to talk you out of them?
- Were you given attention and affection only when you performed a certain way, only when you complied with the spoken or unspoken expectations?
- Did you grow up without much attention and affection?
- Were you punished with physical or emotional abuse—ignored, criticized, demeaned, disrespected, beaten, locked up, screamed at, sexually molested?
- Did you feel shut out from your parents' thoughts and feelings?
- Did you have parents? One? None? Did you grow up in an orphanage, with grandparents or other relatives, or in foster homes?
- Were you caught in the middle of or blamed for an angry divorce?
- Did one parent constantly tell you how bad the other parent was?
- Did you generally see your parents either ignoring each other or fighting?
- Did one parent dominate the other? Was one parent weak and submissive?
- Was one parent or were both parents gone a lot?
- Were you heaped with responsibility for younger siblings or for the household at an early age?

- Were you very poor, sometimes didn't have enough to eat, or dressed poorly and made fun of?
- Did your family ridicule your looks, your intelligence, your friends?

How We Got to Be So Afraid

Human beings are born good, without evil but capable of doing bad things in the protected state that develops from being violated. Also, the essence of all of us is love, which is the God-energy, and if we open to the higher part of ourselves, what we'll find is love, not evil.

Earlier in this chapter we mentioned briefly that people are not born afraid to show emotions. Babies freely express their feelings of pain, joy, sexuality. Unafraid of rejection, we are born open to life, curious, eager to learn. We cried when unhappy, hurt, or afraid. Later, when happy we added laughter to our natural repertoire of behavior and still later, sexual feelings and curiosity were naturally expressed. Everything we did flowed from our instinctual, inner selves and we were one with our natural selves—our outer behavior and inner feelings were harmonious. We were not born afraid of being who we really are.

Soon after birth we started receiving confusing messages which seemed to say that there was something wrong with who we were. For instance, crying may have brought disapproval—"Don't cry" (accompanied by irritation, anger, hitting). As we grew, other judgments were made about our feelings. "You're too sensitive" (said with disgust). "You mean that hurt your feelings?" (said with derisiveness). "You shouldn't let things like that upset you" (said with caring but an obvious message that there's something wrong with you for feeling sad).

Expressions of intense, spontaneous, free-flowing joy and curiosity brought disapproval—"Calm down." "Control yourself." "Relax." "Don't ask so many questions." Expressions of sexuality brought even more disapproval. A great deal of our natural curiosity, openness and sensitivity—fear, sadness, frustration, joy, sexuality, sensuality—were made wrong by those who were most important to us—our families.

How can young children believe they're okay when the constant overt and covert beat of the message is "You are not okay, you need to change who you really are. *If you become what we think you should be, then you will be lovable.*" Disapproval hurts and is frightening since children can't tolerate rejection by their parents. As we chose ways to protect ourselves from these negative feelings, we fooled ourselves into believing that our protections are lovable, that it is possible to feel lovable and get love while we are behaving in unloving ways.

As we grew up, our protections became so well ingrained and automatic that as adults, we are probably unaware we have become protected most of the time. We may become so identified with our protected side that we believe that's who we really are. When protections are lowered (when we fall in love, when we go on vacations) that person you experience may not feel like the real you. Your natural self has diminished to the point where *it* feels like a stranger.

We became approval seekers, afraid to be ourselves, believing that we're not okay, losing touch with who we really are, with our intuitive, Higher Self, looking to others to tell us how to be. We absorbed our parents' beliefs that the universe is a dangerous, unfriendly place and that we therefore must always be on guard, protected. We lost faith in our Higher Selves, in the God within and without. Putting most of our energy into trying to be what we hoped would be an okay, acceptable, lovable, worthwhile person is how we lost touch with who we really are. The poster in our office that almost everyone comments on as their favorite shows a very dejected dog looking out a window and saying, "I've tried so hard to be what I'm supposed to be that I forgot who I am."

It's easy to blame yourself for doing this to your children or blame your parents for doing it to you, but your parents absorbed their fears and beliefs from their parents and their culture; they lacked adequate information, were fearful and insecure, and needed to protect themselves. Their protections set in motion many of the fears and self-doubts you struggle with today, but their intent was not to make your life more difficult any more than your intent is to add misery to your children's lives. They were doing the best they could and so are you. Blaming merely allows the venting of self-righteous anger. You then become stuck in your anger and that's just another protection. No one is to blame.

The nonblaming feeling when considering these circumstances is sadness. Sadness for the love we didn't get. Sadness for the love our parents missed out on. Sadness for the ignorance that created all of this. Sadness for the state of our world populated with people who, because they are so afraid and protected are not loving, caring, respectful. When we stop blaming others, we just feel sad. There's nothing to be done about the past, but we certainly can begin to create a better future.

We are born with a nature that is capable of enormous possibilities and changes within some fixed boundaries. Since we are unique individuals at birth, we each make different choices and have different reactions to any situation. The job of a parent, then, is to get to know the child as an individual, and encourage the emergence of that individual's unique potential rather than attempting to mold him or her into a being which thinks, feels, and acts the way his or her parents believe is right.

The less faith you have in the inherent rightness of children, the more you must attempt to mold your children. Since so much parental behavior comes from beliefs about the basic nature of human beings, this is a central and ongoing focus of explorations. For example, do you believe that:

- Children are lesser because they are smaller?
- Children are blank slates or empty vessels waiting to be filled up?
- Children are born basically wild, uncivilized, and/or evil?
- Children are incomplete, inauthentic, or even potentially dangerous without proper conditioning?
- Children need to be molded to grow up good?

The greater your lack of faith in your children's basic goodness and natural desire to learn and grow, the greater your need to protect. The more approval children get for their natural Higher Selves, the greater their self-esteem. It's that kind of love that teaches faith and self-respect. We all need love for the potential in all areas of our personalities to flower. Only by meeting challenges can we grow; but when afraid of experiencing the pain of failure, disapproval, and rejection, we pull in, afraid to venture forth and test ourselves. The key to being unprotected is being willing to feel pain.

Fears about Feeling Pain

Most of us have a basic fear of feeling and expressing our nonblaming, nonvictimized pain, or of seeing our children in emotional pain. We are afraid of feeling our fear, disappointment, sadness, grief, humiliation, or helplessness. All of these feelings are painful and we have all learned many ways to protect against feeling them (chapter 3).

There are many self-limiting beliefs that create our fear of pain. For example, do you believe that:

- You "can't handle" emotional pain—you'll die or fall apart if you open to your pain, especially your childhood pain?
- Your children can't handle their pain either?
- If you or your child opens to pain, the pain is unending and will go on forever?
- Showing pain indicates weakness?
- If you open to your pain and allow yourself to be vulnerable, your spouse or children will take advantage of your vulnerable state to manipulate you?
- Others around you will not care or will disapprove of or reject you when you are in pain and then you will be in even more pain? (This is the belief when people assume the role of victim, expressing their pain in a way to blame or control others. Then, when others disapprove or walk away because they are protecting themselves from being manipulated, the victim states, "See, I show my pain and they just walk away. They don't care about me.")
- If your child feels pain, he or she will feel unloved?
- There's no point in expressing pain because there's nothing you can do about the situation anyway? ("Don't cry over spilt milk.")

- If your child is in pain that means you are
  a bad parent?
- You are responsible for "fixing" whatever
  painful situation occurs with your child?
- If you open to sharing your child's pain, it
  will open you to your own childhood pain
  and it will overwhelm you?

As adults, your beliefs about your own and your
children's ability—or inability—to handle pain come from
your own childhood experiences of being in pain and
having no one around to comfort you. The truth is that
all of us, children and adults, can handle any deep pain
when we are in a loving environment, and the pain is
intolerable only when we feel alone with it.

Now you may be asking, Why would anyone want
to feel emotional pain? and What's wrong with protecting
against it? No one wants to be in pain and it's never
pleasant. However, there are some critically important
reasons to open to it:

1. The things you do to protect yourself from
pain actually create most of the pain in your
life.
2. You never learn about the erroneous
beliefs that create the pain in your life unless
you open to experiencing the pain that is the
consequence of these erroneous beliefs.
3. When afraid to be in pain you must put
lids on the other two natural feelings, joy
and passion. You can't repress some feelings
without subduing others.
4. If you fear others' disapproval for your
spontaneous expression of feelings, and if
you're not willing to feel and learn from the
pain of that disapproval, then you're always

in a position of having to hold back, to refrain from being your natural self.

You have the strength to tolerate much more pain than you think. You can love deeply, and should you lose that love, you will survive. Should you be rejected or fail, taking responsibility for your part in these experiences and learning from the pain allows you to gain personal strength and create better relationships in the future.

You'll never like being in pain, but used as a learning experience, pain can be a valuable part of your life. Think of it this way: if you were unwilling to be in physical pain you never would have learned to walk or ride a bike. You learned from your falls and felt good about your accomplishment. Another analogy is that if you were unwilling to be in physical pain you could never learn to ski. You must be willing to be in pain before you will take off down a mountain. You may never suffer a bruising fall or a broken leg, but you must be willing for that possibility to occur. The same is true for emotional pain. You will learn that any pain you may suffer you can handle.

To put the difficulty of risking emotional pain in perspective, however, most people would much rather confront physical pain and even death than face emotional pain. This was dramatically demonstrated by an ex-Green Beret Marine we once counseled. This man faced death every day in Vietnam but was unwilling to open to his feelings and be vulnerable with his wife because he feared he couldn't handle the pain.

Many people are afraid to know about the abuse they suffered as children because it would mean acknowledging that they felt unloved or actually were unloved by their parents. If you are unwilling to feel the pain of your childhood, then you have to protect against feeling and exploring all present pain, since feeling and learning about present pain is a doorway to the past.

Also, when you are unwilling to feel your own pain, then you cannot open to your child's pain, as this may tap into your own. As Alice Miller says: "Empathizing with what a child is feeling when he or she is defenseless, hurt, or humiliated is like suddenly seeing in a mirror the suffering of one's own childhood, something many people must ward off out of fear, while others can accept it with mourning.'

Painful situations are a fact of life. You can either choose to protect yourself against them, thus deadening yourself and creating even more pain, or you can open to learning the lessons the pain has to teach you by experiencing the pain and exploring the self-limiting beliefs and resulting behavior that has created much of the pain.

Anytime you choose to love someone you open yourself to the possibility of pain. It can be painful when a loved one is angry with you or ignores you. It can be intensely painful when a loved one rejects you or dies. But if you believe you can't handle the pain of disapproval, rejection, or loss, then you protect against truly loving them and miss out on the deepest joy life has to offer.

Fear of Catastrophe or Loss

The fear of catastrophe creates a great deal of anxiety. We fear we will be unable to handle our own and our children's pain should they become seriously injured or ill, or we fear our children will be unable to handle their own pain. As we said, no one wants to be in pain, but if you have an excessive fear of the pain of accident, injury, illness, or death, you spend tremendous energy trying to control these things.

When open to exploring your fears, you will often find that your childhood experiences with sickness, accidents, or death are fueling your protections. Parents who had traumatic losses as children, such as the loss of a parent or beloved grandparent, often become very protective of their own children. The pain from an early loss is usually an unhealed wound that we fear feeling again. Allowing a child to take risks is frightening for most parents, but for the parent who has experienced the loss of a loved one, it may seem intolerable. Sharing the old pain with a partner, friend or therapist can help heal the old wounds.

We all want to believe that we can prevent catastrophe if only we exert enough control, but this belief is a myth. In fact, it's often the very attempts to control our children that bring about the catastrophe we so want to avoid. Children who don't learn self-discipline because their parents have maintained control are much more likely to make poor decisions like driving drunk than those whose discipline comes from within. While your fears may come true, it's very important to realize that *many of the things you do to protect yourself and your children bring about the very things you fear.*

Overcoming Your Fears

Being afraid is not the problem. Protecting when you're afraid is what creates difficulties. There has been a great deal of misinformation about overcoming fear. The most destructive message comes from those who imply that overcoming fear is merely a matter of deciding to change. Deeply held fears—fears of pain, inadequacy and unlovability—cannot be willed out of existence. These fears, which fuel your protections, thereby running your life, change through a process:

1. Wanting to change
2. Becoming aware—knowing and acknowledging when you are afraid

3. Feeling your fears—learning about and understanding the beliefs causing fear
4. Testing—taking action, being willing to test the belief by doing what it is you are afraid of

Challenging your beliefs and fears by facing them and not letting them beat you is how you become less afraid. And it's love that creates the environment of understanding and caring that helps you venture forth and meet the demons you must overcome to become less fearful.

Wanting to Change

Becoming aware, exploring, and facing fear is not easy. The fuel that generates this, that motivates you to face yourself, is your inner desire for growth and change. This does not mean trying new ways to get your children to change—it means that you want to take responsibility for your own unhappiness and unloving behavior by becoming aware of how and why you create it, so that new choices become available to you, both as an individual and as a parent. This is loving behavior.

Becoming Aware of Being Afraid

Once the desire for growth is there, the next step in the process of overcoming fear is becoming aware that you are afraid. This will be difficult for you if you believe that fears are "kid stuff" and something you're supposed to have left behind by the time you reach adulthood, especially if you're male.

You may fear hearing the typical judgments about being afraid: "You're afraid of that?" "That's dumb." "There's nothing to be afraid of." Many people judge themselves so harshly that they won't ever admit to themselves that they're afraid. "I'm not afraid of women/

men, business meetings, my children, my parents, disapproval, speaking up for myself, my wife/husband, social
situations, rejection, sex." But what happens in these
situations? Do you need to have a few drinks to relax?
Your tension comes from your fear. And who among us
can truthfully say we're not nervous in many situations?
o let's just admit to it, let down our false fronts and agree
that we're all afraid and then get on with the task of
looking at our fears, understanding them and helping
each other to confront them. The more we can stop
judging ourselves for being afraid, the more aware we
will become of what we are afraid of.

Feeling Your Fears and Understanding the Beliefs behind Them

Admitting your fears can be just an intellectual realization,
but deeply understanding fear requires your willingness
to feel the feeling in your body. Feeling releases the
awareness of the beliefs that are fueling your fears, and
the more you understand, the more your fears make
sense. Marilyn, a client of Margie's, provided a good
example of this. She came into therapy with her twelve-
year-old daughter Samantha because Samantha was
becoming more and more angry and resistant at home.
The precipitating event occurred in a restaurant when
Samantha screamed "I hate you!" at Marilyn.

> Margie: You must have some very good reasons for
> being so angry at your mother. Why do you
> feel that way?
> Samantha: Because she's always yelling at me. She
> yells at me for everything and sometimes hits
> me.
> Margie: Tell me about a time when this happened
> recently.

Samantha: Well, the other evening I didn't want to do the reading I had to do for school. It was so boring. Mom told me to do it and I said no. All of a sudden she got furious at me, yelling and hitting me. I don't see why it was such a big deal to her.

Margie: Marilyn, there must be some very good reasons for your getting so angry. What do you think was going on inside you?

Marilyn: I guess I think a kid should do what her mother says.

Margie: Okay, but what were your feelings inside? Your anger was covering some painful feelings. What were you afraid of?

Suddenly as if a dam had burst, Marilyn was convulsed in deep sobs. Her whole body shook as she cried deeply for a few minutes and slowly emerged from her pain.

Marilyn: When I was a child my grandmother would force me to read books out loud to her that were too hard for me. I didn't know a lot of the words and whenever I came to a word I didn't know, she would tell me I was stupid and force stale moldy bread soaked in water down my throat. If I refused to read, she would beat me.

Margie: So when Samantha didn't want to read, it brought up a lot of old fear in you, didn't it? And you didn't want to re-experience that old fear and pain, so you got angry at Samantha to try to get her to stop doing the thing that was bringing up your painful feelings?

Marilyn: Yes. I guess I've been afraid to feel those feelings. They are so intense that I guess I was

> afraid if I felt them they would overwhelm me and I'd go crazy. (Here is an erroneous belief.)
>
> Margie: How do you feel now that you've re-experienced those feelings?
>
> Marilyn: I feel so much better! I guess I can handle feeling them.

While Marilyn was crying, Samantha had gone over to her, put her arms around her and cried with her. Even though it was hard for Samantha to hear Marilyn's story, it enabled her to understand her mother on a much deeper level and to see that Marilyn's anger at her really had nothing to do with her. Marilyn subsequently learned to get through her anger to her pain and fear by hitting the bed with a pillow and yelling at the person she was really mad at—her grandmother—rather than taking it out on Samantha. Samantha learned to remind Marilyn to hit the bed rather than yell at her when Marilyn forgot. Because Marilyn was now willing to face her fear, not only did her own feelings about herself improve, but also the relationship between her daughter and her became more loving and caring.

Understanding the very good reasons you have for your fears is how you gain a greater respect for yourself. Expressing your soft, nonblaming feelings also lets your loved ones know how deeply you are affected and releases caring responses from them. Merely stating a feeling without the accompanying emotion means very little. It's feelings that connect to feelings in others. The words "I'm feeling sad," "I'm feeling happy," or "I'm feeling sexual" mean very little by themselves. Can you imagine making love to a partner who, while hardly moving, with eyes closed, and with no outward signs of enjoyment, keeps telling you, "I'm really turned on right now. I'm really enjoying this. This is great." Or a partner who, in a monotone, deadpans, "I'm really having a good time right now. Boy, this is the most fun I've ever had." It's the same with sadness or any painful feelings. To feel moved we have to *experience* the other person's feelings, not just hear the words. Then we can connect to the other from our hearts rather than our heads.

Words have become our attempts to be safe rather than just feel and let those feelings bubble out. *Expressing* feelings leaves you feeling much more vulnerable than just *saying* feelings. But it's when you are willing to be vulnerable that others respond in a caring way. Because your true emotions were so often met with disapproval when you were a child and because there's no guarantee that you will now get a caring response, it often feels very difficult to risk being vulnerable.

Moving through Your Fears: Testing and Taking Action

When you express fear and understand it on a deeper level, when you become more respectful of yourself and experience the love of a friend or partner that comes from feeling understood, finally doing what it is you're afraid of becomes much easier. This is not to say that these conditions have to be met before you can confront your fears. Many people have been successful in overcoming their fears without this loving process. We are presenting the ideal conditions and the ones that lead to intimacy in relationships.

All the love and understanding in the world will not make a fear go away completely. With this process, the fear can be reduced to a more manageable level, but you must be willing to *do what you are afraid of while still afraid.* Fear goes away only when you are willing to do what it is you are afraid of over and over again. This process is well-described in Susan Jeffer's book, *Feel the Fear and Do It Anyway.* For example, talking about your fear of no longer trying to control when and how your children do their homework will not take the fear away. But understanding the beliefs that have created your fears can lead to your willingness to risk letting go. Only when your children become self-motivated and you see that your fears were not based on reality will your fears go away completely.

Your fears are not based on what is *really* happening in the present, but rather on what you *think* will happen. Fears go away only when you test them out and see that they are a lie to yourself. Tolly Burkan in his firewalking workshop defines fear in the following way:

Ｆalse Ｅvidence Ａppearing Ｒeal

We use:

Ｆalse Ｅducation Ａppearing Ｒeal

·6·

What Do I Believe?

Questioning Beliefs about Values, Expectations, and Responsibility

> *It is not danger that comes when defenses are laid down. It is safety. It is peace. It is joy.*
>
> A Course in Miracles

Ed was twelve when his mother began telling him he would never amount to anything. He was hurt, but didn't ask why she said that. All that Ed could make of it was that his mother wouldn't love him until he was a success, whatever that was. So Ed pushed himself hard and fast as a young adult, rising quickly to the top of his profession. The other thing he did was to keep a safe distance from people, women in particular, so that he couldn't be hurt again. Intimacy was too risky—after all, if his mother didn't love him, who would?

Matthew was four when his father died. Matt had been very angry with his dad shortly before his death. On the basis of this limited but powerful experience, Matt concluded that anger causes people to die. After a while, Matt's mother began to have boyfriends. On more than one occasion Matt saw the boyfriends hit his mother. Matt drew another conclusion this time: if a man likes a woman, he also wants to hurt her.

Christine was the oldest of four children, so her mother relied on her to help raise the family, even to find the alcoholic father in the local bars. By fourteen, Christine was used to phoning around town to find her drunken dad. In addition, the mother repeatedly told her daughter she was selfish. Chris had quite a bit of experience for a fourteen-year-old, and decided in her own mind that her mother was wrong. Christine knew she had done all she could.

There are all kinds of beliefs about ourselves, how we are in the world, what the world and the other people in it are like. There are beliefs about what is right and wrong (these beliefs we usually refer to as values) and beliefs about how people will act if they really love you (these are the expectations generated by the beliefs).

Each and every one of us has countless beliefs, many which we're hardly aware of. All these beliefs are conclusions drawn from our experiences in life. Like the three cases above, we see or hear something happen and draw a conclusion based on that experience. This conclusion becomes a belief, something that we think is true and which extends to everything we think and do.

However, some beliefs coincide with the truth and others don't—in fact they may be downright false, and when they are false, they limit our perception and behavior. Beliefs may be based on partial information, inaccurate information, our personal biases and superstitions, or simply limited experience. One of the simplest examples is the centuries-old belief that the world was flat. The horizon looked flat, so citizens of that day used this much information to form their belief. Only when the belief was challenged by ships going nearer and nearer the "edge" was the belief refuted and the truth known.

Another belief from not so long ago was that women weren't very athletic, couldn't run marathons, play basketball, and so forth. There are countless examples, but the point is this: beliefs may or may not be true. There is no way to know whether they're true until we challenge them, question, test, and learn. When a belief is put to the test and found to be accurate, it becomes a truth or a "knowing." A knowing is the emotional, psychological, or spiritual equivalent of a scientific truth—in other words, a truth which you can't subject to the scientific method, but which, like a measurable truth, is consistent, ongoing, and can't be proved wrong.

The best example of this kind of truth, this knowing, is that you *know* you love your children. You don't believe you love them, you know. There's nothing that anybody could say or do that would have any effect on your knowing you love your kids.

No one will ever (we can suppose) know all the ultimate truths of the universe. However, the problem is not that we don't know all there is to know, but that we spend so much energy defending our beliefs, rather than questioning them and learning from them. When we are in pain, when we are afraid, guilty, angry, or upset as a part of our reaction to the others in our lives, then we need to stop and ask: "What did I expect to happen? What belief led me to that expectation? Is that belief accurate?"

Beliefs That Affect Our Behavior as Parents

We all have very definite beliefs about the right way to do things and when our children behave in ways we believe to be wrong or they do not meet our expectations, we become upset. We look at messy rooms, dirty clothes, and crumpled homework papers and tell our kids they'll never amount to anything. We watch them chew with their mouths open, procrastinate on their schoolwork, or lose their new sweaters, and we call them names—

"sloppy, lazy, stupid," anything that comes to mind at the moment—hoping to make them change their behavior and do things our way. After all, according to our belief, it's the parents' job to make the children do the right thing—isn't it?

In addition to those beliefs about ourselves that were discussed in the previous chapter, all of us have deeply ingrained beliefs absorbed from what our families and culture consider right. Accordingly, there is a right way to do just about everything: walk, talk, look, smell, eat, and dress. There are judgments about moral behavior, manners, etiquette, how to spend our time, our money, and so on.

When your children aren't behaving "properly," you probably feel justified in imposing some type of discipline in an attempt to make them behave. They are wrong because they are not behaving in these ways you believe to be right.

However, what you personally choose to believe is right and wrong is not the major issue here. The second important aspect to this problem of beliefs, and whether they're based on truth or whether they're false and self-limiting, is: what happens when we try to impose those beliefs on our children. You see, exploring your beliefs and the expectations which are extensions of those beliefs, then shedding those you discover are false—these are essential steps in becoming less protected and more lovingly involved with your children. In addition, your personal gains will transcend your family relationships, since this kind of learning is the path toward greater personal freedom and self-esteem.

One of our favorite stories to illustrate the difficulties that can occur when families don't explore the beliefs that are a result of our society comes from that wonderfully exciting, tumultous decade of the 1960s. What

American family didn't discuss the proper length of a boy's hair in the sixties? Back and forth the battle went:

"Your hair's too long. Get it cut!"

"No, I like it this way."

"You look like a girl."

"Yeah, well, why don't you get with it?"

"Martha, I won't tolerate a son of mine looking weird. Make him get his hair cut."

"I'll move out of this prison before I'll cut my hair."

"This is my house and as long as you're living here you'll do what I say. Now get your hair cut!"

"It's my hair and you have no right to tell me how long it should be."

"You can't talk to me like that. Trouble with you is you've never learned any respect."

Today this dialogue probably wouldn't happen. The younger generation won the battle and now long hair is generally not an issue. Every generation, however, always finds beliefs and values to challenge, and as long as parents are invested in the "right" way to do things, there will be battles. Only the issues will change.

Neither parent nor child learns anything from battling, and there is always so much to learn. Instead of just making their children wrong, the parents of the sixties could have learned a lot by asking: Why do we believe long hair on men is wrong? What are my beliefs about masculinity and femininity? Are my upsetting feelings coming from my fear of what my family, neighbors, friends might think? Why am I so concerned with what others think? Why am I so afraid of disapproval?

Children could also have questioned their responses to their parents' attempts to control them: Is this what I really want or am I just reacting to being told what to do?

Do I think my hair looks better or am I just going along with my friends? What do I really want?

These and many more questions could produce important learning for everyone in a conflict:

- Why am I afraid of being wrong?
- Why do I need to make others wrong when they don't agree with me?
- What happens when I try to control others?
- What are my fears of not being in control?
- Why don't I have more faith?

But, you may ask, isn't it better to be neat, and isn't something wrong with people who aren't? Isn't it better to be mannerly and isn't it rude to ignore social customs? Isn't it better to work hard in school and get good grades than to waste time? Two people arguing these questions could each find reasons to support their points of view. However, in a debate, the objective is not to learn anything or to understand the other side, but to prove your side right and the other side wrong.

Parents often try to make their children wrong because of another false belief—that making them wrong is an effective way to get them to change their minds. What often happens is that the children become resistant and entrenched in their position, stuck in a power struggle. Even children who were seemingly compliant become extremely rebellious during adolescence. As the old saying goes, "As soon as you try to make your daughter break up with her boyfriend, you might as well send out the wedding invitations."

Another irony appears when parents try to make children wrong for their own beliefs: all too often the adults model the very same behavior that they're trying to teach their children is wrong. As Alice Miller states in *For Your Own Good,* "In order to teach the child these almost universal values (not to lie, deceive, or hurt others) which are rooted in the Judeo-Christian tradition, among others, adults believe they must sometimes resort to lying, deception, cruelty, mistreatment, and to subjecting the child to humiliation."

All of us have values, that is, beliefs about what is right and wrong, and most often these are sound; living up to them would definitely be beneficial. *But when your intent is to learn, the point is not to decide whose values are right or wrong, but rather to understand the important reasons each of you has for believing as you do.*

Still, you may wonder, are there *no* universal values? We (Jordan and Margie) personally do believe there are universal truths, all centering around the Golden Rule, that it is wrong to intentionally harm another human being. This is probably the only rule found in every major religion. But all other beliefs—yours and ours—are arbitrary decisions. Further, when your primary intent is to learn about yourself and others, the question of affixing the judgment of right or wrong, other than related to the Golden Rule, just isn't relevant. *We can only learn when we are willing to suspend judgments, putting aside our beliefs of right and wrong, while we explore the compelling reasons behind our beliefs.*

Does this mean that you should give up your values? No. Your own values may change because you have learned new things, but giving up beliefs out of fear, obligation, or guilt is to lose a sense of yourself.

Trying to influence your children's values is not the same thing as imposing your values on them. Part of parental responsibility is to offer your views to your children, but they can be offered openly: "Here's the way I feel about it, but you may see it differently. Let's talk about it."

Before this all starts to sound like pie in the sky, or too theoretical, too liberal, or whatever, let's get practical for a minute. Being open and discussing values with your children is really the only chance you have to influence them, unless you want them to do just the opposite of what you'd hoped, or unless you happen to have children who choose to agree with you. Politics and religion provide plenty of examples for this case. Just ask the local Democratic leader whose daughter registers Republican, or the Republican precinct worker whose son works in an opposing campaign. Another example is the youth raised as a Catholic who leaves the church of his youth to join a commune, or the fundamentalist Protestant adolescent who follows the currently popular guru. Sometimes we forget that Americans are born and raised on freedom and we're all eager to exercise our rights, the freedom to think as we choose heading the list.

The next objection you might raise is also a question of practicality: How can I possibly have a thoughtful conversation exploring differences with my children every time conflict comes up? You can't. There are times when a conversation is just not realistic. But there are two things you can do immediately and on every occasion. Both involve a shift in your consciousness, a shift in intent:

> 1. You can avoid, whenever possible, making the other person wrong for disagreeing with you.
> 2. You can ask yourself in each situation: What is the loving thing to do? (This unique way of thinking is the focus of parts 3 and 4.)

Questioning Our Beliefs

The thousands of beliefs or values can be divided loosely into categories: behavior and the outcomes of behavior, feelings and thoughts, and expectations. Behavior has to do with cleanliness, neatness, manners, being on time, spending money. Beliefs about the outcomes of behavior center around the question: What will happen if . . .? Beliefs or values about feelings and thoughts have to do with whether it's right or wrong to think, feel, and/or express certain feelings, i.e., fear, sadness, joy, anger, sexuality, masculinity, femininity. Expectations come from our beliefs about what people should do . . . if they really love us.

Beliefs about Behavior

Did you know that not everyone believes children should keep their rooms neat? Some parents even let their kids go to school with socks that don't match. Some parents require a bath every day. Others think that two or three times a week is adequate. Is one group of families right and the other wrong? In questioning these beliefs, you'll find that no matter what you personally value in the way of behavior, there are always consequences and any time we choose a way to behave, we give up certain benefits and gain others.

For example, suppose your child jumps into things spontaneously without giving them much thought, and you're the kind of person who's more methodical. You would approach a swim in the ocean by taking one step at a time, carefully measuring the depth and temperature, but your child runs and dives as far out as he or she can. Being cautious certainly has some positive benefits. You avoid many difficulties. By jumping into situations, your child may encounter some difficulties and have to do some fancy swimming to survive. If a person were to jump headlong into a dangerous situation without being adequately prepared to handle the special challenges, we would certainly question that person's judgment. On the other hand, protecting ourselves from problems keeps us from feeling competent to handle problems and work our way out of them. People who jump into situations often encounter problems, but also increase their opportunities for learning. Is one way better than another? Each is just a different style and each has positive as well as negative consequences. Each person has compelling reasons for his or her behavior. Is one person wrong and the other right?

Any behavior can be looked at the same way. Your children's behavior may have negative consequences for you and for them as well, but making them wrong is never helpful. Understanding your own reactions and the good reasons your children have for their behavior defuses the situation and leads both to involvement and growth.

Beliefs about the Outcomes of Behavior

We have many beliefs about what will happen if you . . . pick up your babies any time they cry, let your children play in the rain, spank your children, don't spank them allow them to be responsible for remembering their own lunch money or sweater.

There is so much to learn when your child wants to regulate his or her own bedtime, or go without a jacket when you think it's too cold. Questions you can ask are:

- How did I come to believe this?
- Am I willing to check out my belief with others? If not, why?
- Why am I afraid to let my child test out this belief?
- What's the worst thing that could happen?
- What purpose might I have for keeping this belief?
- What does my intuition tell me? Is it something different from my belief?
- Why don't I trust my intuition?
- Why don't I trust my child's intuition?
- Why am I afraid to let my children learn their own lessons?

Beliefs about Feelings and Thoughts

What do you believe are the rights and wrongs, the goods and bads of feelings? As a child you probably heard many judgments about your feelings; you may already have passed on to your children phrases like "There's nothing to cry about," "Big boys don't cry," "Don't be so sensitive," or "Don't be silly (stupid, ridiculous)."

Other beliefs about feelings that many people have absorbed are:

- Strong people don't show their sadness, disappointment, etc.
- Being too emotional means that you're weak.
- Angry feelings are wrong, especially toward parents, siblings, teachers, other authority figures.
- Having certain sexual feelings or thoughts is wrong.

Whenever your children express feelings and you're upset by them, you have the opportunity to look at a value that you have regarding the feelings. When you're open to learning, not only can you avoid passing on to your children the false beliefs you got as a child, but you can free yourself from the limiting effects of these beliefs in your own life.

Questioning Expectations

All beliefs and values generate expectations. However, the ones we really cherish are the expectations we have about how our children will behave if they really care. Each of us has fantasies about what it means to be really appreciated and cared about—often with subconscious scenarios that serve as unexpressed expectations. The following are some of the common expectations of our children, "If you really loved me, you'd . . . "

- celebrate me on Mother's Day, birthdays, etc.
- never do anything that upsets me
- agree with me
- lose weight or gain weight
- eat right and take your vitamins
- never be angry with me
- always feel affectionate toward me
- do well in school
- always tell the truth
- dress and comb your hair the way I think you should
- appreciate all I do for you
- do your chores willingly, without being asked
- love the things I buy for you

Having these expectations is not the problem. It's making your children wrong when your expectations aren't met that creates the difficulties. Realizing fully that your disappointments are caused by *your* expectations is an important awareness.

When your son forgot your last birthday, what did you do? Did you—

a. reprimand him?
b. cry to make him feel guilty?
c. give him the cold shoulder/silent treatment for several days?
d. ask him in a sincere, nonblaming tone of voice if he knew it was your birthday and what were his thoughts about celebrating birthdays?

There are always options for you to choose. In this case, if you chose *a*, *b*, or *c*, you chose to make your child wrong, to blame him, to make him feel guilty, hoping to make him want to meet your expectations for loving you. Curious choice if you look at it that way. In option *d*, however, you have shifted from protective to loving behavior, the behavior that promotes the emotional growth and personal responsibility of both you and your child.

Taking personal responsibility as the parent means learning that your children are not wrong for failing to meet *your* expectations, since these come from within yourself. An intent to learn from upsetting feelings opens the door to exploring expectations.

- Why isn't my child meeting my expectations?
- Are my expectations realistic?
- What do I do when my expectations aren't met?
- When reactions are protective, how does my child respond and what happens between us?
- When my expectation isn't met, is it really because my child doesn't care about me or is he or she resisting my attempts to be in control? Are we in a power struggle?
- Is my child's response really a reflection of not caring about me or is it the fear of losing him/herself?
- Why do I have these expectations and what purpose is it serving to continue them?
- What am I afraid of finding out if I believe that my child has good reasons for not meeting my expectations?

A Fascinating Journey

Learning from your beliefs and expectations takes you on a fascinating journey which will lead you to question values widely held by the culture, your family, and friends. Discovering that almost all values are arbitrary, and not universal or God-given truths, brings you to a transformational awareness: Nobody has the answer for you. The truth lies within each of us. Giving up looking to others to tell you simple rights and wrongs leaves you with the inward search to discover the truth. People you seek help from will be those who help you discover the truth for yourself. *And your role as a parent would not be to give your children your "truths," but to help them discover the truth for themselves.* This means giving up making your children wrong when they don't live up to what you believe is the "right" way, and giving up making yourself wrong as well.

To do this, you must be willing to face your fears and beliefs. The exciting part of this process is that as you do this, you learn some very important lessons about faith and about who you really are.

Some of the questions to ask in this process have already been stated throughout this chapter. Here are some reiterated and some added:

- Am I open to learning about my beliefs, values, expectations?
- What are my fears of opening to this learning?
- What do I believe are God-given values? How do I know this?
- Why do I need to impose my beliefs on others?
- Why do I make my children wrong when they go against what I think is right?
- Why am I afraid of being wrong in someone else's eyes? In my own eyes?
- Am I open to talking to people whose values differ from mine and learning why they believe as they do? If not, why?
- Are my beliefs the same or opposite from my parents? Have I complied or rebelled without questioning what is right for me?

Beliefs about Responsibility

One belief and one corresponding expectation deserve special attention because they lead to countless difficulties in all primary relationships. The belief is that you are responsible for another's happiness or unhappiness and that others are responsible for yours. In the parent-child relationship this means that you are responsible for your children's happiness or unhappiness and they are responsible for yours. The corresponding expectation is that when you love your child and your child loves you, neither of you will do anything that hurts or upsets the other.

We make our children wrong when we believe they are directly responsible for our upset feelings. We blame them, saying things like, "You make me angry . . . or miserable . . . or crazy . . . or sick." But the truth is that your feelings—of hurt, disappointment, fear, and anger—are the result of your *own* beliefs. Your children's behavior merely taps into these beliefs. If you didn't have them, you wouldn't get upset.

When children go past *your* tolerance level, why are they automatically wrong? Your tolerance level is set by your fears, values, and expectations. Another parent, having a higher tolerance level because he or she has less fear or different values and expectations, would not be affected in the same way. Your children's behavior will always have an effect on you. *The question is whether you make them wrong for your feelings, or you assume personal responsibility by wanting to learn from your feelings.*

Blaming your children for what they've done is a separate issue from allowing them to enjoy or suffer the consequences of their actions. Let's say your young daughter has decided not to take your advice to wash her hair before school. A parent's comment "You drive me crazy," only produces guilt. But if this girl returns home tearful, saying that the other kids said she looked dirty, the shoe probably will be on the other foot. She will very likely blame her upset on you: "Why didn't you make me!" If you accept the blame for her feelings, you also are admitting responsibility and will feel guilty.

The guilt that drives people through a lifetime of unresolved misery arises from the parental injunction: "When I'm upset, you're wrong." Letting go of this notion isn't easy since it's been so deeply imbedded. *But you can only be responsible for what you do, not for how others feel and behave in reaction to what you do. Your happiness or unhappiness results from your freely chosen actions and reactions and the same is true for others.*

Although usually a subconscious wish, most parents want children to believe they're wrong for upsetting them. The hope is that instilling guilt and fear in children will effectively maintain control over them. Of course, that only works until they don't feel guilty or afraid any more.

When parents take responsibility for their children's feelings and behavior, there are equally negative side effects. Children learn to avoid personal responsibility. They learn to blame their parents, teachers, or society for their own unhappiness or problems. Believing that, they become helpless victims, blaming others for their own destructive or self-destructive behavior.

It's hard to believe you aren't wrong for actions that upset another. You've been told just the opposite so many times. How do you make sense out of this apparent contradiction? *Intent* is the key. Consciously and deliberately abusing a child physically, emotionally, or sexually is wrong. But doing something for yourself that does not physically or emotionally violate your child and is not *against your child* is not wrong. There is a big difference between doing something for yourself that upsets your child and doing something *against* your child.

If you believe that you should never do something for yourself if it upsets your child, then you will have to give yourself up whenever your child is upset by something you want to do. Or if you go ahead and meet your own needs, then you'll feel guilty. You can't win. If you don't do what you want, you lose yourself. If you do, you feel guilty. A vintage Catch-22.

For example, your four-year-old son doesn't want you to go out to dinner with friends. If you go, leaving him screaming at the door, and if you believe that it's your responsibility to make him happy, you'll feel guilty. If you stay home, you'll feel trapped and resentful. And it's your *belief* about responsibility that is causing your feelings, *not* your child's outburst.

What Are You Responsible For?

After this discussion about looking inward, examining beliefs, and questioning them, it is an easy mistake to view this attitude toward parenting as somewhat narcissistic and passive. On the contrary, the main point of looking inward is to free up outward behavior, that is, to be able to be loving in ways you weren't able to before. And far from passive parenting, the process recommended here is all about *doing,* not just feeling. But, your intuition tells you, "I'm the adult, I'm the parent, I'm responsible for the health and welfare of my child." To this we would say, "Of course! You brought these children into the world. You are entirely responsible for caring for and nurturing them, safeguarding their health until they are able to do these things for themselves."

One of the most essential messages of this book is to clarify what is for the health and welfare of the children and what, disguised as "for their own good," serves the protective purposes of the parent. Now that you know how to separate these two—protective, unloving behavior from loving behavior—you are charged with the responsibility for your own behavior.

Judging behavior right or wrong is never helpful. Nevertheless when you behave protectively you are *responsible* for the consequences. For example, if you spank, yell at, ignore, or criticize your child because you believe these are good ways to teach and your child becomes angry, resistant, rebellious, or destructive, *you are responsible* for your part in creating this unhappy environment and the pain it causes. Therefore, if you want things to change, you are responsible for doing something about your part of the problem and for helping your child with his or her part of the problem.

You are also responsible for recognizing that you are stuck in habitual responses and you are not a helpless victim. You are responsible for your choice to be unloving, uninvolved and protected, or to be loving, involved, and open to learning when you or your children are in pain.

Once you become aware of your protections and the fact that they are unloving, you are responsible for choosing to open to learning and doing what you must to overcome your protections so you can be a more loving parent, thus giving your children more of what they need in order to feel worthwhile. You are responsible for the consequences should you decide to remain protected.

You are responsible for how you choose to react to your children's protections—whether you react with your own protections, or open yourself to learning and being affected by their protections.

You are responsible for the fact that your protections have an effect on your children—the pain, insecurity, and self-doubt that may result from making them wrong or shutting them out. In other words, you are responsible for your children's pain when it is a direct result of something you've done to them—hitting, yelling, ignoring. When taking care of your own needs—working, resting, spending time with friends, mate, doing a hobby—upsets them, you are not responsible for their unhappiness, but you are responsible for how you react to their unhappiness. Do you react unlovingly, telling them not to feel their feelings, or lovingly, wanting to learn about their feelings?

You are responsible for your children's feeling unloved if you use the above activities to exclude them from your life because of your need to protect yourself from your fears of being involved with them.

You are not responsible for your children's difficulties that result from *their* choices to behave in uncaring, destructive, or self-destructive ways, but you are responsible for what you have done that contributes to this behavior. And you are also responsible for whether or not you offer to help them work through their problems in a way that promotes their personal responsibility.

Although we could debate whether or not little children are responsible for the ways they learn to protect themselves from their fears—fears of losing love and/or losing their integrity and individuality—there is no doubt that, as they grow up, they are responsible for their choices to remain in their protective patterns or to do whatever they need to do to increase their feelings of self-worth, take more personal responsibility, and become more loving human beings.

Caring without Taking Responsibility

Since feelings and responses always arise from our beliefs about values, fears, and expectations, it is impossible to be responsible for our children's reactions or for them to be responsible for ours. This does not mean that we will be unaffected and uncaring about our children's feelings. To do what we want without caring about how our children are affected is very unloving.

When you meet your own needs, and in so doing, *unintentionally* upset your children, you can care about them, even feel bad that you hurt them, *without* feeling responsible and guilty. You will feel guilty when you feel wrong for doing whatever you did for yourself. Being able to distinguish between feeling sad and feeling guilty is crucial. Feeling sad is an appropriate, open, natural feeling. Feeling guilty is self-blame, self-condemnation; it gets in the way of being open to learning, personal growth, and intimacy.

More about Personal Responsibility

Many current philosophies interpret concepts of responsibility as nothing more than excuses for self-indulgence which totally frustrate learning and intimacy. The most destructive aspect of these philosophies is their simplification of responsibility into "I'm not responsible for you, you're not responsible for me. Therefore I'm not going to be affected by you and my behavior shouldn't affect you." We are all affected by those around us, especially by those people who are most important to us. The only time it's possible not to be affected is when the other person doesn't matter to us.

Each human being has freedom of choice over his or her own actions. All of us, including very young children, are accountable for our choices and the resulting consequences. No other person can be responsible for the feelings that result from our choices, whether they are happy or sad.

When parents make responsible attempts to see family problems as clearly as possible, they also want to understand how their own protections create these problems. According to traditional usage, the behavior we are calling protective—anger, withdrawal, bullying, laziness, and any other form of manipulation—is bad and irresponsible. *However, we would claim that the fundamental or primary irresponsible behavior is the choice to protect yourself and then blame your children or others for the unhappy consequences your unloving behavior has created.*

When parents are not willing to take personal responsibility, through modeling they encourage the same unwillingness in their children. An extreme consequence of this can be seen in the increasing number of young people who do not take responsibility for their behavior. They lie, steal, cheat, drive drunk, take drugs, or do poorly in school and then they blame their parents for their choices, seeing themselves as victims of their parents' choices. Their parents see themselves as victims of their children's choices and blame their children for the unhappiness that results from their own unloving behavior.

This section on responsibility may be difficult for you to read because the word "responsibility" is frequently considered to be synonymous with "blame," "wrong," or "fault." When your parents said accusingly, "Who's responsible for this?" what they meant was "Whose fault is this?" It may take a lot of work for you to take responsibility for yourself without feeling like you are wrong and accepting blame.

A Transformational Awareness

Personal responsibility means trying for greater harmony between our outer behavior and our inner nature—expressing in action and words the way we really feel inside, under our protections. Outer behavior, when protected, is a part of the personality constructed in order to be accepted in the world. This part of us, called the "ego," is based on our original fear of rejection and disapproval, then perpetuated by our false, self-limiting beliefs. When our intent is for ourselves alone—thus operating within the confines of our egos—we are closed and unloving, and we initiate a chain of negative consequences represented by the left side of the chart, "The Path of the Unloving Behavior (Ego)," in chapter 2.

We can't achieve the harmony we're after by trying to fix our protections, i.e., to find better ways to protect. We can only choose to let them go. When we make that choice, we make a transformational shift from our ego to our Higher Self—our real, inner, loving nature. Our intent has changed from trying to *get* love to wanting to *give* love. The chain of positive consequences is represented on the right side of the chart as the "Path of Loving Behavior (Higher Self)."

When we make this powerful change and open to our strong and gentle, loving nature, we and our children can care very deeply without hiding our feelings behind protective behaviors. We no longer need to live in pain and fear or be kept in line by guilt.

We have the choice of treating others lovingly or unlovingly. When we become aware of what makes us feel truly good and worthwhile, we can see that behavior which hurts another *never* makes us feel better about ourselves.

Much has been written about self-esteem and how to attain it. Many people believe self-esteem is achieved when you accomplish certain goals—make a certain amount of money, have a certain number of children, look a certain way. Yet most people continue to feel inadequate even after achieving all their goals. The reason is that self-esteem comes from feeling lovable, and *you can never feel lovable when you are acting in unloving ways.* Your happiness and unhappiness come from your choice to be open and loving or protected and unloving. That is why no one can be responsible for your happiness or unhappiness—it is truly a consequence of your intent, to protect or to learn, to be unloving or to work toward being loving which is in itself loving.

The same is true for your children. The more they copy your unloving behavior, the worse they feel about themselves and the unhappier they are. The more they copy loving behavior, the more self-esteem they have and the happier they are. The best way to raise happy, successful children is for you to be a model for them. When they see you taking personal responsibility, and when they experience you gradually behaving in more loving rather than protected ways and reaping the benefits of self-esteem and joy, they will do the same.

We often read about social responsibility as if it could be legislated or forced down the throats of the unwilling. But real responsibility cannot exist in a society until it grows and flourishes in the individual. Granted, being open, willing to risk and to learn takes energy and courage. But it is the way you and your children can break down the barriers that get in the way of love.

Part 3

If I Really Loved You

. . . It is the courage to be open and loving which is the manifestation of underlying strength and power. And it is only in embracing the possibility that you have a Higher Self that knows how to love, that knows the truth within, that *is* truly powerful, that you can begin to face and dismantle the false beliefs of the protected self, the ego. You can't begin to look at these and deal with them if you don't believe there's anything else. You can never move into the feeling of personal power unless you recognize truly that there's a place within you that is already there that doesn't have to be developed and doesn't have to be fixed.

·7·

What Do I Do Now?

Changing the Focus to If I Really Loved You

Once we realize there is no right or wrong procedure, we can turn to love in complete confidence.

–Dr. Gerald Jampolsky
Teach Only Love

In the Old Testament of the Bible, there is a story of a good man named Job who suffered greatly, apparently without just cause—basically a "when bad things happen to good people" case in point. Job's plea was to have an answer for the unanswerable question "Why me?" but he was never to know. At least one accepted reason why Job never got an answer, whether his predicament is viewed from a religious or philosophical point of view, is that his question was *irrelevant.* In other words, the answer wouldn't have helped him. Regardless of the situation that Job or any one of us has to face, the significant question to be asked is not "Why me?" but rather "What shall I do now?"

To elaborate a bit, this moment that we live in, the Now, is the only time in which we move and breathe. It is the only time we can directly act on. And so it becomes the only opportunity we have to exercise our freedom to make a choice. In the case of human relationships, it is our moment, our opportunity, to choose to be loving or unloving. And short of physical survival, this is probably the most important choice we have to make in our entire lives.

The first half of this book was preparation for making this choice. In the beginning we talked about parents with loving feelings, but children who didn't feel loved. We talked about families who spend much of their time struggling against each other, but without wanting to or understanding why. Confusion, sadness, and unmet expectations existed where there had been hopes for personal fulfillment and satisfaction with warm and joyous family feelings. At first it seemed like conflict itself was the obstacle in our course, but then we discovered it was, instead, the way we understood conflict along with our reactions to it that kept us from reaching our most cherished goals.

Chapters 1 and 2 discussed conflict and the two choices that are possible for us to make when we are faced with conflict—to protect ourselves, which results in unloving behavior, or to be open to learning and loving. Chapters 3 through 6 discussed how and why we learned to protect ourselves from those we love and the inevitable consequences of choosing the protected path in our relationships with our children, whether we try the authoritarian or permissive approach. In either case there are negatives—feelings, words, behavior—for both the parents and the children. All this was indicated as the path of unloving behavior on the left side of the chart, "The Paths through Conflict." From this point on, we want to focus on the right side of the chart, which includes the choice to be open, to learn and to assume personal responsibility for our own fears and beliefs—the path of loving behavior. So, then, what *is* loving behavior? What does it look like? What does it feel like?

Walking on Air

Just as you know when you are "in love" by the way you feel, so does loving behavior have a feel—a lightness, a sense of peace and personal power that is missing when you are reacting out of fear. Like the family with the handicapped boy who walked in space in chapter 5, when fear is overcome in favor of love, both parents and children have a sense of walking on air.

Loving behavior can be felt in the muscles and seen on the face. There's no mysterious theory here, just a simple observation. When your young child spills the milk (a conflict) and you scream, "What's the matter with you! I told you to be careful!" how do you feel afterwards? Happy or sad? Strong or weak? Proud of yourself or remorseful? How does your body feel? Tense or relaxed? And while you were screaming, what do you suppose your face looked like to your child? What was the expression on your child's face? What do you imagine your child felt inside?

We all have screamed in irritation and anger at times because we're all human, so we need not blame ourselves for not being perfect. But we can act as observers of our own interactions to see if we feel good about what we're doing. If we try to visualize, we can step off the stage of our daily lives and see ourselves rather clearly. So when you react to the spilt milk by caring for your child's feelings instead of your own irritation, and with a calm tone of voice say something like "That's too bad. A paper towel would be good to clean up the mess," you can clearly see and sense the difference. How do you look and feel now? And which behavior was loving is obvious.

Actually, the age of the child is scarcely significant. You might have used the same words—whether loving or unloving—to an older child in the same conflict. The only difference is that the younger child will likely absorb the anger like a sponge while the older child may fight back.

Since there is an infinite number of situations in which conflict can occur, there is no possible way to specify what is loving and what isn't for each case, but rather we will point out a constellation of "symptoms" which are characteristic of loving behavior.

Loving behavior is always consistent with what makes you feel best about yourself. The more you behave consistently with who you really are inside, the more often you are loving. The real you, your Higher Self, loves your child with every ounce of your being. The yelling, anger, blame, and criticism are not true reflections of how you feel about your daughter or son. Those behaviors come from the defense mechanisms which you constructed to protect yourself from feeling hurt or afraid, from real and imaginary emotional dangers. Because this protected self is a construct, we call it the ego. While in traditional psychoanalytic theory, the ego mediates between the id, or instinct, and the superego, or conscience, we are choosing to use ego as defined in Eastern philosophy. This ego is the constructed, protected self, which is created out of fear of rejection and based on the self-limiting belief that one is unlovable, defective, inadequate. The purpose of the ego is to protect against the pain of disapproval and rejection and to gain love. The self with loving feelings and an innate ability and desire to love others we call the Higher Self. The Higher Self is the spiritual aspect of ourselves. There is no fear in the Higher Self because it does not carry self-limiting beliefs. It just gives and receives love. It is love.

The truth we seek as parents— *and as people in any kind of loving relationship*— lies within each of us, in the Higher Self, available for us to know when we want to tune into it. When you want to determine what the loving response is in a given situation, all you have to do is ask yourself, "What would be loving behavior here?" No child psychologist or other outside expert is needed to tell you that yelling at your children produces negative results. *However, the power to choose to do otherwise comes from understanding that the behavior is not just negative, not just harmful, not just protected, but it is unloving. Once you attach that label, your choice not only becomes clear, it also becomes possible.*

The Case of Jack

When Jack came to us as a client, he was miserable. Being the father of two strong-willed teenage boys was driving him into a depression. At our first meeting he was very honest from his level of understanding. The conversations that follow have been shortened to highlight the illustrative comments.

> Jack: I want my kids to do what I tell them to! That's all. Simple request, isn't it?
>
> Jordan: How old are your children?
>
> Jack: They're 16 and 18.
>
> Jordan: They're becoming young men. Maybe they're in a power struggle with you.
>
> Jack: They might be, but kids need to know who's boss.
>
> Jordan: When you do get your way, how do you feel? And how do the kids feel?
>
> Jack: Well, I don't feel good because it's been such a struggle. The kids don't like it. They're angry—slamming doors, putting fists through walls—that kind of stuff. But I can't stop them physically because they're too big.
>
> Jordan: What would happen if you stopped trying to control them?

Jack: I guess they'd run wild. They'd probably never come home at night. They'd never help around the house. They'd never clean their rooms.

Jordan: Do they do those things now?

Jack: Uh, well, not very often.

Jordan: What if you tried something different then and let them make their own decisions?

Jack (head dropped to his chest and eyes downcast): But I'm scared to let go. Aren't fathers supposed to be in control?

In subsequent meetings Jordan and Jack discussed protections and the issues of power. Jack realized that in his own mind, he didn't feel like a powerful person. He thought that he would feel power when he finally gained control over his boys. It was his belief that life should be that way. He wasn't really satisfied with his wife either, because she had a job outside the home. He really preferred that she stay home in the more traditional homemaker role, but she refused. He didn't yell at her. He just silently withdrew.

Jordan: Does your wife know how you feel about her job?

Jack: Yes, but she says I can choose between a working wife and an unhappy wife.

Jordan: Her job must be very important to her. How do you feel about her doing what she wants?

Jack: I wish she wanted what I want.

Jordan: Does withdrawing from her make either of you happy?

Jack: No, but I can't help that.

Every person wants and needs a sense of personal power. When a person doesn't feel powerful, he or she necessarily feels weak and fearful of being overtaken—of losing himself or herself, losing even the appearance of power. But as Jack tried desperately to protect himself, he felt less and less powerful. It was clear, however, that he didn't know any other way to behave or any other way to be. His definition of personal power meant power over others. And he thought that being protected and controlling were positive—how else could he deal with the situation?

In the next session, Jordan asked Jack to describe his wife and boys. It became obvious as tears filled his eyes when he described his family that Jack felt a deep, abiding love for all of them.

> Jordan: It sounds to me like you really love them.
>
> Jack (softly): Oh, of course I do. They're my life.
>
> Jordan: Let's talk about your kids for a minute. Let's take an example of a recent conflict with one of them. Tell me about it.
>
> Jack: Well, Rob cut school last Friday.
>
> Jordan: Okay. Now, remembering that you love him, what would be the loving thing to do? What would help Rob learn the most?

Slowly a look of something like surprise came over Jack. His understanding seemed to come from a different, new level of awareness. After a few tentative answers which he rejected himself, Jack decided what he'd do.

> Jack: I guess it would be to let him deal with the school on his own—to take whatever penalty there is.
>
> Jordan: Which would be more likely to get Rob to stay in school—facing the school authorities himself or facing you, say if you yelled at him and imposed some sort of punishment?
>
> Jack: Well, I did that last time he cut and now he's done it again.

Jordan: How would you feel about yourself if you chose the behavior you described as loving? Would you feel strong or weak?

Jack (laughing a little): I'd feel stronger. I wouldn't be letting him run over me, for one thing.

Jordan: It seems to me that feeling strong would give you a sense of personal power. Is that how you feel?

Jack (smiling): Yes.

Jordan: Then it seems to me that this loving behavior of yours—what you decided to do instead of yelling or threatening or arguing—is more powerful than being unloving. The other ways you tried hurt both of you. Behavior which you chose when you remembered that you love him helped you both—your son to become more personally responsible and you to feel more powerful. Would you agree?

Jack: Yes. But it won't work every time.

Jordan: That's your old definition of "work." But how would you feel about yourself as a father if, every time you got into an upsetting situation with one of the boys, you asked yourself, "What is the loving thing to do?" Would you feel strong or weak? Powerful or not? Miserable or happy?

Jack: I'd feel pretty good about it.

Jordan: Where does it feel like the answers come from when you ask yourself "What is the loving thing to do?"

Jack (thinking for a minute): From somewhere within.

Jordan: When "works" means feeling good about yourself, every time you behave in a loving way, it will work.

As the sessions continued, for the first time Jack could remember he began to feel good about himself as a person and as a father. He learned how much of his behavior was not compatible with his true feelings about his family. And he learned to believe in the answers that came from within, from his Higher Self. When he came into therapy, he saw no alternatives; he was stuck knowing only one way to be. In our terminology, Jack believed that his protected self, his ego, was powerful and could be in control, not realizing that protections are based on fear and you never feel powerful when you feel afraid. By the end of his sessions, Jack reached two important awarenesses:

Being loving is more powerful than being frightened.
Being loving is more powerful than being unloving.

No one gets healed through fear. People are healed through love. Last we heard from Jack, he no longer described himself as miserable and out of control. Basically, he felt at peace with himself and his family.

More about the Higher Self

As we have defined the central spiritual lovingness of the Higher Self, it is evident also that this is God within you. They are one in the same.

Most people come into therapy not knowing they have a Higher Self, not having faith in their own innate goodness and worth, not trusting their own sense of what is true. If you don't believe in yourself and have respect for yourself, then there's got to be fear and protection, because as far as you know, there's nothing else to rely on. The fear eclipses the love you have to offer, and blocks self-esteem and personal power. There seems to be strength in the protections, but this is a facade; it is not true. You wouldn't feel the need to be defensive if there wasn't an underlying fear of powerlessness.

In contrast, it is the courage to be open and loving which is the manifestation of underlying strength and power. And only by embracing the possibility that you have a Higher Self that knows how to love, that knows the truth within, that *is* truly powerful can you begin to face and dismantle the false beliefs of the protected self, the ego. You can't begin to look at these and deal with them if you don't believe there's anything else. You can never move into the feeling of personal power unless you recognize truly that there's a place within you that is already there that doesn't have to be developed and doesn't have to be fixed.

The Higher Self is also powerful because it is not coming from false beliefs. When you are attuned to this Self—who you really are and what the truth is for you— you can never be taken advantage of, used, manipulated, or run over. People are manipulated when they feel wrong, inadequate, guilty. It is in these cases that people are liable to give themselves up. Giving yourself up is what weakness is. Not giving yourself up and yet still loving and being loved—that is real personal power. And it's a great feeling. It's like walking on air.

Steps toward Loving Behavior

None of us humans is perfectly attuned to God within us. Even knowing what you know now, you may still rant and rave, trying to control, or get cold and withdraw, or comply out of fear. As parents, you have the double duty of taking care of yourselves and the welfare of your children. Those children you love so much can present every imaginable kind of conflict as they struggle to grow and develop. Also, there are numerous circumstances of your own which make it difficult for you to act and react as you would like. Being tired, overworked, or under different kinds of stress, being raised in a protected family—any of these and a myriad of other factors get in the way.

However, there are two steps you can take which will always help you shift from the path of unloving behavior to the path of loving behavior. One step is to deliberately, consciously move into the intent to learn. A client, Judy, expresses it this way: "When I am through with my need to be angry, I put that aside and look at him. I think of why he did what he did, what he was thinking about, and the block between us goes away. Then I can even see how my own reaction was, well, sort of silly. The whole problem just goes away." While Judy was talking about her husband, the dynamic is the same whether the loved one is a spouse or a child.

The other step you can take to tune into your Higher Self and the behavior that expresses your deepest, real feelings is simply to remember that you love the person. To remember this activates the feelings of love and diffuses the protections. A friend, Diane, describes it this way: "When one of my daughters has done something that upsets me—forgotten her homework again or left her dirty clothes in the hall—I say to myself, 'I love this child' and it softens my anger and irritation immediately. My face relaxes from a tense frown into a smile, recalling the sweet and wonderful person my little girl is."

Many, many times as a parent you have to make decisions quickly. There's much confusion, many demands, little time to weigh alternatives, pick and choose behavior. These are the times when you have to ask yourself simply, "What is the loving thing to do?" The answers will be clear and fast. Your Higher Self will never say, "Let's call him names and see if that works." Or "Maybe if I undermine her self-confidence and ask her what in the world she thinks she's doing, she'll do things my way." Instead, in the act of asking "What's the loving thing to do?" your face and tone of voice will soften, and your focus will shift from how upset you are to how you can be of help to your child: "That's too bad you spilled the milk. A paper towel would be good for cleaning up the mess." Or "I agree that homework can be boring, but it won't help you learn your spelling words if I look them up." Or "I know it's frustrating to lose things. If you retrace your steps carefully, you'll probably find the car keys."

Intent Is Always the Key

Every so often someone speculates, "What if we lived in a world where everyone could read our minds?" For most of us, the reaction is that this is a pretty frightening thought. But a second thought might generate another question, "Why? Why are we so afraid to have someone else know our true feelings?" Of course, there are the obvious answers about hurting someone's feelings—if we think a person isn't pretty, handsome, etc. But on a more reflective note, the message underlying our words reflects our intent and if others knew our true intent, they'd know when we intended to manipulate them in order to protect ourselves rather than to learn about them, or to deceive them rather than be honest which might be risky.

As always, intent is the key which determines whether a behavior is loving or not. And verbalizing what is in our minds as well as on our lips is one way to test this out. Giving praise, being generous with money, giving in to your children's desires, offering encouragement, discipline, giving information which you believe to be important and helpful—these are just a few examples of behaviors which need to be looked at in the light of intent to see if they are loving or not. For example, when you give in to your children, is it because after thinking through the request, you decide a "yes" is in their best interests—or is it because you are afraid they'll be angry or won't love you if you say no?

Unloving behavior—all the behavior that follows the intention to protect—is more easily understood than loving behavior. We're not used to thinking in terms of loving behavior and have rarely seen it modeled. The following list of loving behaviors or attitudes with the corresponding unloving behaviors may help clarify what is loving:

UNLOVING	LOVING
Criticizing, putting down, judging	Wanting to understand
Persuading your child to see things the way you do	Wanting to understand how your child sees things
Attempting to get love	Giving love
Making another wrong, blaming	Respecting another's choices
Trying to make another change to do what you think is best	Opening to understanding why you are upset by another's behavior
"I know what's best for you."	"I'd like to help you discover what's best for you."
Trying to hold on and have control	Letting go and being willing to deal with the fears generated when you let go
Trying to hold others back when their behavior causes you discomfort	Encouraging, supporting, being happy with another's choices, and exploring your discomfort

Believing you alone know what's best	Having faith in your children's ability to find what's best for them
Trying to impose your suggestions or ideas	Offering suggestions or ideas freely with no strings attached
Trying to make others behave	Modeling behavior
Caring only about your feelings	Considering another's feelings
Caring only about another's feelings	Considering your own feelings
Trying to make someone change to make yourself feel better	Making yourself happy
"You belong to me."	"You're your own person, an individual, a unique expression of God."

Loving Behavior in the Real World

The real world of family life involves many, many issues which to all outward appearances have very little to do with love: television, school and homework, clothes, hair, mealtimes, manners, getting up in the morning, friends, drugs and alcohol, curfew, and more. However, if you think about it, these are some of the issues which create the most conflict between parents and children. Most of us are very loving until we're crossed, upset, or frightened. At these times—in situations of conflict—we get unhappy. That's when we "lose it" and create the problems in our lives. And we become critical or cold or whatever behavior we choose. Then people around us get the message: "I'm only going to get love when I do what my parent wants." That doesn't feel like being loved, because the love feels conditional on never doing anything that upsets mom or dad.

So, it is primarily in the nitty gritty of our daily lives, "in the trenches" so to speak, where children will be convinced that they are loved by the most important people in their lives. And if they are loved, *if they are really loved,* by these central, original figures, they will almost always feel good about themselves. In other words, they will have self-esteem, which brings us as parents to our first-chosen goal for our children.

Stories from Real Life

Peggy and Brook

First-grader Brook didn't want to do her homework. Her mother Peggy offered her special treats if she would; then Peggy tried limiting privileges like television. In desperation, she put Brook in her room at night, but still Brook refused to cooperate. In fact, she became less and less cooperative. Brook got defiant and Peggy got angry. Finally she sought our advice. We suggested that Brook was old enough to be responsible for her own homework and probably sensed that Peggy had a great investment in the issue, so Brook knew she had her mother over a barrel. Peggy went home for another try.

> Peggy: Let's talk about your homework.
>
> Brook: You can't make me do it.
>
> Peggy: I know I can't. I just wondered why you didn't want to do it. When I was little I loved school.
>
> Brook: I love school too.
>
> Peggy: Then I'm still curious why you don't want to do your work?
>
> Brook: Because I want to do my own homework by myself, not for you.

Peggy: Are you old enough to do that now?

Brook said that she was. The next night Peggy said nothing at all. Brook opened her backpack right after dinner, spread out her papers, and did her work start to finish. After that, except for Peggy's occasional reminders that she indeed was in charge of her own schoolwork, Brook continued to work on her own without resistance.

Mike and Robert

The report cards arrived in the mail. Mike opened the envelope marked "To the parents of Robert" and found to his complete dismay that his son had gotten an F in Spanish. Robert arrived home shortly after and found his father, head in hands, bent over on the couch.

Robert (softly): Why does my F in Spanish bother you so much? It's my grade, not yours.

Mike: I guess because it embarrasses me, for one thing. And I know you're capable of passing, so it makes me think you just didn't try.

Then Mike stood up and went about his business. Two or three times throughout the rest of the day, Robert walked passed the report card which lay on the coffee table and commented aloud: "Boy, those are the worst grades I've ever gotten." The next semester he opted not to participate in an after-school sport and proudly displayed his final grades to his father—all A's and B's.

Margie and Sheryl

Sheryl, age twelve, got irritated easily and Margie didn't like being with her when she was like that. Margie tried different things. First she got irritated back, but that didn't help. Margie felt bad and Sheryl got more irritated. Margie asked Sheryl why she was irritated, but Sheryl felt attacked, and felt like Margie was making it all her fault.

Margie finally decided what to do: whenever her daughter was irritated, Margie would just get up and walk out. Since confronting Sheryl didn't work, at least Margie would be taking care of herself. So, whenever Sheryl acted that way, Margie would just get up and leave.

Finally after Margie did that a number of times, Sheryl followed her into the other room:

> Sheryl: Mom, did you leave because I was irritable?
> Margie: Yes.
> Sheryl: Oh, I'm sorry. I don't like being that way. I'd rather you said something to me.
> Margie: But when I've said something to you, you've gotten upset with me. And I just don't want to be with you when you're like that.

After that direct experience of the consequences of her behavior, Sheryl became irritable a great deal less.

In each of these cases the parents had to feel their way, make mistakes, learn what doesn't work, and finally come to a decision on what would be loving to themselves and how best to help their children in the given situation. The parents learned and the children learned—and ultimately assumed responsibility for themselves.

It is another one of the essential paradoxes of life—in the same way that trying to prove power is evidence of powerlessness—that choosing loving behavior with your children actually brings about more positive change in the behavior of your children than any amount of coercion, persuasion, or other method of control.

This chapter has attempted to define and illustrate loving behavior and to show that when we do, however imperfectly, work at fostering our own and our children's emotional and spiritual growth and personal responsibility, it works better both for ourselves and each other. In the next chapter we'll discuss general situations where conflict is likely to occur. Hopefully, this will give you a taste of the possibilities for learning about yourself and your children. Since no one has written the complete book of learning, you have a lifetime to build on the information offered here.

·8·

What Does Loving Behavior Look Like?

Learning about Loving Behavior in Some General Situations

> *Children who are truly loved unconsciously know themselves to be valued. This knowledge is worth more than gold . . . The feeling of being valuable—"I am a valuable person"—is essential to mental health and is a cornerstone of self-discipline. It is a direct product of parental love.*
>
> —M. Scott Peck, M.D.
> *The Road Less Traveled*

When we live with people we love, our lives touch each other's every day in countless ways. To make living together easier and more comfortable for everyone, families often set rules. In previous chapters we have tried not to suggest what your rules should be, but rather show you what will happen when you react in certain ways if there is conflict over broken rules or anything else. And as we said earlier, since there is a whole world of possible situations which can arise, we can only describe what loving behavior is in general. However, there are some potential problem areas which are common for most people. In this chapter we will talk about some of those aspects of conflict situations which all of us have to deal with. Our hope is to add to your learning by sharing some of the information we've learned about being loving in some general situations.

Learning about Respecting Children's Needs

As unique individuals, children often have needs and rhythms which differ from their parents. For example, babies, guided by their Higher Selves, know exactly when they need sleep, food, or attention. When parents believe they know what's best they often get into power struggles, even with a baby. Children tend to be fed on their parents' timetable, forced to eat the amount of food their parents think is right, dressed by their parents' metabolism and expected to sleep according to what their parents think is the correct amount of sleep. Unloving behavior imposes the parents' needs and feelings on the child without learning about the child's needs. Loving behavior respects a child's individuality.

After years of receiving one of the most destructive messages children get—"You don't know your own mind"—is it any wonder that an overwhelming number of adults have lost touch with their inner knowing? After receiving the messages that we don't even know when we're cold or hot, tired, hungry or full, many adults often have to look for a higher authority to tell them what they think, feel, need, and want.

An example of how destructive this can be occurred during the 1930s and 1940s when physicians (mostly male) decided that babies should be fed by the clock. Millions of mothers, not in touch with their own inner knowing or not trusting that knowing, followed the "authorities." Babies were left to cry until the appointed hour arrived for their feeding. Some mothers, even though they agonized over their babies pain, still refused to go against the orders of their doctors. Others trusted enough in their instincts and intuition not to pay attention to such nonsense.

Advice-givers abound in our culture, but any way that steers you away from your own inner knowing is ultimately unhelpful.

When we were new parents, we got advice on how to do everything. For example, many people advised us not to always pick up our babies when they cried. Their rationale was that we would spoil our child with too much attention. Thankfully that was advice that Margie knew was false and we attempted to meet our children's needs as much and as soon as we could. We even put plug-in intercoms around the house so we could always hear when a baby was crying and needed us.

Responding to babies' cries lets them know they have some power and that someone cares. Children whose needs are met develop an inner security that doesn't occur when they are in need but their cries are left unheeded. There is an important distinction here between responding to babies' cries and predicting their needs so that their needs are met before they ask. When parents are overly indulgent, children don't learn how to ask for and go after meeting their needs, but rather wait for someone else to meet them.

Certainly, it is possible to spoil children, but never by meeting their very legitimate needs for love and attention. *Spoiled children are the result of parents who give up themselves, and thereby the children don't learn to respect others' needs.* Infants and young children, though, need to have their needs met in order to feel loved and learn trust.

With an infant it is loving for parents to put aside some of their own needs for sleep, time alone, or hobbies to meet the needs of this totally dependent being. However, as children grow and become capable of meeting more of their own needs, they must learn to shift from their self-indulgent, center-of-the-world position to one of nurturing and caring about others. This learning process can begin from the time they understand language, as parents slowly shift from focusing all their attention on their children's needs to meeting more of their own.

Children can quickly learn manipulative, irresponsible behavior to get their way. So loving behavior would be for parents to explore their own reactions, to learn about the reasons for their children's behavior as well as to learn about themselves.

The following is an example of only one of our struggles to discover the most loving behavior.

MARGIE:

One night about 2:00 a.m. when Eric was six months old, he woke up crying. I went into his room and held and rocked him. This had comforted him in the past but this time his difficulties were not satisfied by this kind of comfort. Out of desperation and exhaustion I carried him into the den and sat down in front of the TV. Eric immediately calmed down and in a few minutes I was able to put him back in his crib to sleep. The next night Eric woke up again and this routine again quieted him. After two weeks of this I began to suspect that he was deliberately waking himself up in order to watch the fascinating lights of the TV. The next night when he cried I went to his room, picked him up and sat down in the rocking chair. He continued to cry and point to the door. Nothing I could do would soothe him. I realized that he had learned to wake himself up in order to watch TV. When he realized that I wasn't going to go to the television he calmed down.

For the next few nights he kept waking up and I would rock him in his room. Finally I realized that, if I wanted him to sleep, I would have to not go into his room at all. The first night he cried for about an hour. The second night it was about twenty minutes. The third night it was for only five minutes, and after that he stopped waking up. Hearing his screams was one of the hardest things I've ever had to do, but I was pretty sure I was right and I needed to test out my belief.

Children who are overly indulged become spoiled and may never learn to give. Children whose needs aren't met and don't feel loved usually become protected out of their fear of being unloved; they never learn to trust others or be loving and nurturing. Children best learn this important balance between too much and too little from parents who love and respect the children without giving up themselves.

BELIEFS TO QUESTION:

- Responding to a child's needs is wrong.
- Children get spoiled by getting too much love and attention.
- Crying is good for babies; comforting spoils them.
- Babies need to cry in order to strengthen their lungs.
- Meeting your children's needs for love and caring makes them dependent on you.
- Giving a child too much love makes them greedy for love.
- Tenderness is harmful.

Learning about Saying No

Children's explorations, an essential part of learning, activate many erroneous beliefs and resulting fears for parents. The usual result is a barrage of No's! Sometimes saying no is the most loving thing you can do. Certainly in matters of health and safety a parent must make certain decisions for a young child. But saying no usually accompanies a behavior which the parent believes to be wrong. Making children wrong occurs thousands of times without parents questioning their own behavior and its effects.

No can be said firmly *and* lovingly (without blame) when you don't believe the child is wrong or bad for his or her behavior. An irritated, hard tone of voice, reflecting a parent's belief that the child is bad, erodes a child's self-esteem and therefore is very unloving.

JORDAN:

One afternoon we were walking to our car after a day at Disneyland. A family was by their car getting ready to leave. Their small boy, about three years of age, was tired and he lay down on the asphalt next to the car. His father came over, grabbed his arm and yelled at him, "Get up off the ground. You'll ruin your jacket!" The child started to cry, and then the father yelled at him to stop crying. Obviously, the father believed he had to make his son wrong to have any impact. Yet it would have taken the same amount of time if the father had lovingly picked up his son and said simply and calmly, "Jackets can get ruined on the hard ground." The boy would have gotten the message without feeling wrong.

Sometimes the no is to "protect" the child from making a "mistake" or failing at something. But what's wrong with failing? A great deal of important learning goes on by trial and error and the child's emotional and spiritual growth is not impeded by failure. It's only when failure has negative connotations put on it that children become afraid to make mistakes.

Reserving no for only really important things like health and safety issues and saying it without making the child wrong give a much better chance of your wishes being met without injuring the self-esteem of your child. In addition, the greater the barrage of "Don't touch that" and "Don't do this," the greater the likelihood that requests will begin to fall on deaf ears. As parents get frustrated by their children's resistance, they often resort to louder no's or stronger punishments. This usually leads to deep scars, awful power struggles, and an increasing emotional distance.

Reducing the number of times you say no is a challenging project. Many can simply be reduced by modifying the home environment. You can child-proof the house so that children can explore as much as possible without harming themselves or infringing on your rights. Many parents believe that a child must be punished to learn to be careful and not touch valuable items. However, we've seen that when children have been treated with respect, in time they learn to respect people and objects. As they grow they can naturally learn, through modeling, not to touch or break things. They do not have to be taught this at ages one or two. Until that time, reducing the possibilities of needing to say no eliminates many problems later on. If it's a question of which is more important, your convenience or the child's curiosity and emotional development, the loving behavior is obvious.

Another loving way to substantially reduce the no's is to examine your own beliefs and fears. The less *you* fear, the less need you'll have to say no.

Learning about Time Alone for Them and Us

Children feel important and loved when they know that their parents want to spend time with them. Time alone has always been important for our children. We've made unfailing efforts to set aside time to be with each of them on a consistent basis. We learned to establish a set time, because we realized that unless we planned for time alone it usually didn't happen.

When the children were younger, this was a part of our daily routine. Time to play games, read, hold and cuddle, or just lie on the bed together and talk. A time when we didn't answer telephones, take care of our chores, or deal with the other children. This was that child's special time, a time when we focused on him or her alone. Only extreme emergencies were allowed to interfere. We found things to do that both of us liked and that also gave us the space to talk about whatever came up. Sometimes we'd do things out of the house, but usually our time was spent in the children's bedrooms. As they got older, they didn't seem to need as much time with us but we continue to enjoy and value time together.

Giving the children that special time helped them at a very early age to understand and respect mom and dad's need for time alone with each other. They could understand our need for time alone once they realized how much they enjoyed it and how important time alone was for them. "Our relationship needs special time without being interrupted" was easily understood and respected once they understood what special time was.

Learning about Feeling Loved

There are some specific things that most people, children and adults, need to feel deeply loved: 1) to feel seen, understood, and valued for who they really are; and 2) to know that their behavior has an effect, or in other words, that what they do matters to the important people in their lives.

To feel understood children need to feel respected for their feelings, thoughts, dreams, interests, desires, and behavior. Ask your children if they feel respected by you, especially when they differ from you in the above categories. If the answer is no, a good place to start is to ask them why they feel disrespected—what do you do? The next step for you is to deal with why it's hard for you to respect your children when their beliefs differ from yours. We keep coming back to the same place, don't we?

When children feel understood and respected, they feel supported emotionally. They feel you have faith in them. *The more you need to control them, the less faith they feel you have in them.* When children do not feel their parents' faith in them, it is not only devastating to their self-esteem, but they will never feel loved.

To feel loved children also need to know that they are important enough to have an effect. Knowing that their needs and feelings matter is one way of experiencing this. Knowing that their parents are affected by their behavior is another. However, our children cannot see these effects unless we are willing to be vulnerable. Protected responses like getting angry or irritated don't give them the sense of the deep effect. Your reaction probably doesn't register anyway since they've probably protected themselves from your attack and are not thinking about you. When the shield of protection goes up, we all see only our own pain. Also, we usually can't see into other people and care for their pain unless they let us see how they feel. Letting our children see how they affect us is difficult for most parents.

JORDAN:

The time had arrived to leave for the Segals' bar mitzvah and Eric and I were in the middle of a huge battle. Although we were still furious with each other when we arrived at the temple, we stuffed our anger like "good boys" and entered the temple with polite smiles frozen on our faces. During the reception we mingled with peers pretending not to notice each other. At the end of the day's activities each person gathered for the ending ceremony was asked to read a short passage from a prayer book. Eric, who was eleven at the time, read beautifully and I was so proud my anger melted and a real warmth and openness went through my body. As the ceremony ended, I lovingly put my arm around him, but he shrugged my arm off his shoulder and kept on walking. My body immediately stiffened as I thought, "You little jerk, you'll pay for that."

The ice returned to my veins and he got the message. On the way home he tried to bridge the gap, but I felt hurt and now he would have to pay. He made further attempts after we got home but "he needed to be taught a lesson." Agonizing minutes went by that seemed like hours. I felt awful and headed for the bedroom to lie down. Margie came in and lying down next to me said, "Let's talk."

Our exploration led me to realize that I had been unwilling to let Eric see the hurt I felt when he shrugged off my attempt to patch things up. With that awareness I softened and said, "I guess it's hard for me to let anyone see my hurt, but especially my own child." I explored my difficulty in letting anyone be important enough to affect me, and my masculine image training which taught me that it was weak to be sensitive and emotional. As my protections melted, I realized the pain I had caused Eric with my coldness and felt very sad. I went into Eric's room, put my arms around him and shared my feelings. Eric softened in my arms as we talked and wept together.

Disapproval can hurt, especially from a person who is important to you. If you're not affected by your children, they will probably conclude that they are unimportant. The nonverbal message sent is, "You're not important enough to matter."

BELIEFS TO QUESTION:

- I give my children what I think they need and that should be enough for them to know that I love them and to feel loved.
- Never let children see that you've responded to them with hurt or fear.

Learning about Respect and Caring

We want our children to be respectful and caring about us and others. However, if you believe children should respect you just because you're older or because you're their parent, then you will probably try to teach them to respect you using punishment, lectures, threats, insults, criticism, etc. As we said earlier, you cannot teach your children to respect you by behaving disrespectfully towards them. They may learn to *act* respectfully out of fear or guilt, but that will last only as long as they fear you or feel guilty. Genuine respect flows from feeling understood, cared about and respected. Genuine respect and real caring are learned together and become part of a person's way of being in the world.

Children are much more likely to care about your needs when you request rather than demand or command. Demands create power struggles in which the child resists out of fear of being controlled. Children will not care about you when they are protecting themselves from your control. A true request can be refused without any negative consequences being imposed. If you impose negative consequences when a request is refused, then the "request" was really a camouflaged demand.

BELIEFS TO QUESTION:

- Parents deserve respect just because they are parents.
- Parents have a right to demand respect from their children, regardless of how they treat their children.
- Parents cannot survive being offended by their children.
- Respect must be taught through discipline.
- Children are wrong if they are disrespectful. There are no good reasons for being disrespectful.
- Children are undeserving of respect just because they are children.
- What does it mean to be respectful and why do I think so?
- A feeling of duty produces respect and caring.
- A pretense of gratitude is better than honest ingratitude.
- Hatred can be done away with by forbidding it.
- Respect and caring can be created by demanding them.

Learning about Fighting in Front of the Children

Although we have been worried that fighting in front of the children would be harmful to them, we've done it anyway. To our surprise we've found that as long as they also witness our explorations and resolutions, they can handle our fights. They've experienced a picture of conflict, protections, and learning—a total picture. If children only see fighting, they draw the conclusion that conflict always just leads to fighting and unhappiness. If children never see interactions over differences, they never learn that it's okay to have differences, and that people can work out their problems in mutually satisfying ways. Our children know that when we've worked through a difficult situation, we feel better and more loving. While we wish very much to be at the point where we can always go directly into learning when there is a conflict, we're not yet there and so we do sometimes fight before we open to learning. But because our children know that we will always explore until we resolve our difficulty, they're not unduly afraid of conflicts.

BELIEFS TO QUESTION:

- You should never fight in front of children.
- Children should not know about parents' difficulties.

Learning about Failure

Many adults suffer from the belief that only perfection is acceptable. Failure has a negative connotation. The fear of failure is so great that people either avoid any chance to fail, thereby greatly limiting their growth, or they hide anything that may be considered a failure. But failure is impossible when you believe there are always good reasons for behavior. Whatever happens, there is always something to be learned.

We have tried hard to help our children not be so hard on themselves. Mistakes are to be learned from. Hugh Prather put it so well when he wrote, "You are not a mistake just because you made one." This is a hard concept in a culture that makes failure or mistakes wrong. Even in school when a question is missed, instead of being welcomed as an opportunity to discover what we don't know, it is given a bad mark. We have to hide our mistakes or what we don't know out of the fear of being made wrong, being a failure.

BELIEFS TO QUESTION:

- It's bad to make a mistake or not know something.
- Making children wrong helps them learn.
- Making children wrong increases their motivation.

Learning about How Children Learn

How children learn is another important area where self-limiting beliefs create many difficulties. A basic belief to question is, "Children must be taught."

Human beings are born with an innate curiosity and desire to learn. In fact, it is widely known that during the first few years children learn more and at a faster rate than during any other time in their lives. When they do not fear failure, children are led by their curiosity into many new and fascinating areas. When children are made wrong, fears begin. Afraid of making mistakes, being disapproved of, or failing, children start to hold back and the accelerated learning that accompanied openness becomes slower and slower. The more disapproval, the more fear. The more fear, the bigger the blocks to learning. School, by attempting to motivate through fear, manages to kill most of what is left of our natural joy of learning. When Jordan was teaching high school, on the first day of school he would occasionally say to his tenth grade class, "Learning is fun," and get back thirty pairs of eyes doubting his sanity.

Where does motivation come from? How do children learn? What gets in the way of that learning? What really has to be taught? Do *you* have to motivate children to learn? What happens when you attempt to motivate learning by instilling fear? Although these questions and many others will be dealt with in a subsequent book (probably to be titled, "Do I Have to Give Up Me to Be

Taught by You?'') some of them are particularly important for parents to consider.

When you trust children's innate drives, it isn't necessary to make the decisions on what to teach your children. Instead you can be eager to help them learn when they ask, and you can enrich their environment so that their curiosity can be encouraged. These are things we try to do. We suggest and we model the behavior that we think is healthful. We try to stay out of power struggles. We try to stay aware of the problems that are created when we don't behave in the above fashion and deal with what's getting in the way of following these ideas. We try to keep the faith and deal with our fears when we lose it.

It's so difficult for parents to let go of trying to control the outcome with their children because most parents have very little *faith* in the ability of their children to make good decisions and take good care of themselves. Lack of faith comes from beliefs about people in general—about whether we, as human beings, are inherently motivated to learn and do well, or we have to be pressured into it. The less faith you have in your children's own desire to learn and grow and do well, the more you will attempt to control them and the more they may resist you. Parenting becomes a much easier task when you come to have faith in your children. You can then realize that they do not have to be taught, and that more than anything they need your love, support, understanding, and adequate modeling. Then they will be just fine.

You may be asking the very legitimate question, ''What's wrong with teaching?'' Nothing, except when you attempt to teach what your children don't want to learn. When they want to learn, some will ask while others may just want to learn from watching. Sheryl loves to be taught and is a great student. Eric and Josh have always hated to be taught and would rather learn it themselves. Attempting to teach when a child doesn't want it often winds up with them resisting. Then, the more you want them to learn, the harder they resist.

In junior high school, Eric used to give us papers that he had written to look over. We'd eagerly jump in to make corrections, giving him suggestions on his style, content, grammar, and spelling. He'd usually wind up irritated and inevitably a battle would ensue. After many battles we learned that he felt invaded when we just plunged in with our ideas as to how things should be. Sometimes he just wanted general comments—whether or not we liked the paper and whether we thought he was on the right track. We realized that unless he invited us in, we were violating him. It was hard but we had to learn to ask, "Do you want corrections or not?" before reading his paper. It was even harder not to correct when he said no, but we did finally learn to give him what he wanted and to have—you guessed it—faith. We certainly could tell him we had some ideas we'd like to share on content, or that there were mistakes that needed correcting, and then wait to be asked to help. It took us a while to give up what we thought was the best way to be and to tune into what this particular person wanted and needed. When we did, everything went much more smoothly and his interest in writing expanded.

BELIEFS TO QUESTION:

- If children are not forced to learn, they won't.
- Motivating children by fear is an efficient way to teach.
- If children are not interested in learning, they should be forced to learn.

Learning about Sexuality

Personal responsibility for sexuality is another major trouble spot in people's lives. Many adult problems stem from the enormous number of erroneous beliefs we have about sex. False beliefs lead to the sexual irresponsibility that creates a great deal of pain. We have worked very diligently with our own sexual beliefs and are constantly finding erroneous beliefs that have to be cleared away.

Although we've been very open in talking to our children about sex, we've felt sex between parents to be a special and private sharing. They know that we love each other and enjoy our sexuality together as an outgrowth of our love. When appropriate, we've shared many of our thoughts and feelings about sex, including the difficulties we've had throughout our lives because of our sexual misconceptions and fears. We have talked freely with our children, when it has been appropriate, about our problems—our feelings and experiences as teenagers, our first sexual experiences, masturbation, our marital adjustments, and what we've learned about male-female sexual relations. We've had many talks about sex and love and shared with them why we feel that sex without love and caring can be an empty and unfulfilling experience.

Although we've read excellent books about sex to them when they were younger, and they've read some excellent books on their own, it's probably been our willingness to be open about ourselves that has taught them (and us) more than anything else. As in all important areas of life we want to influence them, but are very careful not to get into power struggles that close them off to us and push them away.

Their own sexuality is something we've always been available to discuss when they wanted to. We've given them information about sex and never criticized their questions or behavior. Like any natural feeling, this is a very tender area and one which needs a great deal of care. Negative messages about natural feelings create much self-doubt and confusion which leave deep scars and have a tremendous impact on future relationships.

Sex is a beautiful way to express love and can be used as a very powerful, positive force in our lives. Sex is also a physical need. Understanding these two aspects of sex and integrating them into one's life is a task that most people find difficult. We don't want our children to be used sexually by others nor do we want them to use others sexually. We don't want them to use sex to meet other psychological needs, such as the need for affection or the need to be accepted. Establishing a healthy sexual attitude is best accomplished when parents have a loving sexual relationship, and children feel the freedom to discuss their sexual feelings openly.

BELIEFS TO QUESTION:

- Sex is wrong/bad unless one is married.
- Sex is wrong/bad unless it's for making babies.
- Masturbation is wrong.
- Sex play between children is harmful.
- Children will grow up promiscuous unless they feel guilty about sex.
- Seeing parents nude will cause problems for the children.
- Nudity within the family context is always/ seldom sexual.
- Children should/should not know that their parents make love.
- Parents should/should not talk about their sexuality or their sexual difficulties in front of their children.

Learning about Teenage Rebellion

One of the most common misconceptions that we hear over and over again is that teenage rebellion is normal. Teenage experimentation is normal, but rebellion only exists when there are power struggles in the parent-child relationship. Rebellion becomes a part of a protective way to establish a separate identity when teenagers fear domination.

The teen years can be a wonderful experience when parents are open to the learning that goes on as a part of an experimentation process. Probably there will be too much alcohol consumed at times; there may be some frightening experiences with drugs. Almost certainly there will be experimentation, overindulgence, lack of sleep, and sexual confusion. Teenagers need to talk about their experiences. They will want to talk to you as long as they feel they'll be respected and not punished. To sort things out and learn from their experiences they will need to dig deep into their fears and beliefs. They may just muddle through like most of us had to do and later on undo the beliefs and habits formed in adolescence, but parents can help their kids a lot if they remain open.

We've really enjoyed our children's teen years. They're going through a lot and there have been some difficult times, but our family bond has grown closer. After hearing all the horror stories about family relations during teenage years, it's actually been easier than we expected. The time and energy we put into the early years has paid off.

Is It Worth Your Time?

People are always concerned about how much time this process of loving interaction takes. Telling children what to do does take less time at first. However, the problems occur when they never learn to take responsibility for their own lives and always have to be told what to do, or when they rebel against your attempts to control them. Also, having to be a police officer, be on guard, and be in control becomes very wearing and is not much fun. Being in a constant power struggle leads to fights about almost everything and family relations become very unpleasant. The effort and time you spend become worth it as children develop personal responsibility and don't need to rebel. Because personal responsibility is the cornerstone of being a loving person, we have separated it from this chapter into a chapter of its own.

·9·

What Am I Responsible For?

Learning about Personal Responsibility

> *Distinguishing what we are and what we*
> *are not responsible for in this life is one*
> *of the greatest problems of human exist-*
> *ence. It is never completely solved; for the*
> *entirety of our lives we must continually*
> *assess and reassess where our responsibil-*
> *ities lie in the ever-changing course of*
> *events.*
>
> –M. Scott Peck, M.D.
> *The Road Less Traveled*

Would you breathe a huge sigh of relief if you knew your children were responsible human beings? For most parents that would be the key to not worrying and not having to be in control. But has anyone helped you learn how to teach children to be responsible? Or more to the point, has anyone helped you understand what you may be doing that is contributing to your child not learning to be responsible? Most parents in their well-meaning attempts to teach responsibility, bring about the opposite result.

When people don't take personal responsibility they become protected behind compliance, control, resistance and/or indifference. They believe they are helpless victims, reactors to other people's choices. Believing that they are unable to make themselves happy, they try to get others to change their behavior so they can be happy. A victim blames others and blaming is never loving.

Since emotional and spiritual growth is dependent on becoming more personally responsible, anything that promotes a child taking personal responsibility is loving. Conversely, anything that interferes with a child learning to become more personally responsible is unloving. Fixing your children's problems—and also taking their pain away—does not allow them the opportunity to learn to work out their problems and deal with the pain in their lives. *Allowing children to handle their problems, with guidance when asked for, conveys the message that you have faith in them. That's the loving way to help them grow into self-respecting, personally responsible adults.*

Before going much further we need to define what we mean by personal responsibility. In general, personally responsible behavior is always loving behavior. More specifically, personal responsibility involves recognizing and accepting that you are free to make choices and that your choices cause your happiness and unhappiness.

Also, when you choose unloving behavior in a certain situation—because no one can be perfectly loving all the time—you are being personally responsible when you recognize that you are accountable for your actions and for the consequences of your actions. In addition, taking personal responsibility means you would explore what kept you from being loving to yourself and your children and learn from that.

Another aspect of personal responsibility concerns choosing to develop the various parts of your being— physical, intellectual, emotional, sexual, social, and spiritual. How does this relate to personally responsible and loving behavior? The areas in which you feel weak or inadequate are the areas where you're likely to be fearful and protective. So if you feel inadequate in athletics, for instance, you may avoid physical activity out of fear.

That's not loving to yourself. And when your children take up sports you may be too invested in their performances. That's not loving to them. Sports are an easy example, but there are many others. An overweight parent may insist on the child being too thin. An adult who has never felt attractive to the opposite sex may be too concerned that the son or daughter be popular and have dates. A parent who didn't do well in school may place too much emphasis on getting good grades. In all these cases, the adults' feelings of inadequacy translate into unloving behavior toward themselves and their children. Personal responsibility means taking steps to remove the blocks to loving behavior.

You may be thinking, "Your definition sounds okay to me, but I'd be happy if my kids just took out the garbage, cleaned their rooms and did their homework." Of course, they need to take care of business and responsible people do that. People in rebellion don't, angry people don't, people who don't care don't. So, if your child is not taking care of business, you now have the chance to learn what is getting in the way of your child's living responsibly. And you can learn how and why the ways you've been trying to teach responsibility are not working.

It would be ideal if our children had an internal discipline guiding them throughout their lives. The question is, "How do you best help children develop that?" Overly controlling parents usually produce children who lose that sense and either rebel or conform. Children who come from permissive backgrounds don't develop it either since they never learn respect for the rights of others. Does discipline or punishment teach responsible behavior? What do they teach? These are crucial questions which we'd like you to consider.

Ideally when parents respect their own and their children's rights, when children are allowed to suffer the consequences of their choices, and when explorations are a part of family life, discipline and punishment are almost never necessary. Natural limits are set for children when parents respect their own rights. That's not to say that we have never disciplined our own children. At young ages children occasionally need to be isolated when they get out of control and are being manipulative. Putting children in their rooms, for brief periods of time, *without being angry at them and making them wrong,* may be appropriate. Children must learn that they cannot run over the rights of others. But what do you teach when you run over their rights by punishing them? When you accept the premise that all behavior has important reasons motivating it, then you will question your right to run over your children, or anyone else. And what do you teach them about caring when you don't care enough to explore and understand the good reasons they have for their behavior?

When people feel respected, cared for, understood and open to learning, solutions for conflicts can always be found. When punishments and threats are used to keep children in line, it is almost impossible to find mutually respectful solutions. When discussion, explorations and learning are a part of problem-solving, discipline and punishment are simply not necessary.

Babies are the most responsible of all human beings. Growing infants develop all the areas of their being with great tenacity and focus. They are able to respond and their response ability (responsibility) is perfect. If we allow them to suffer the natural consequences of their choices, (other than issues concerning their personal safety when they're young), model loving, personally responsible behavior by taking personal responsibility for ourselves, do for them, for the most part, only what they are incapable of doing for themselves, help them only when they need help, and treat them with love and respect, they will maintain their naturally high level of personal responsibility. This requires that the parents have the faith not to control, to learn what their children are capable of doing for themselves, and to learn about themselves so they can model the behavior that they want for their children.

For example, you wouldn't think of lifting your babies to a standing position every time they attempted to stand. Your willingness to allow your children to struggle and finally stand up is an important accomplishment. They learned to take responsibility for their need to stand up. That's an obvious example. But how about setting the alarm clock in order to get up on time in the morning? Choosing what clothes to buy? Choosing what clothes to wear? Getting dressed? Taking a shower or bath? Becoming toilet trained? Eating meals? Manners? Doing homework? Cleaning their rooms? Getting enough sleep at night? Giving up the bottle? Giving up nursing? Stopping thumb sucking? Learning how much alcohol they should drink? Managing money?

How many of these decisions have you made or attempted to make for your children? What have been the results of your making those decisions? Have your children learned to be personally responsible or do you have to police them? Have power struggles developed around these areas? Are your children gaining a greater sense of self-worth and trust in themselves?

What are your fears of allowing your children to find their own way, to learn from their mistakes? Why is your role that of a doer rather than that of a helper? Most parents do for their children long past the time children are able to do for themselves. Sometimes it's nice for you to do things even though they're capable of doing them themselves, like making their school lunches. But doing too much or trying to get them to do things on your timetable, by your standards, inhibits their learning to be responsible.

Like most parents, we learned many lessons with
our first child that greatly benefitted the other children
and the area of "Whose responsibility is this anyhow"
was a really important one. To illustrate we'll share the
before and after of Margie and Eric's routine for getting
ready to go to school.

MARGIE:

Getting three-year-old Eric ready for nursery
school began every morning with a hassle. Beginning at 7:00 a.m. I would give him gentle
reminders of what he had to do to get ready. He
was spaced out in front of the TV, and my
suggestions fell on deaf ears. By 7:30 my
reminders were not so gentle. "Eric finish your
breakfast . . . You've got to brush your teeth." By
7:45 I was getting frantic. "Eric your carpool will
be here any minute, you've got to get your clothes
on." Eric dawdled and by 7:55 I was angrily
pulling on his socks and tying his shoes. The
carpool came and he still wasn't ready. "Eric,
where's your jacket?!" (To Jordan) "Hon, go tell
the carpool we'll be right there." (To Eric dragging
him out) "Come on, they're waiting for you!" (To
Jordan, returning from outdoors) "I'm so mad at
that kid . . . . Oh no, he forgot his lunch." (To
the rear of a disappearing station wagon) "Wait, he
forgot his lunch!" (Bedraggled and now muttering
to myself) "I can't take this, I feel like crying." I'd
been up for only an hour and I felt exhausted.

After realizing that Eric was perfectly capable
of performing all of these tasks by himself, I
started to consider my part of the difficulty. I
talked with Jordan, who was not as emotionally
involved in this problem and he helped me get
some clarity. I realized that Eric, being a very
independent child, was in a power struggle with

me. Therefore, I had a responsibility in creating this difficulty. Eric was not wrong. I took a look at my controlling behavior, my beliefs about parental responsibilities, and what I feared would happen if I let go of trying to control his behavior. I realized that Eric was capable of getting himself ready and that nothing could be worse than the ordeal I was going through. I decided to let go.

I told Eric lovingly that I realized that I was taking too much responsibility for his getting ready in the morning and from now on he would be on his own. I would tell him when it was 7:30 and that was all. After that he would have to get himself ready. If he wasn't ready when his carpool came, I would gather up his clothes and transport them and him out to the car where he could finish getting dressed.

The next morning when he wasn't quite ready when the carpool arrived, I *lovingly* handed him his shirt, shoes and socks and escorted him to the car. We allowed him to experience the logical negative consequences of his choices. That was the last time we ever had a problem with being ready and my mornings were sure a lot nicer.

Children learn to be responsible from the consequences of their actions when allowed to experience them. Children are not fools. They know or can quickly learn how much sleep they need and when their stomachs are full. Hungry children will not tell you they don't want to eat unless they have an overriding need, such as the need to be in control of their own bodies. When you tell children over and over to take a jacket because it's cold or an umbrella because it might rain, you communicate that you don't think they have enough sense to come in out of the rain. Multiply that message ten thousand times and it is debilitating. The message is, "You don't know your own mind. I, your parent, in my infinite wisdom, know what you need. I know when you're cold, how much sleep you should get, exactly how much you should eat (when you finish the amount of food I put on your plate you will be full), how much you should study," etc.

What are your fears of your children learning their lessons by getting wet, being cold, not handing in their homework on time, failing a test, being late?

Imposing consequences is not the same as natural consequences. Restricting television watching when your children don't do their homework is not the same as letting them deal with the consequences of not doing their homework. Imposing a bedtime or curfew is not the same as allowing them to suffer the tiredness or other problems associated with not getting enough sleep. When you impose consequences, you are the controller and sentencer. Your children may learn only to be angry and blame you rather than take responsibility for their lives.

The above examples are for behavior that directly affects only the child. When their behavior affects you directly, letting them experience the logical negative consequences is more difficult. For example, when Eric was a young child he would leave his toys all over the house. This caused us a great deal of inconvenience because we had to clean up the mess. First we calmly tried to explain to him that he needed to pick up his toys and put them back in his room. When that didn't work, we got angry and imposed punishments. But that didn't work either. When we picked up his toys and put them back in his room we felt like we were being taken advantage of. We needed to find a way of handling this problem without giving up ourselves or trying to get him to give in—we needed to do something for ourselves when his toys were left around without trying to control him.

We decided that if a toy was left in some room other than his own and we picked it up at the end of the day we would put that toy in the trash can. We told him this without blame or hardness. At that point the problem ceased being ours and was his. If he didn't retrieve the toy it would not cause us any further difficulties and we would not replace it. He then had the choice to go outside to the trash to retrieve his toy or he could put it away at the end of the day. This was a logical consequence of parents reacting to a situation by taking care of themselves and being personally responsible without "imposing" negative consequences. While you cannot instruct in personal responsibility, you can model it. We were being personally responsible because we were taking care of our own happiness without harming anyone.

Taking Responsibility for Children

When you take responsibility for children, you can look for two results. First, there is the child who will resist doing what you want, thus creating power struggles. Second, there is the child who will docilely do what you want, and wait for further orders. Neither of these children has learned responsibility.

A responsible person knows what needs to be done and does it. Jordan recalls seeing many high school seniors who had been closely watched over by concerned parents flounder terribly their first year in college because no one was there to tell them what to do. Some of these kids learned to take responsibility after doing very poorly, some of them didn't.

Giving teenagers responsibility for their lives when they've been tightly controlled is frightening. The decisions they have to make are much more serious than those that have to be made at six or ten years old. It's scary to think of kids who haven't been allowed to make any major decisions for themselves having to make major decisions. Kids who have practice with decisions don't have so much trouble. We would rather have our kids start to make decisions at earlier ages when the consequences are not so important and to learn from the consequences of their decisions. When children have a chance to practice making decisions, they are better equipped to make the more important decisions as they get older.

For example, would you rather have your children waste their time until they failed the third grade or learn that lesson in college? Would you rather have your children learn to get the amount of sleep they need to get by being very tired in the first grade or on their first important job? Children need to learn from the consequences of their actions and one of the most difficult things for parents who love their children is to see them unhappy. But if you try to "fix it" or help them avoid their unhappiness, what do they learn? They either learn that they can do whatever they please and mommy and daddy will make it better or when things don't work out they can blame you. When you are prepared for them to be tired, hungry, or overweight, or to fail, get sick, be late to school, oversleep, then you can let them suffer the consequences of their choices at an early age so they can learn how to be responsible for themselves.

What Is a Parent's Responsibility?

For children to take responsibility for their lives, parents have to let go of that responsibility. That doesn't mean not being involved. On the contrary you will be very involved but in a very different way. *Loving parents are concerned, available as information-givers and as guides and helpers for children to learn from the consequences of their actions.* And loving parents model personal responsibility. Actually, *modeling personal responsibility is the parents' primary responsibility.* If parents give themselves up and then feel resentful and taken advantage of, they are not modeling personally responsible behavior because they are not making themselves happy. They are teaching their children to manipulate by being martyrs, compliers, placators. They are teaching their children to believe that other people, rather than themselves, are responsible for their happiness.

If parents take responsibility for their children by trying to control them, they are not modeling personally responsible behavior because they are not learning about their own fears or trying to understand their child. And they are again teaching the child the belief that others are responsible for their happiness, because implied in control is "If you change I will be happy and if you don't I will be unhappy. You are responsible for my feelings."

Protective behavior, then, is never personally responsible. We therefore have the responsibility of dealing with our fears, beliefs, and protections, so that we can model personally responsible loving behavior for our children.

Obviously when we talk about not taking responsibility for a child we're not talking about matters of safety. You don't allow your three-year-old to run in the street to learn that cars are dangerous, or touch a hot stove to learn about fire. But what about matters other than safety? Whose decision is it as to when they should give up their security blanket or give up taking piano lessons? What are the fears and beliefs that lead you to making decisions for them on matters pertaining to *their lives?*

One of the hardest things to know is what to realistically expect from children, what they are capable of at certain ages. Expecting too little diminishes them; expecting too much frustrates them and sets the stage for power struggles. Children at six months of age are not capable of the sphincter control necessary for bowel or urinary control. Expecting them to be toilet trained too early is bound to cause difficulties. On the other hand, children are capable of taking responsibility for many things in their lives far earlier than parents allow them. *Not allowing children to assume what they're capable of inhibits the child learning to take personal responsibility.*

Children's Domain vs. Parents' Domain

Parenting is made much harder than it need be by your beliefs that lead you to take responsibility for areas of your children's lives that, in reality, only they can be responsible for, such as how they do in school, eating and sleeping habits, or how they dress. Parents need to take responsibility for making sure their children have clothes in their closet and healthy food in the house and on the table, but they complicate matters greatly when they try to force their children to eat or wear what they're "supposed" to. You can put them in their rooms at night and close the door, but you can't force them to go to sleep. You can force them to sit at their desks, but you can't force them to learn. The more parents infringe on the child's domain, the more power struggles are created and the harder parenting becomes. *We believe that you are responsible for meeting your own needs, giving your child love and respect, supplying your child with food, clothing and shelter, and for modeling loving and responsible behavior—and that's all!* Attempting to own your children's problems creates many problems for them and for you as well.

BELIEFS TO QUESTION:

- I can't be happy if my child is unhappy or upset.
- I shouldn't feel happy when my children are unhappy.
- When I'm hurt or upset by my children's behavior, they are wrong.

- It's my children's responsibility to make me happy.
- It's my children's fault when I'm unhappy.
- I shouldn't do things for myself that make me happy if my child is upset about it.
- I can make my children be open and loving.
- I can make my children be responsible.
- I can get my children out of their protected behavior.
- It's my responsibility to make my children happy.
- When my children are unhappy it's my fault.
- It's my responsibility to make sure that my children don't fail.
- If I don't take responsibility for my children's happiness and unhappiness, I'm not a caring person or a good parent.
- I don't deserve to make myself happy; therefore, my children (or my mate) have to take responsibility for telling me it's okay to do what makes me happy.
- If I take responsibility for my own happiness, I'm being a selfish parent.
- It's selfish of me to be happy unless my children are happy.
- There are certain areas of my children's behavior that as a parent I have the right to control.

·10·

What Do I Do When...?

Loving Behavior in Some Specific Conflicts

> *If we are each equally weak and equally strong, as good and as bad as one another, then what is left to us? We must learn that each of our lives can itself become a spiritual pilgrimage.*
> —Sheldon B. Kopp
> *If You Meet the Buddha on the Road, Kill Him*

To become personally responsible, children need to find their own limits based on their unique needs and rhythms. A loving response then is anything that helps them accomplish this and unloving responses are those that inhibit this. Like everyone else's, our own protections get in the way of always being loving with our children. We have, however, given our children a lot of freedom to make their own decisions and assume personal responsibility. In this chapter we will share many of our own experiences in giving our children responsibility for their lives. Please keep in mind that we have continually explored our fears and beliefs and we are in a never-ending process of reevaluation and learning. We don't presume that our beliefs are right. We're trying to find ways that work best for everyone.

In the specific conflicts we will describe we are not looking for a right or wrong way to deal with these conflicts but only trying to find the most loving response.

The criterion is whether the response is fostering both the parent's and the child's emotional and spiritual growth. For children, this means helping them become more personally responsible. Although it's hard to describe on the printed page it's crucial to remember that whatever we did or said was only loving if it was accompanied with loving, respectful feelings. Acting loving when you're not feeling loving is not loving.

In this chapter we'll look at just a few of the hundreds of possible conflicts. Some of the ideas may disturb you. They might frighten you and challenge your beliefs but, as always, you can choose to learn or protect.

Conflicts over Bedtime

Because we want our children to know how much sleep they need and make appropriate decisions for themselves, we did not set bedtimes for them when they were young. Instead, we told them that we would be available to put them to sleep at 8:30. That usually meant that at about 8:15 we'd come into their bedroom to tuck them in bed, spend some quiet time, read a story, talk, listen to music. At 8:30 we'd kiss them goodnight and turn out their light. If they were not tired, they did not have to go to sleep, but they couldn't watch TV or disturb anyone else, and we would not be available later to tuck them in. They almost always chose to go to sleep at that time because having that time with us was very important to them. However, at those times when other things were more important, they were free to make another choice.

Our needs for a quiet house and time for ourselves were met, so everyone got their needs met and there were no power struggles over bedtime. As our children got to be six or seven years old, they would generally be the ones to come to us and say, "I'm ready for bed." Friends of ours would be shocked to see a child come in and say that. They were so used to children resisting bedtime that they couldn't believe a child might want to go to sleep because he or she was tired. As our children got older and needed less sleep, then we became more flexible about when we tucked them in. Our main objective has been for them to know when they are tired and be responsible for getting the sleep they need, rather than relying on us to tell them.

When our children became teenagers, we chose not to place a curfew on them. They had learned how much sleep they need to function well and it became their responsibility even more to take care of themselves. To quiet some of our anxieties we have asked them to tell us what time they expect to be home as well as let us know where they're going. We have rarely had problems with either of these requests, but then our children know we trust them and will not forbid them or punish them. When we have been concerned, we have discussed our concerns with them and we have all learned valuable things from these talks.

Conflicts over Eating and Food

In our house dinner has always been served at a regular time and whoever was around and wanted to eat with us was certainly welcome. Those who weren't around or weren't hungry had their food put in the refrigerator and could retrieve it whenever they wished. This has been true from very young ages.

We've always wanted the dinner table to be a special, fun place. So dinnertime was not the time to air gripes or place many restrictions. The kids almost always made it to the dinner table and dinnertime has usually been fun. We talk about things that are important to them. Manners have not been important and language has never been an issue. Digestive disturbances have been a constant source of hilarious scenes; spilt milk has been a "no big deal" accident that needed to be cleaned up. No demands have been made about what or how much should be eaten.

Because we've never wanted to police our children, we only keep in the house food we want them to eat. What they eat outside of the house is totally up to them. Because of the severe contrast between healthy food and other types, they've learned the effects on their moods from eating many junk foods, especially sugar. We've shared with them our beliefs about healthy eating, but we've never taken responsibility for what and when they decide to eat. The snacks we keep are always healthy and available. If they eat a lot of these snacks before dinner and are not hungry for dinner, that's their problem, not ours. A limited amount of snacks are bought for the week and apportioning them out is the kids' problem. We've had many family meetings to try and find equitable ways to settle that one.

Without power struggles our kids have eaten well and we've all had fun. We haven't needed to threaten them to keep them in line. They eat well because they don't need to rebel in order to escape from tightly constructed rules. They come to the table because the table is a fun place to be. They eat good, healthy food at home because that's all there is to eat. (Also, we've never tried to control their eating habits outside the home.) If their internal clocks are not ready to eat, they can get their needs met when they're ready. We've had faith that they know how much to eat and when they are hungry. These ideas may seem too radical to you, but it's not important whether you do all or any of these things. What is important is to understand the attitude behind what we do and the results.

When our children were very young, we rarely took them out to eat at restaurants or into homes that weren't childproofed. The restaurants we did take them to were always casual, family restaurants that didn't mind having a young child wandering in the aisles. Very young children have a hard time sitting in one place for very long; so, rather than trying to impose restrictions on them and making all of us tense and miserable, we just waited until they got to be three or four and then there was no problem. We often see anxious parents and screaming kids in restaurants and wonder why they are willing to go through all that misery. Do they believe they need to teach their children to behave in restaurants? Again, they may have no faith that as children grow they will naturally learn appropriate behavior in a restaurant.

We followed the same guidelines when we wanted to take a young child to friends who were particular about their homes or had valuable objects displayed. Because we didn't think it was fair to our children to be constantly saying no, we chose to wait until they were a little older for those outings.

When children don't behave, or eat well, or they overeat, the loving response is to assume that they have good reasons and to attempt to learn what these are.

Conflicts over Manners, Cleanliness, and Neatness

Would you believe that we've never attempted to teach our children any manners and yet none of them has ever embarrassed us at even the most elegant events? Our children have learned manners naturally by imitating others. Wanting to be like adults, they started playing with eating utensils while still in their high chairs and by trial and error they found ways of eating that bore an amazing resemblance to ours. We've never told our children to say thank you when getting a present or after spending a day with a friend, but they do. Remembering times we were embarrassed by our parents' nudges and whispers loud enough for everyone to hear—"Say thank you"—we resolved to find a better way. Every time our child got a present, or left a friend's home, we said,

"Thank you," and our children eventually learned this behavior. What do you remember about your experiences as a child or the experiences with your own children as you attempted to teach them to say thank you? Most people eventually learn to say thank you, but hard feelings aren't necessary to accomplish this simple response.

Cleanliness and neatness bring up all kinds of interesting issues for parents to deal with. So many families have awful power struggles over baths, neat clothes or rooms, and the like. Our children certainly don't have the same ideas about neatness and cleanliness as we do. In fact, getting the boys to take regular baths was another source of constant struggle until we pulled out of it. We finally got a commitment that they would bathe at least once a week "whether they needed it or not." They seemed willing to commit to that one. But at puberty they seemed to realize the importance of showering more frequently and without our telling them, they became daily showerers to our relief. They probably would have reached this no matter how we handled it, but until they did, we certainly avoided the unhappiness and power struggles that many families have to go through. We have needed to question our own beliefs about cleanliness and how important it really is and why. Did we want our children clean to protect ourselves from the judgment of others or because we thought it was healthier?

When children admire their parents and aren't in angry power struggles, they will emulate many of their parents' values. They will also need to blend in their own unique contributions. They will not be exactly like you, but, we believe, your highest qualities will be passed on.

BELIEFS TO QUESTION:

- Manners must be taught.
- My children must behave the way I think is right.

- The way you behave is more important than the way you really are.
- It's wrong to be messy.
- It's wrong or unhealthy not to bathe every day.

Conflicts over Language

When certain words make you cringe or you believe that certain words are bad, whose problem is that? Are you willing to take responsibility for your discomfort or are you convinced that the person saying the words that are upsetting you is the perpetrator of a crime? It is very difficult not to make others wrong when you're upset, isn't it?

Not judging words as right or wrong to use is one of the things that has made it very easy for our children to talk to us. However, this wasn't always our attitude; we were raised with the idea that certain words are bad. But questioning our upsets has changed many beliefs that had caused us many problems. Life is much easier, less uptight, and more fun without worrying about many of the words we were brought up to believe were "wrong."

That attitude may frighten you. You may even be feeling very judgmental (if you haven't already felt that way). But what's wrong with this attitude? What terrible things do you fear happening to you or others who give up worrying about words? Will you be less good, less loving, less spiritual? By whose definition? Will you be producing children who are irresponsible or unloving?

Words are a good example of the need to question values and the results of making people wrong. In every generation words that were unacceptable in the last generation are acceptable in the following one. Since this is so arbitrary, how can you be so sure that you are right? Think about the concept of making someone wrong because they say a word. A word is not an action. If you didn't have the beliefs you have about the word you wouldn't be feeling the pain it causes you, unless the *intent* behind the word was to cause you pain. Focusing on intent rather than on specific words is far more enlightening and growth-producing. How can another person be wrong because of your beliefs?

If your children don't want to cause you pain and if you tell them about your sensitiveness and own it as your problem, they will probably try not to say things that tap into your pain. But if you make them wrong rather than take responsibility for your difficulties, there's a good chance they'll get defensive. And then, since you attacked and hurt them, they may want to attack and hurt you and be much more likely to swear or talk back. They won't care about you, but you haven't cared about them. It certainly would be nice for you to care about each other; then neither of you would be hurt.

If you don't like your children using certain words, then be sure you are not using them yourself. If you make them wrong, then they may get back at you and do the opposite of what you want. If you can work with yourself to the point where you don't react with judgments in response to their swearing, then the chances are they will swear a lot less.

In our house words have never been an issue because there aren't any words that cause much of an emotional charge in either of us as parents. Our children can say whatever they please, but they don't use swear words very often. We've helped them to understand and care about other people's sensitivities and they rarely use words around others they know would upset them.

BELIEFS TO QUESTION:

- There are bad words.
- It's the words themselves that are bad or wrong, rather than the intent behind them.

- There are words children should not say.
- It's okay for parents to swear but not okay for children.

Conflicts over School Complaints

When your children complain about school—or about anything else, for that matter—the loving response is to assume there are very important reasons for their feelings and to be caring enough to hear them out. This can mean putting a great deal of credence in children's complaints about school and specific teachers. Complaints about boring or unfair teachers, or the boring irrelevance of what is taught in school are often accurate. Once your child feels understood, a loving response might be to help him or her find possible solutions. When there are no really good choices, just knowing you've cared enough to try and just being listened to and understood will often ameliorate the problem. Feeling understood is often all children need to help them learn how to make a miserable situation much more acceptable.

Attempting to convince children that something is true when it isn't is unloving. Much of education is boring, irrelevant and unnecessary, especially for older children. So when they feel homework is meaningless and stupid, trying to convince them otherwise is impossible and a put-down as well. You may need to know the very important reasons your children have for feeling as they do before you can support them. That's loving. It's never helpful, and therefore is unloving, to make them wrong for their feelings.

One of the most common misbeliefs is that if you empathize with a person's unhappiness he or she will have a harder time. So parents often try to talk children out of their feelings, which usually doesn't work and only succeeds in leaving them feeling frustrated, misunderstood, uncared for and unmotivated. The more children allow themselves to be talked out of their feelings, the greater grow their self-doubts. The greater the self-doubts, the greater the fear of failure. The more children fear failure, the less motivated they will be.

BELIEFS TO QUESTION:

- Empathizing with your children's unhappiness will only encourage it and make it worse.
- Teachers are usually right/usually wrong when they complain about your child.
- Children exaggerate their unhappiness with school and teachers.
- Children complain about their teachers just to excuse their poor performances.
- A child should be expected to do well in school even if the teacher is boring or the child is not interested in the material.
- There are no excuses for doing poorly in school.

Conflict over Illness

Because the mind has such great power to create and to cure disease, children will benefit from using that energy as much as possible. The more they enjoy school and life in general, the less chance they have of getting sick. Children can learn to use illness to avoid responsibility or to manipulate attention. In our house there's never been a payoff for being sick. We've always told our children that a sick child needs to stay in bed and rest. Since TV has never been allowed during the day, and since there are no TV's in bedrooms, they couldn't use TV as a way out. We would always do what we could to help them be comfortable and get well as quickly as possible, but they never got special attention for being sick; they just got the same love and acceptance they always got.

Of course, there are times when children do need a lot of special attention, as when they are seriously ill, for example. However, when children don't take responsibility for eating well, getting enough sleep, or when they've learned they can use illness as a way out of school or other problems, the loving response is to help them explore their reasons and feelings rather than coddling or judging them.

Conflicts over Lying

Honesty is one thing that's always been important to us. Once when Jordan found out that Eric had lied to him, we were very upset. Jordan asked him why he had lied and Eric replied, "Because I was afraid if I told you the truth, you would be angry with me." This was the beginning of our realization that if we wanted our children to be honest, we had a responsibility not to punish them for telling the truth. Certainly most people would lie if they thought they were going to be punished. Clearly we had to choose between hearing the truth and being in touch with our children's behavior, or being lied to, with no chance to offer input and guidance. That was our choice. Jordan told Eric that he would work on his part of the difficulty, not getting angry, but he would also like Eric to work on his willingness to be honest even if negative consequences might be imposed. Jordan also let him know that we were in this difficulty together, and that none of us was to blame.

As parents, do you really want to know the truth? Why? Do you want simply to be in control or do you want to help your children learn to control themselves? Are you really interested in knowing about your child's feelings and behavior? How will you handle things you believe to be wrong? Why should your children tell you the truth if they will be punished? Again, do you really want to know whether they're cheating in school, taking drugs and/or drinking at parties; having sex, with whom; stealing?

If you think you want to know but punish your child when you hear the truth, then you don't really want to know. It's certainly understandable if you don't want to know. Knowing often creates a great deal of fear. But if you really don't want to know, you don't have to ask. And if you want to know, you can be ready to deal with your fears and beliefs, again.

BELIEFS TO QUESTION:

- It's wrong to lie.
- There are never any good reasons
  for lying.

Conflicts over Watching Television

There are very few inventions that have the capacity to do as much good and evil as television. Very few people can withstand the spell of TV's hypnotic effect. Once in its clutches nothing else seems to matter. It can be used to tranquilize the pain and boredom of our lives with seemingly no physically harmful effects. It's legal and you can even drive after having ingested huge quantities. Yet, in addition to the hypnotic effects, there is some wonderful entertainment and to the discerning viewer some exciting learning opportunities. But for children it's like giving them a dose of an addicting drug every day. Our society has yet to realize the impact of an entire generation of children being raised by television sets. Television programming shapes our values and saps our initiative. A parent has to work hard to overcome the effects of TV, but limiting television watching is essential.

Even though we don't watch television ourselves, we noticed our children in their elementary school years relying more on the TV to fill up their lives. Playing, reading, and creative pursuits were dwindling away and being replaced with greater and greater amounts of time in front of the television. The longer they spent in front of the TV, the more unhappy and irritable they seemed to become, but they seemed unable to do anything about it.

Although we had given our children freedom to make their own choices, this did not seem to be working out well and we got more and more frightened. We tried talking with the kids to no avail. We felt this was not an area where they were capable of making a healthy decision for themselves and so we had to make the decision for them. This was one of those rare times we saved for imposing our wishes over theirs.

We decided to take an essential tube out of the TV and told them we would not replace it until we saw that they had found more productive ways to handle their free time. We did everything we could to help them with this, such as taking them to a hobby store to help them find new interests. They started to read again, draw, play more indoor and outdoor games, and become more involved with each other. After two months of no TV, we found that our entire household was calmer and happier. The kids were getting along better with each other, and they were feeling much better about themselves because they were learning and accomplishing new things.

Before we put the television back together, we had a family talk. We pointed out how positive things were in the house, and the kids agreed. Together we came up with a plan for television watching that felt comfortable for all of us. They agreed to limit their television watching to one-half hour in the morning before school and one hour in the evening on weekdays. On weekends we established a more flexible schedule but still with definite limits.

That was one of the best decisions we ever made. The television has a place in our lives and some of us watch it more than others, but it doesn't seem to get in the way of anyone's initiative, creativity, learning or our family relationship. To us that's the criterion to judge the effect of television on your life.

BELIEFS TO QUESTION:

- Television has a relatively minor effect on children.
- Television has a relatively minor effect on the family.

Conflicts over Homework

Conflicts over homework plague most families. Parents are worried and want their children to do well. Believing that encouragement, praise, explanations, tutors, setting limits, and even threats and anger are well-meaning, deserved, necessary and loving, parents begin many interactions with their children that lead to a number of difficulties. From the time our children began school we took the radical position that their learning was their responsibility. We let them know that we would always be available when they needed our help, but it was their job to let us know when they needed help or if they just wanted us to sit with them and keep them company while they studied.

We've rarely asked our children if they have homework or if they've done their homework. We've never told them they couldn't do something until their homework was finished—watch TV, play, go to a friend's house. They've always known that we value and appreciate it when they do well, but that we want them to do well for themselves, not for us, so we've never offered them rewards such as money for good grades. We want them to get their own internal rewards and to learn to be personally responsible.

This position has worked very well for us and our children. They all do well in school and they assume complete responsibility for their work. They are examples of what we believe is natural—that children like to do well and are self-motivated when they receive love and acceptance from their parents and are not in a power struggle. We have spoken to hundreds of families on this issue of schoolwork: over and over again when the power struggle is broken, children learn easily and beautifully.

Many parents who have understood the importance of modeling have been perplexed when their children turn away from many of their important values, especially education. This is almost always the result of a child resisting being pushed to study. When education is important to parents and they push a child to study, this is often an area in which a child resists. Many school problems are the result of this power struggle. Of course, school problems may be due to other things such as boredom, poor teaching, physical problems, etc. But when the power struggle is taken away, like magic, most problems disappear.

This is usually a difficult area for parents to let go of their attempts to control. To do this parents need to make it okay for a child to fail and continue to love that child. The attitude must be, "I will love you even if you fail. It's your decision to do well or not." As usual, parents need to explore many of their beliefs and fears to reach this point.

Our friend Karen tells this story about her own learning. Believing that she was responsible for motivating her fifth-grade son, Tim, to do his homework, she reminded him constantly. Tim did not work faster and better. Instead, he worked slower and with increasing reticence, although he was a very bright boy. One weekend Tim had an essay assignment, so Karen sent Tim to his room on Saturday morning, saying he could come out when his essay was finished. Alone in his room, Tim dawdled the time away. By mid-afternoon with no progress, Karen's frustration and anger were building, so she began visiting his room every so often making a variety of threats and demands. Still Tim made no move to write. Karen slept poorly that night and awoke Sunday morning more determined than ever to get Tim to write his paper, admittedly afraid of the consequences if he didn't. By Sunday evening she had spent most of the weekend in and out of Tim's room with various ploys— yelling, anger, criticism—trying everything she knew how to do. Finally, in tears of frustration, anger and fear, she gave up. And as she did, Karen tells us, she was forced to come face to face with her beliefs about what she could and could not control as a parent. Also, she was forced to consider alternatives, since what she was doing wasn't working.

Monday after school Karen and Tim met with Tim's teacher. "I just wanted you to know," Karen said to the teacher, "that Tim will now be in charge of his own work. I won't be helping him or reminding him. Whether he does his homework or not will be his choice." All three of them agreed on this new plan. "The teacher was a little surprised," Karen laughed, "but I felt strangely relieved and Tim was obviously happy." The biggest surprise was the change in Tim. The difference in his attitude was like night and day. For the rest of the year Tim did his assignments without being asked, most of them done very well. Tim felt the pleasure of being personally responsible and Karen learned a lot about what she could do to be the best help to her son.

BELIEFS TO QUESTION:

- Parents need to take responsibility for their children doing homework.
- Getting children to do well in school is the parents' responsibility.
- Parents can make children learn.
- Unless forced to do so, children won't learn.

Conflicts over the Use of Drugs, Alcohol and Tobacco

The number of alcohol and drug-related problems in this country is staggering and so, for good reason, this is one of the most frightening areas in a parent's life. Caring parents do not want their children to abuse drugs, or alcohol, or to smoke cigarettes. The thought is terrifying. So what can parents do? Most of the advice given suggests ways to try to control children's lives—punish, forbid, lecture, set limits for them. But the evidence is really growing thin that these methods are effective. Attempts to control usually backfire and bring about the thing we're most wanting to avoid. Since most kids will experiment with drugs, alcohol and tobacco, *the focus needs to be on what leads to substance abuse.* After working with parents and children for over twenty years, it is our opinion that the only real hope you have that your kids can avoid problems with these substances is to raise them with high self-esteem.

People who have high self-esteem and who are open to dealing with their feelings, in general, do not do things that are detrimental to their well-being. So drug and alcohol abuse prevention for our children really must start in the crib with the loving relationship between parent and child. We take great exception to those programs that want to place responsibility for children's abuse problems with society or with their peer group. Withstanding peer pressure is difficult and the society certainly encourages drug and alcohol consumption, but not everyone *abuses* these substances. We must take responsibility for our part in parenting children who do not have a strong enough sense of self to withstand peer pressure, who cannot come and talk with us about their concerns, who need to escape from their reality. We don't believe anyone is to blame. We all do the best job we can with limited information and lots of fears, but we need to attack the problems from their depths or they'll never go away.

Our involvement with drug abuse began in 1967 when Jordan and a teaching colleague began a drug rehabilitation program at their high school. The program became one of the most successful in Los Angeles and was copied successfully in many other places. It was a program of caring, listening, and helping kids discover their needs and feel respected for their feelings. It is relatively simple for others to give this kind of caring to your children but unless you as a parent get yourself to the place where you can give this kind of involvement, you'll always be living in fear. Something new will always come along to fear—marijuana, LSD, cocaine, alcohol, downers, uppers or some undiscovered drug. Education is always important, of course, but parents can never relax until they trust that their children have enough strength of character and enjoy life enough not to succumb to the allure of mind-altering substances.

MARGIE:

I had picked Eric up at school and we were on our way home when he said, "You know, Mom, we can smoke at school if we get permission from our parents. If I asked you would you give me permission?" I was a little taken aback. No one in our family smokes and everyone had always expressed strong negative feelings about tobacco. I repressed my immediate urge to say, "Of course not!" and said, "Well, I'd have to think about that. I guess if it was something very important to you I would give you permission, but it sure would be difficult for me. You know how important good health is to us and I sure would be worried about you. I wouldn't want you not to do this just because of my being upset. If it's what you want I'll have to deal with my feelings but I do want you to know how I would be affected by your decision. I'd also want to talk with you about what was going on in your life that was leading you on that path and I sure would like to keep an open communication with you. What are you thinking?"

"Well," he replied, "I'm really not thinking seriously about it, I just wanted to know how you would react."

As parents our job is to educate, model, stay involved, be affected, and then, back off. Easier said than done? Then ask yourself, where are you having difficulty? What can you do about it?

BELIEFS TO QUESTION:

- All alcohol and drug use is bad.
- The way to prevent children from using drugs is to forbid it and punish them if they're caught.
- Experimenting with drugs is bad/normal.

Of all the possible conflicts, one of the most disturbing and persistent for most families is the problem between siblings. The next chapter will take a look at the dynamics of sibling relationships. There is a loving path even through this kind of conflict.

·11·

I Can't Stand Their Fighting!

Conflict in Sibling Relationships

Teach them to consult their own inner lights, rather than try to please everybody else and live their lives as approval seekers, as blamers rather than doers.
—Wayne Dyer, Ph.D.
What Do You Really Want For Your Children?

Our sons Eric and Josh were in one of their seemingly endless and constant battles. Josh came crying that Eric had just hit him. We flew into the next room and found Eric vacillating between his fear of our being angry at him and his resentment for Josh. We reacted with our typical responses, being angry at Eric, trying to comfort Josh, and lecturing both of them to try and work out their problems and try to get along better. Although these methods were definitely not working we didn't know anything else to do. We felt helpless.

Because sibling conflicts are so misunderstood we have taken a separate chapter to discuss what parents can learn about their part in this most important relationship. Having our children love, respect, and get along with each other is very important to us. The relationship between Eric and Josh was a deep and continuing source of frustration and pain. Learning from this conflict, like many others, has taken us on a fascinating journey into understanding the roots of sibling rivalry and the process necessary to help our children lovingly develop a caring, respectful relationship with each other.

The sibling relationship is unique and complex. To begin with, two or more people, often of very different temperaments, are forced to live together. When you consider the difficulties that adults have after consciously making *the choice* to live together, sibling difficulties begin to make sense. Add to this the resentment and fears that accompany an unwanted intruder taking away time, plus a lack of help in understanding and dealing with these feelings and with conflicts in general—is a continuing battle and growing distance any wonder?

Bringing about a peace and love that comes from respect and caring does not come about through attempts to impose caring behavior—punishment, demanding respect, lecturing. Sibling difficulties arise from complex and subtle beliefs and fears. Real resolution for problems comes about through learning why the children are relating as they are, how we as parents are contributing to the difficulties, and helping our children understand and take responsibility for their own individual part in creating the difficulty. A lack of loving feelings between siblings comes about from the same protected ways of relating that erode the love in any relationship. Creating love and intimacy takes the same process of opening to learning as well.

Sibling Power Struggles

Making one child wrong and responsible for a relationship difficulty denies the fact that each child has a part in creating the problem. An ongoing problem cannot exist unless both children participate. One child may seem to be more responsible for the problem, but that is usually very deceptive. Eric, being the older child, was an easy target to blame. After all, he was bigger, stronger, and more verbal. Poor cherubic Josh, smaller and weaker, seemed only to be asking for help against an unreasonable oppressor. We didn't understand power struggles then.

Sibling difficulties are a result of how each child reacts to a conflict. One may be bored or angry and tease the other. The other reacts in some way that hooks him or her into the interaction and the struggle is on. It's easy to see one child as wrong unless the interaction is seen as a protective circle. Eric learned to used his strength and verbal ability to attempt to get his way and have control over Josh. Josh, in order not to be controlled by Eric, learned how to passively resist. Josh's resistance was harder to identify, but it would drive Eric crazy. By continually defending Josh, we encouraged his non-responsible, manipulative behavior and left Eric feeling uncared for, misunderstood and even angrier at Josh. Is it any wonder that their relationship got worse and worse?

Roots of the Power Struggle

Power struggles are rooted in the fears of being open to vulnerable feelings. Older children often fear being wrong and therefore unlovable and rejected. Needing to be right to prove their adequacy and fearing losing their place, older children often fear younger children may be better at almost anything—academics, looks, games.

Second children often develop a passively resistant personality, to a large extent due to their relationship with an older sibling. The older sibling's approval is very important to younger siblings and much of their behavior fluctuates between giving up themselves to get approval or avoid disapproval and resisting to avoid losing their integrity. For many older children the withholding of approval becomes an important tool in their arsenal for maintaining control.

Older children often feel the need to control others when they have experienced a parent's need to control them. Parents are often much more controlling with the first-born child. Not knowing much about what to expect from their child, parents tend to go overboard in carrying out what they believe to be their responsibility to mold their child. Parents tend to be a lot less rigid with subsequent children, but the first-born, having received a large dose of controls from parents, often becomes very parental with the second-born.

Touching Off the Power Struggle

The fears of being controlled and losing oneself and of losing love are the very good reasons that keep power struggles going. There are also very important reasons that begin the power struggle both for the child who initiates and the child who responds. With children who can and will explore, looking for these reasons can be a focus for explorations. Sometimes, however, a parent has to attempt to figure out what these reasons might be. We will comment only on a few of the more common reasons.

- Children may pick on their siblings as a way of getting back at their parents for trying to control them. Kids know parents get upset by their battles and their fighting often reflects an unconscious desire to do to the parent what the parent is doing to them.
- If a child feels pushed aside or shut out, fighting with siblings may be a way to get parents' attention.
- When children have a fear of their parents' fighting with each other, they may be fighting as an attempt to direct the parents' attention toward themselves.
- When children are bored, fighting may be a way to involve the parents and/or create

chaos to avoid taking responsibility for doing something about their boredom.

- The instigator of a power struggle may be expressing anger at his or her sibling for getting more of the parent's attention or for being the "innocent victim."

Helping Children Learn From and Resolve Power Struggles

The more you understand about your own power struggles with your mate, parents and children, the more you will be able to help your children with theirs. You can learn a lot about your own power struggles and theirs by becoming a relationship observer.

Start looking for the power struggle dynamic in all relationships around you. Watch other parents and their children in doctors' offices, supermarkets, their homes or yours. When one person asks another to do something, look for the subtle, and sometimes not so subtle, reactions that indicate a power struggle—a tightening of the jaw and face, a hard, disgusted look accompanied by a turning away, any angry or irritated response, any resistant response that indicates, "Don't you tell me what to do!"

Focus on the interaction rather than the issue of the conflict. Start to become aware of who initiates the attempt to control and how they do it. Who resists and/ or instigates in passive-aggressive ways? How does the interaction progress? Who usually gets blamed? Who is usually the tattle tale? Which child plays the role of "innocent victim"? Usually it's the younger child who has learned to instigate in very subtle ways to get the older child in trouble. Josh once came into our bedroom to tell us that Eric had just pushed him down. Usually that would have been enough to send us angrily off to find Eric and settle this problem immediately. This time, however, Margie calmly asked Josh, "Why are you telling us this?'' He thought about that for a few seconds and without a word turned on his heels and walked out.

In the past, rather than help them understand their difficulties we had been sucked into the problem as the judge, jury and executioner. We subsequently let them know that we were willing to help them understand each of their parts in any difficulty, but they were each responsible for working out their problems. Blaming one of them, telling them what to do, or even helping them problem-solve never helped them to understand and take responsibility for their part of the power struggle.

The Exploration Process for Power Struggles

Exploring power struggles with children is accomplished most easily when children understand that your intent is to learn about yourself and to help them learn about themselves rather than to judge, criticize, blame, or lecture. To resolve sibling difficulties, siblings must be open to learning about themselves. To help children open to learning about themselves parents must be open to learning about themselves.

The primary question when you're open to learning about yourself is, ''How do I contribute to my children's power struggles?'' The questions following your intent to learn are:

- Do I withdraw and shut my children out? If so, how, why, and what are the effects?
- Do I teach them to control or resist through my own attempts to control and/ or resist? Am I modeling power struggles for them as a way of handling my conflicts with them and/or with my partner?
- Do I allow their battles to suck me into taking responsibility for them, thereby reinforcing their behavior? Do I try to settle

their battles for them rather than help them settle their own?

- What are my beliefs about my responsibility in these matters?
- Do I take sides? Do I blame one child most of the time?
- How do I really feel about each of my children? Do I give one more attention and approval than the others, thereby fostering jealousy between them? Am I feeding their anger at each other by how I treat them?

Another important question to ask yourself is, "What beliefs, fears and pain get touched off in me when my children fight?" Some of the questions that follow your intent to learn are:

- Am I afraid their battles mean I'm not a good parent?
- Do I feel unloved by them when they fight and they know I don't like it?
- Do I believe they should always love each other?
- Do I believe they are fighting just to "get" to me?
- Do I ever let my children see the sadness I feel when they hurt each other's feelings so deeply, or do I just protect myself and get angry when they fight, trying to have control over getting them to stop?

Starting the Process with Your Children

You might start the process of helping your children explore their power struggles by sharing your own pain caused by their being so uncaring with each other. Parents often hide the deep pain resulting from children not liking each other or treating each other badly. When your children fight, expressing your protected feelings—anger, frustration, or any feelings that blame and make them wrong—will probably touch off your children's protections and they won't see the deep effects of their behavior. They often conclude that their behavior doesn't matter because they never see your pain. A note of caution: If your pain comes from a victim place—"poor me, look what you're doing to me"—your children will probably respond defensively to that as well.

A major shift began in helping our children deal with their relationship began one evening when Jordan let himself feel his deep pain around Eric's and Josh's constant battles. He spoke to both of them through heartfelt tears, saying he realized how important the family's getting along well was to him, how he had dreamed of his boys liking each other and being good friends, and how their interaction was a constant source of pain in his life. This kind of sharing must be done with a great deal of awareness, however, as it can be nothing more than an attempt to manipulate through guilt. Jordan was very clear that expressing his feelings was not attached to any outcome. He told the boys that he knew they had important reasons for their behavior, he didn't expect them to change immediately, and that he wanted to know what part he was playing in perpetuating their difficulties. Sharing non-manipulative feelings gives children important feedback as to the facts that their behavior does have an effect on others.

When you're open to learning about yourself, an important question to ask your children is, "Is there anything I'm doing that makes it difficult for you to want to share your feelings?" You can find out if they feel you to be partial, unfair, judgmental. Or if they're afraid you'll punish them, be angry, or get withdrawn if they say something you don't like.

When your children are open to learning about their roles in the power struggle, you can help them learn with each other or separately. At some point learning with each other is vital because you want them eventually to be able to do this process without you. You can also help them understand power struggles with their friends and deal with them as well. The exploration process in chapter 13 describes how as a parent you can actively listen to each child and then explore the very good reasons behind the power struggle and help each child see and understand his or her protections and the consequences.

Concepts Children Can Learn

At very young ages children learn ways of behaving in a conflict that become deeply ingrained. Interactions with authority figures, women/men, important people in their lives, or someone from whom they want approval tap into these patterned ways of reacting. Learning about power struggles can be invaluable in helping them take more personal responsibility in their lives and fashion more meaningful and satisfying relationships. First of all, they need to learn what a power struggle is so they can recognize when they're stuck in one and the consequences of being in one.

Important learnings that come from understanding power struggles include:

- The concept of equal responsibility—By understanding and taking personal responsibility children can learn from every difficulty they find themselves in. Without understanding that each person has a part in creating every relationship difficulty, it's easy to become a helpless victim.

- The concept of important reasons—The most crucial concept to developing good self-esteem is to not make oneself wrong. The most crucial concept to avoiding power struggles and continuing open communications is to not blame one's sibling. Both of these concepts require the belief that all behavior is motivated by very important, compelling reasons. Helping children understand power struggles is an important contributor to learning this concept.
- The need to be right and win—In dealing with power struggles you can help your children understand how their need to be right comes from their fears of being wrong and feeling stupid, inadequate, unlovable or their fears of losing themselves. Working with these fears helps them develop faith in themselves while increasing their self-esteem.
- Understanding protections—Helping children learn about their protective behavior when they're frightened, sad, or disappointed helps them have more control over their lives. Rather than just being carried along by behavior that comes from their subconscious fears, they can become more aware and therefore more in control of their lives. Learning about protections includes learning what protections are, how they protect, why they protect and connecting their protections with the negative consequences that follow them.

Eric, Josh, and Sheryl are in the process of learning all of these things as a result of dealing with their sibling difficulties. The more they understand, the better their relationships have become. When they first began working on their relationships, they used to come to us and say, "We're in a power struggle, can you help us?" As their understanding has increased they haven't needed our help as much in dealing with their power struggles. With the power struggle less of an issue they have much fewer conflicts.

The sibling relationship is one of the most important relationships shaping our personalities. Everyone is well aware of how interactions with parents affect children but not much has been discussed or even written about the dramatic effect the relationship with one's siblings has on our feelings and behavior as adults. For example, when you have an overwhelming fear of disapproval, consider your interactions with an older sibling as a source of your feelings. Are you a person who needs to be in control much of the time? If you're an eldest child, think about the birth of your brother or sister and the interaction that ensued. How much does your need to be in control of your adult partner stem from your feelings of helplessness, or being replaced, or parroting your parents' attempts to control you? If you're a younger sibling, think about your passive resistance, your rebelliousness, or your compliance and the interaction with your older sibling's attempts to have control over you. Think about your need for your older brother's or sister's approval, the pain you felt at not getting it. Consider how that relationship shaped your personality, i.e., how you react to your adult partner today when he or she attempts to have control over you, and/or how you go about attempting to gain his or her approval.

Understanding the sibling relationship and building it into a loving, supportive friendship is one of the keys in creating loving relationships and thereby increasing joy and satisfaction in your life and the lives of your children.

Part 4

Exploration: A Process for Becoming More Loving

You will know what to do if you listen to the Higher Self within, rather than to the ego's voice of fear and protection. And when you don't listen to your inner truth, it's because you haven't come to the understanding that you are choosing between being loving and unloving. It is this awareness that brings the power to choose to learn, to be open, to risk, to love.

·12·

What Do I Ask Myself?

A Process for Learning about Ourselves

*I am satisfied with feeling that I have
moved closer to God and therefore I have
moved closer to myself which is the key to
moving closer to you. And that is what I
want to do. The feeling is that I truly love
you but that love is locked within a
prison of fear. My fear is the lock. But
God is the key.*
— Dwight Wolter
"For Adult Children of Alcoholics"

When two people really want to learn about themselves
and each other, the process we call exploration can begin.
An exploration is spending time learning about fears,
beliefs, protections, and consequences. Exploration is
how we learn what is the loving thing to do in a particular
situation and what fears and beliefs are getting in the way
of giving that love. The intent to learn is loving behavior
in itself and it also leads to additional loving behaviors.

What does it mean to be in process? Essentially, it
means to be engaged in a system of operation. In our
solution-oriented culture, process is often a foreign and
difficult concept. In a conflict, process involves letting go
of the frantic search for solutions and having faith that
understanding yourself and your child on ever deepening
levels, and becoming a more loving person, will lead
away from problems and toward meaningful resolutions.

An understanding of process is essential to understanding the primary message of this book.

In life, anytime you enter a process, you know it will take time. The process of becoming formally educated that begins with entering kindergarten and continues through high school or college is an example of a long process. When we enter this process, we do not expect to learn everything in one year. When we decide to learn to play a musical instrument, we don't expect to be proficient after the first lesson. We know it will take much practice before we're really competent. The same is true for the process of exploration. It's a skill that takes much practice. Reading this book is like a first lesson—it just gets you started. For the process to work, you must become skilled at it and this effort takes time.

Unlike problem-solving, the goal of exploration is not just resolution, but learning and growth. Resolutions are a natural consequence of the learning that occurs through the process of exploration. Putting aside the immediate importance of resolution and focusing on understanding and learning about our self-limiting beliefs is one of the major problems people have with exploration. *The resolution and changes emerge from becoming aware of and challenging, through loving behavior, the beliefs that create your fears and protections. As beliefs change, everything changes.* It's very difficult to have the faith that resolution will actually occur with this process when you've never seen it or had any personal experience with it.

We had to go through hundreds of explorations with ourselves and our children before *knowing* that it would work every time. This process has *never* failed us, but it's taken many experiences to really trust it. That's another reason practice is so essential—you can't come to trust something until it works for you over and over again. And by "work" we do not mean that we always reach a resolution. That, as we have said, is not the goal. Some problems, like power struggles, are so complex that actual resolution may not come for years. But the more you explore and learn about the beliefs and fears that lead to your power struggles, the more open and loving you will become. Your protective behavior may never stop completely, meaning that you may never become totally open and vulnerable, but as long as you continue to pursue learning through the process of exploration, the more you will move toward being less protected and more loving and the better your relationships and your life will become.

The less complex the problem, the faster it will come to resolution, but again, the resolution is only the by-product of the learning process. It is the process of exploration itself and the willingness to challenge your beliefs that create your own emotional/spiritual growth as well as the love and intimacy between you and your children, you and your mate, or between you and anyone you are in a relationship with. *It is not the resolution that creates loving feelings, but rather the open sharing and understanding of oneself and each other.*

Becoming Aware of Intention

Exploration involves both a method and a spirit—the intent to learn. There is often difficulty, however, in recognizing intent, because it is expressed on a level of communication that is usually ignored. Communication always occurs on two levels: 1) *What* you are talking about, i.e., the issue itself, and 2) *How* you're talking, i.e., the intent—whether you are protected or open to learning.

On the first level you're talking about things like being late, hitting a sibling, messiness, homework, etc. You can talk about an issue with either the intent to protect or the intent to learn. Talking about the issue when one or both people are protected will always lead to negative consequences and there's really nothing to be gained by that. Once you really believe that, you will understand why dealing with *how* you're talking to each other is the key to better communication. Once you drop your protections and open to learning, then discussing the issue can be very productive.

It is the second level, then, the level of intent, that determines the course and outcome of an interaction. The following classic question provides a good example:

"Why didn't you call me?"

The tone of voice, expressing intent, carries most of the meaning of the words. The speaker could be simply asking for a reason, or blaming the other, or trying to manipulate with plaintive wheedling—all depending on the tone and accent on different words.

You cannot explore yourself or your child when either of you is protected. People sometimes complain to us that exploring doesn't work, but when we've observed their explorations, we've always found that they were trying to explore while being protected. This is not an exploration since there is no intention to learn. Since you can't be open and closed at the same time, it's impossible to explore when protected. The first step, then, before attempting to explore yourself or your child, is to become aware of your own intent.

Tuning In to Your Intent

You can become aware of your intent by tuning in to your body and the feelings that you feel in your body. When protected you will generally feel a tightness somewhere in your muscles. Your stomach may feel tense, your chest, throat, forehead, or jaw may feel tight. The muscles around your eyes or mouth may feel stiff and tight, your hands may be tense, as well as your shoulders. Or, you may be feeling nothing in your body. Your body may feel empty and dead. You might feel a heaviness in your head or around your eyes that makes you feel as if there is a weight pressing down on you. You may be aware of feeling angry, upset, critical, defensive, righteous, frustrated or resentful. If you're crying, it's about someone else's behavior towards you. You may feel like a "poor me" victim.

If you are feeling that your child is responsible or to blame for your upset feelings, then you are in a protected state. You may feel a hardness inside, or hear a hard edge in your voice. Your body and the sound of your voice reflect your intention. You may be talking softly, but if there is a slight edge or a condescending tone in your voice, then you are protected. Anytime you believe that your child or anyone else is wrong for whatever they've done, you are protected. This belief will always be reflected by a judgmental tone in your voice. You cannot hide your protective intention. Your children will always accurately experience your protective intention and will generally respond with their own protections. *Noticing your child's response to you,* then, is another way of becoming aware of your own intention.

When you are protected, and you don't know that you're protected, you have no way of making another choice. You can't choose to be open if you think you are open, but are really protected. *The belief that you're open when you're not is one of the major causes of communication problems.* If you believe you're open and you see that your child (or any other person you're in a conflict with) is not open, then it's so easy to believe that the problems in communication are his or her fault.

When you are willing to become aware of when you're protected (and this will be very difficult, if not impossible, if you believe it's wrong to protect and you judge yourself for protecting), then you have a choice. You can continue to protect, which you may want to do if you are afraid to feel your soft and vulnerable feelings, and continue believing that you can win and have things your way. *Or* you can choose to open.

You will know you are really open when you feel soft, vulnerable, curious, available, and accepting. The tension drains from your body, your heart opens, and you feel loving feelings towards yourself and your child. If you're sad and/or crying, you feel no blame towards anyone for making you feel that way. You feel a deep desire to understand your own beliefs and fears, as well as your child's. As long as you and your child, or you and anyone else, remain in this open state, learning will take place in an atmosphere of love and closeness.

Staying in this open place is very difficult, however. If your child says something that hurts your feelings, disappoints you or frightens you, you may instantly protect against experiencing the pain or against knowing the truth in what your child is trying to tell you. Explorations, then, rarely run a smooth path. Rather, they wind in and out, up and down, hitting many bumps and curves along the way. The goal will eventually be reached if you keep in mind what the goal is—awareness of the erroneous beliefs and resulting fears that underlie any conflict situation, and of what the loving behavior would be.

How to Get Out of Protecting and into Learning

Most of us, even when we do become aware that we are protecting, do not just instantly open to learning. We generally need to go through a transition to discharge our blaming feelings or break through the wall of indifference before we can get to the nonblaming, vulnerable feelings of fear and sadness that always lie under our protections.

As parents, it is vitally important that you do *not* take out anger and other blaming feelings on your children. Your children's self-esteem is eroded *every time* you become indifferent or make them wrong, whether you do it with hitting, yelling, scolding, lecturing, explaining, criticizing, or any other method of control.

When you are upset with your child, you need to find some way of releasing those feelings other than dumping them on your child. Below is a list of ways we have found helpful in moving from protecting into learning:

1. Express your anger physically by taking a pillow or a rolled up towel and hitting the floor, the bed, or a chair while yelling, screaming, calling names, blaming, etc. Continue hitting until you're exhausted. When the tension is gone from your body you will be open. Do this while you are alone or with another adult, such as your partner, a friend, or a therapist. *It is not appropriate to do this with a young child present.*

2. Roll up the windows in your car and scream out your anger where no one can hear you.

3. Engage in some physical activity, such as running around the block, working out at a gym, gardening, or taking a walk. Anything that reduces tension will help you to open.

4. Engage in an activity that gives you pleasure, such as reading, listening to music, playing with a pet, or taking a nap. Oftentimes, after a night's sleep, you may find yourself in a much more open place than you were the previous night.

5. Tune in to and remember the deep love you have for your child. Remembering the close and warm times can help you dissipate the angry and blaming feelings you may be experiencing towards your child.

6. Tune in to your body and feel the pain, fear, and sadness that are there. Allowing yourself to make sounds and move your body with a rocking motion will often open you to experiencing your pain. Once you can cry and really feel how bad it feels to be protected, you will open.

7. Explore your protections with your mate, a friend, a therapist or by yourself, using the Format for Exploration on page 271. Explore until you open to your own vulnerable feelings.

8. Write. Write out your anger and blame, your fear and pain, your wants and needs. We use a format for this that we call a Learning Letter (see Appendix A). We have found this to be one of the best tools available for releasing protections and helping to take a look at what we want to learn about ourselves. It is an excellent tool for children to use as well.

For any of the above methods to work, you have to *want* to shift your intent from protect to learning. If you say you want to, but you really want to remain "safe" (the safety is truly an illusion) behind your protections, or you really believe you are right and you're going to prove it, or you really want to teach your child a lesson by withholding love, then none of the above methods will make a dent in your protective barriers. So the first question to ask yourself in any conflict situation is: "What do I really want *most* right now? Do I want to win, be right, have control, not feel, or do I want to learn about myself and my child?" When you truly want to open, you will find a way to do it.

The Conditions for Exploration

The concept of learning about yourself and your child in a conflict may seem like a simple one, but it is very challenging because of two conditions which must be met—you must believe that there are always compelling reasons for behavior and you must be willing to feel your vulnerable feelings.

Compelling Reasons

In order to learn, you must believe that both you and your child have important, compelling, valid, respectable reasons for your feelings and behavior. If you believe that you have no good reasons for your feelings and behavior, that you are just wrong or that you're just a bad or inadequate parent, then you are blocked in exploring the fears and beliefs underlying your protective behavior. When we talk about good or compelling reasons for behavior, we are not talking about excuses or justifications, but about the beliefs that lead to the fears and resulting protections. We are not wrong or bad for having these self-limiting beliefs.

Linda came into therapy with Margie because she was having problems with her six-year-old daughter Carrie. She described Carrie as an angry and resistant child, who was afraid to try anything new. Linda loved Carrie and was blaming herself for Carrie's problems. Linda would often fly into rages at Carrie's anger and resistance, screaming at her and hitting her. She would then feel awful about herself, questioning her own worth and even her sanity. She would say, "How can I behave that way toward my daughter whom I love so much?" She felt insecure, inadequate and judgmental of herself.

Margie introduced Linda to the concept that she must have some very good reasons for her behavior, that she was not a bad person, and that some fears and erroneous beliefs were creating her unloving behavior.

> Margie: Linda, what do you feel inside when Carrie gets angry at you or resists you?
>
> Linda: I guess I feel that she doesn't love me.
>
> Margie: You believe that if she is angry with you or won't do what you say, that means she doesn't love you?
>
> Linda: Yes, if she cared about me she would want to do what I say (one of Linda's self-limiting beliefs).
>
> Margie: So what do you do when you feel uncared for?
>
> Linda: I guess I get mad (protecting against her pain).
>
> Margie: What do you hope will happen when you're angry?
>
> Linda: I guess I think if she sees how upset I am, she'll care and do what I want (another self-limiting belief).
>
> Margie: What actually happens?
>
> Linda: She gets madder and won't let me near her (the negative consequences of Linda's protections).

Often when parents try to get children's love and are rageful at not getting it, it is because they were inadequately loved as a child and are hoping to get the love from their own children that they never got from their parents. When the parents have not dealt with their own pain at not being adequately loved, they often take it out on children, because they are an easy target, just as the parents were when they were young.

Margie and Linda explored Linda's childhood, and it soon became apparent that Linda was filled with rage at her mother. Her mother was an angry, highly critical, manipulative, cold woman. Linda never remembered being held or told anything positive about herself. She was constantly told how bad she was, how inadequate and unlovable she was. And she was never allowed to be upset about this or she would have been punished for being disrespectful and for not loving her mother.

It took Linda many months to begin to remember bits and pieces of her childhood. She had blocked out most of it because it was so painful. As she began to remember and express her deep pain over having been so unloved, she was able to see that her rages at her daughter were really about her mother. As she released that rage in the safety of the therapy sessions, she was more and more able to accept and be loving towards her daughter. And, of course, as this happened, her daughter became more loving towards her.

As Linda was able to understand the good reasons behind her unloving behavior, she was able to release the fears and beliefs that caused this behavior. Had she gone on judging herself, she would have remained stuck in her angry behavior.

The Willingness to Feel Vulnerable Feelings

The second major condition necessary for exploration is that you have to be open to feeling and experiencing your soft, nonblaming, vulnerable feelings—fear, pain, hurt, grief, disappointment, sadness. When you are unwilling to feel these feelings, then you must protect against them. Since you can't explore when protected, being willing to experience these vulnerable feelings is basic to being open.

We've all been brought up with many erroneous beliefs about pain. Rather than teaching us that our pain is trying to tell us something important, our parents, reflecting the beliefs of the culture, conveyed the belief that pain is to be avoided at all costs. But just as our physical pain tells us that something in our bodies needs attention, so our emotional pain tells us that we need to examine our beliefs and fears in order to understand the choices we are making that are creating our pain. *The emotional pain we suffer in our lives is always the consequence of our own choices, and these choices stem from our erroneous beliefs and resulting fears.* When you are willing to feel your vulnerable feelings rather than protect against them, they will lead you into an ever deepening knowledge of how and why you make the choices you do, and of the consequences of those choices.

For example, Joan came into therapy with Margie because she felt alienated from her teenage children, and especially from her oldest daughter, who always seemed angry at her. As Joan and Margie explored, it became evident that Joan deeply believed that her children would not learn, would not accomplish anything, and would fail in life if she wasn't constantly on their backs reminding them to study. Joan had no faith in the inherent desire of children to learn because her parents had been controlling with her and she attributed her success in life to their prodding.

As a result of her constant nagging, Joan's children were angry at her most of the time. The oldest daughter had complied, which is probably why she was the angriest. The middle boy was resisting and doing quite poorly in school. He too was angry at Joan, but expressed it mostly by being sullen and withdrawn. For some reason, Joan had let up on the youngest daughter and she had the best relationship with this child.

Joan was in pain about her children and her pain was the consequence of the protections that arose out of her false, self-limiting beliefs about them. As Joan examined her beliefs and understood where they came from, she made the choice to test out whether or not they were accurate. She decided to stop nagging her children about their schoolwork and to see what would happen. This was a very frightening thing for her to do because she was sure that they would all stop working, but she knew she needed to find out the truth.

The first couple of months were very difficult for her. As the children realized that she wasn't going to nag them anymore, they became more lax with their work. They were probably testing her to see if she really meant it. While it was extremely hard for her, Joan stood her ground. She told them that they had permission to fail, that it was their choice whether or not they wanted to do well. Within a few months the two daughters were doing as well as they were before and the son had made some improvement. In addition, the relationship between Joan and her children was rapidly improving.

Originally, Joan had believed that her pain was caused by her children. Through the process of self-exploration, Joan came to realize that her pain was the consequence of her choice to protect and that this choice came from her beliefs and fears. *By paying attention to her pain,* Joan learned what she needed to learn to make new choices.

In order to learn, we have to be open to learning the truth about ourselves, even if the truth hurts. It was painful for Joan to recognize that, not only was she creating her own pain, but that in choosing to try to control her own children, she was being unloving to them and causing them pain. Most of us protect against knowing that our protections inflict pain on our children, and likewise, that their protections are painful to us. We want to convince ourselves that we can yell, criticize, withdraw, ignore, or hit our children without hurting them, and so we lie to ourselves and do not allow ourselves to be sensitive to our own and our children's pain. When you really want to understand how your protections affect your child, try this brief exercise. Visualize yourself as a child at the receiving end of your own protective behaviors. Do it until you can really be him or her and feel all that your child feels being so little and having your parent reject you. See yourself through your child's eyes.

Once you realize the pain that your protections inflict on your children, then how do you deal with them if you no longer want to protect? You explore.

How to Explore Yourself

When you are having a conflict with your child, the first thing you need to do to begin to understand and resolve the conflict is to explore yourself. This means wanting to learn about your beliefs that create your fears, values, expectations, and protections and the resulting consequences. It means looking into the past to understand where you got these concepts, and looking into the present to understand the effect they have on your life today. You can do this exploration with yourself by writing, or with a partner, a friend, a therapist, or your child if he or she is old enough and wants to do that with you. You cannot explore yourself with a young child.

The awareness you can gain from an exploration is both intellectual and emotional. You need to gain an intellectual understanding of your protections and their consequences, and of the fears, values, and expectations that always lie under your protections. And you need to gain facts about your childhood to understand where all these came from. Emotionally you need to release your blaming feelings—anger and hurt—so that you can move into your nonblaming feelings. You need to experience and express these feelings as they relate to both present and past. Knowing facts about your childhood is important, but experiencing the feelings from childhood that still remain locked in your body is vital to true awareness and subsequent change. Likewise, knowing the facts about how and why you protect and of the consequences is important, but experiencing the present fear that underlies your protections and the resulting pain of the consequences is essential for meaningful change.

People often say that awareness alone is not enough to bring about change. This is certainly true if the awareness is only intellectual. *Transformational changes come about when you explore intellectually and emotionally, and then test out the truth about your fears and beliefs through loving behavior.*

Questions to Ask Yourself When You Want to Explore

Below is a Format for Exploration that we have designed that can serve for any self-exploration:

FORMAT FOR EXPLORATION

1. What is the situation that I am unhappy or upset about?
2. How am I protecting in this conflict? (Refer to checklists pp. 78, 79, 82, and 84.)
3. What do I hope will happen as a result of my reacting in this way?
4. Is it working? What is the actual result of my reacting in this way to the conflict? (Refer to checklists pp. 111, 112, and 113.)

5. What am I afraid will happen if I don't protect in this conflict?

6. How do I feel about myself when I react this way?

7. What fears led me to protect in this conflict? (For example: Fears of rejection, being a bad parent, facing my own feelings of helplessness.)

8. What beliefs created these fears?

9. What has happened in my past relationships that created these beliefs?

10. What are the worst things that could happen if I let go of these beliefs?

11. Am I now willing to test out the accuracy of these beliefs by doing what it is I'm afraid of? If not, I have just made the choice to stay stuck with my unhappiness. To get unstuck, I must explore those beliefs and fears that have led to my unwillingness to test out the above beliefs.

12. What, exactly, do I do to test out these beliefs? *In other words, what is the loving behavior*—the opposite of how I've been protecting? What behavior would support my growth and make me happy as well as support my child's emotional growth and spiritual growth? (This is the key question and will require a lot of creative thinking.)

Other Questions to Ask Yourself during the Exploration

1. Why do I believe that?
2. What does that mean to me?
3. How do I feel right now?
4. What am I feeling about that?

5. What are the good reasons I have for feeling this way?

Below is a brief example of how an exploration with yourself might go. Let's say that you are having a conflict with your son over keeping his room clean. The conflict degenerated into a power struggle with you attempting to get him to clean up by withholding TV privileges. Now he's really angry at you and he's still not cleaning up his room. When you want to learn about yourself, you could go through the following exploration:

Q. What am I upset about? (What is the conflict?)

A. I'm upset because I can't get him to clean his room.

Q. How am I protecting myself in this conflict?

A. I'm getting angry and critical.

Q. What do I hope will happen as a result of my getting angry?

A. Well, I guess I hope he'll finally hear how important it is to me and do it.

Q. Is it working?

A. No.

Q. What is the actual result of my getting angry?

A. He's angry too and we keep fighting. Maybe we're in a power struggle. Maybe the reason he won't clean his room is because my anger is an attempt to have control over him and he's resisting being under my control. It's possible that the angrier I get the less chance I have of getting him to clean his room.

Q. What am I afraid will happen if I don't try to get him to clean his room by getting angry?

A. I'm afraid he'll never clean it.

Q. Why do I believe that?

A. I guess that's how my parents got me to clean my room. It worked with me but it sure doesn't work with him.

Q. How do I feel about myself when I get angry and critical?

A. I feel frustrated and unhappy and I feel like a lousy mom. And I end up feeling hurt and sad and rejected. I feel so uncared for.

Q. What does that mean to me?

A. I guess I believe that if he really cared about me he'd see how important it is to me and he'd clean his room. But I guess it's hard for him to care about me when I'm angry so much. He must feel that I don't care about him when I'm angry and critical so much.

Q. What are the fears I have that lead me to be so upset about his room? Why is getting him to clean his room so important to me?

A. I just think kids should keep their rooms clean.

Q. But why? What are the good reasons I have for feeling this way?

A. What will people think of me as a parent if my child's room is a mess? Oh . . . .I guess I'm afraid of what other people would think. I also believe he needs to learn to be responsible and this is a way to teach that.

Q. What belief created the fear of others' disapproval?

A. I guess I believe it's right to be neat and wrong to be messy and also that if I do something wrong that other people will think less of me and won't like me. And I believe that I have to teach him to be responsible or he'll end up being irresponsible.

Q. What has happened in my past relationships that has created these beliefs?

A. My mother kept our house immaculate and was always worried about what people would think if everything wasn't spotless. I guess I picked that up from her. And she would get mad at me and not love me when I didn't do things her way. Oh, my God! That's what I'm doing with my son. But I think I would have been a responsible child even if she hadn't been angry. Maybe he will be too.

Q. What's the worst thing that could happen if I let go of these beliefs?

A. Well, maybe my friends would judge me according to how my house looks or how my son's room looks, but now that I think about that, I don't think they would. But my mother would. So I guess the worst thing that would happen is that my mother would judge me and be upset with me. But maybe that wouldn't be as bad as I think it would. It might be better than having these hassles all the time with my son. And maybe my son would become even more irresponsible. But he really is a good kid, so maybe that wouldn't happen.

Q. Am I willing to test out the accuracy of these beliefs by doing what it is I'm afraid of?

A. Yes. I guess I'm willing to face her judgment and rejection rather than continuing this power struggle. And I guess I'm willing to see if he would become irresponsible in other areas.

Q. What, exactly, do I have to do to test out these beliefs?

A. I guess I need to stop nagging my son and try to understand his side of things and just close his door if his room bothers me. And if my mother's upset, I'll deal with it. And maybe my son will become more responsible, or at least more caring about me if he sees I care about him. Well, we'll see. I'll try it.

The above is a fairly short and glib example—in reality it may take a lot longer to come to the awareness necessary for change, but hopefully it gives you some idea about what we are talking about.

Obviously, if you just believe that your child is wrong when you are upset with his or her behavior, then you will just try to get the child to change rather than explore yourself. And the consequences of that will probably be a power struggle as well as unloving feelings between you.

The Format for Exploration can be used any time you are unhappy or upset about anything. You always have a choice—to be protected and try to change your child or to be loving by learning about yourself and your child.

·13·

What Do I Ask My Kids?

Process for Learning about Our Children

We parents sometimes feel that the inter-ruptions, hassles, and inconveniences of parenting are standing in the way of our growth. We don't realize, however, that the constant change and adjustment are teaching us every moment. They propel us forward as human beings, strengthen-ing our ability to love unconditionally and bringing forth our true greatness. As we endeavor to teach our children, they are the ones who are truly teaching us.

–Joyce and Barry Vissel
Models of Love

Exploring with children can be an exciting adventure, and is the key to learning how you and your children are creating the problems between you. Also, you can help your children discover how they are creating their own problems.

An exploration is not always called for when there is a problem. Sometimes a solution is needed and it would be the most loving thing to do for you as parents to decide on it. But most parents greatly overuse this method and make decisions for their children that the children are capable of making for themselves. Children will not usually resist occasional parental decisions in one or two areas that you consider to be of vital importance, but when you frequently use your authority in many areas, your children may resist and may not cooperate with any of them.

There are many situations where exploring with children is not appropriate, necessary, or loving. Oftentimes children just want to be listened to and understood and are not interested in or do not need to understand any of the fears and beliefs that underlie their feelings. With our own children, in our zèal to explore and understand the roots of their feelings, we've often probed when they didn't want to be probed, and our attempts received an irritated "I don't want to talk about it anymore." We finally learned that that meant they didn't want to explore, they just wanted to be listened to.

Understanding Children's Feelings

It is thoroughly mind-boggling how the misconceptions about children's feelings began and are perpetuated. Children are often treated as if they don't have any feelings. In some homes animals are treated with more respect than children.

What gives parents the right not to respect children's feelings, invade the sanctity of their bodies, and do to them what they don't want done? What gives anyone the right to invade the sanctity of anyone else's physical or emotional being? Invading someone else's body sexually is called rape, but what is it when another person's body is violated in ways other than sexual and who has the right to do that? Does anyone have the right to hit, pinch, or do anything, even be affectionate, if another person does not want that?

Children are like delicate flowers. Without defensive walls which build throughout childhood, feelings get deeply hurt and they'll even show you, if you care to see.

JORDAN:

Sheryl was the child who, because of her willingness to be open, most opened me to learning about feelings. One day when she was about four years old I said something to her in what I considered to be only a mildly irritated tone. She looked up at me with tears in her eyes and in a quivering voice said, "Please don't yell at me, Daddy." "I'm not yelling," I snapped back sternly. "Yes you are," she said bursting into tears. I looked at her with disapproval, shaking my head, and left the room thinking, "What's the matter with her? Why is she so sensitive? She makes such a big deal out of everything."

It took me a while to realize that there was *nothing wrong* with her. Being hurt when a parent is hard and disapproving is a very appropriate response. My definition of yelling was a loud outburst, but to little Sheryl a cold, disapproving response was yelling.

All of us under our protective shells are as sensitive as little children. Only our cultural conditioning has convinced us that adults shouldn't be sensitive. But our sensitivity is our humanity. *It is only when we lose touch with our own sensitivity that we can hurt others or infringe on their rights.*

Many children stop sharing their feelings when they feel disapproved for them. But it's not only critical responses that tell children their feelings are wrong. Discounting feelings—"It's really nothing to get so upset about"—or trying to make feelings go away—"Don't feel bad, tomorrow we're going to get you a new puppy"—also communicates to children that their feelings are wrong. Allowing children to feel their feelings deeply while nurturing them communicates that "Your feelings are okay, it's okay to express them, and we have confidence that you can feel them deeply and be all right." All other responses communicate to children that their feelings are not okay and are to be feared. As adults, the fear that our feelings are not okay and/or that we can't handle them leads to repressing the feelings we need in order to feel alive, and create joy, intimacy, and love in our lives.

BELIEFS TO QUESTION:

- Children can't handle strong feelings.
- Children will outgrow their sensitive feelings.
- Disapproving of children's feelings is not harmful to them.
- Disapproving of children's feelings will not injure my relationship with them.
- Children need to have their feelings disapproved of in order to teach them right from wrong.
- Certain feelings are wrong. (You can explore which ones you believe are wrong and why you believe that way.)
- Your children will appreciate you for training them properly.
- Parents must prepare their children to bear frustration by teaching them to repress their feelings.

Active Listening

When you and your child are having problems between you, or your child is having a problem that has nothing to do with you, to be of help you must first get yourself into the intent to learn. Once you are open, then your first step with your child is to attempt to understand your child's feelings, behavior, and point of view. This is best accomplished by using "active listening," a term coined by Thomas Gordon in *Parent Effectiveness Training*.

This technique, originated by Dr. Carl Rogers, is an excellent tool for helping both you and your child understand your child's feelings. With active listening, you let your children know that you understand their feelings by putting the *feelings* that are under their words into your own words and feeding them back to the child with empathy. Being empathic, i.e., feeling into your child's feelings, feeling *with* your child, is the most important aspect of active listening. You encourage your children to express all of their feelings, both positive and negative. When active listening, you don't ask your children *why* they feel a certain way—you just accept their feelings. Your sentences might start off with "Sounds like you're feeling . . ." or "I'm hearing you say that. . . ."

It may be easier to understand what active listening is by describing what it is *not*. It is not:

asking leading questions
giving advice
disagreeing
explaining
discounting
changing the subject
denying the child's feelings
denying your own feelings
    or behavior
getting angry
judging
telling own stories, feelings
telling child how he/she
    feels
problem-solving
lecturing
giving lip service
condescending
looking away, being
    distracted or bored
showing the error in child's
    thinking
placating
making helpful suggestions
joking
exaggerating
giving examples of others'
    behavior
comparing
defending
interrogating
excusing
analyzing
parroting the words
adding your interpretation
adding your feelings or ideas

In other words, any time you respond protectively, you are not actively listening. When you get defensive, try to problem-solve, or attempt to talk them out of their feelings you miss a wonderful opportunity to learn more about your children and your children miss an important opportunity to learn about themselves.

Children's feelings always have meaning and an important source. The cries and sounds of a pre-verbal child communicate something important and need attention as well as do the verbal expressions of a toddler or an older child.

Along with children's sensitivity goes an uncanny perception. There are always good reasons when a child says, "I don't like him or her," "I don't like school," or a particular teacher or even a parent. Children are very sensitive to being manipulated and seldom like to be around manipulative people. They may not like that saccharine sweet aunt you want to have over for dinner any more than they like your overly critical mother. Trying to talk them out of these feelings will communicate to them that there is something wrong with their feelings or that they can't count on you to be loving unless they agree with you. They may learn to suppress these feelings and begin to lose trust in themselves as they lose trust in their intuitive knowing, or they may secretly retain their feelings but refrain from sharing them with you.

When you listen to your children's feelings, you will often be confronted with difficult situations or feelings, such as: fears relating to the job you're doing as a parent; possible problems in your marriage; your ability to handle a particular situation; facing your own feelings that may be similar to your child's feelings. Out of fear, most parents act like ostriches.

When you find that you can't actively listen to your child, you need to explore and learn about what's getting in your way, what fears and beliefs are being tapped into. Are you afraid your child's emotions will touch off your own? Do you believe your child is not capable of resolving his or her problems? Do you believe it is your responsibility to solve your child's problem? Are you afraid your child can't handle the painful feelings that might come up? Do you believe it will take too much time?

Active listening gives children the feeling of being understood. Enough cannot be said about the importance of feeling understood. It's one of the best feelings in the world, like a breath of fresh air, or a sigh of relief that accompanies, "Somebody understands me."

Feeling understood is an important part of feeling loved. Not feeling understood almost always keeps protections in place. Once children feel understood, protections often dissolve and they are open to the deeper awareness that comes through exploration.

BELIEFS TO QUESTION:

- Children exaggerate their feelings.
- Children's feelings, perceptions, and intuition aren't accurate because children are too young to know what's real.
- The best way for children to learn to handle difficult situations is to leave them alone.
- Children's feelings go away and are forgotten in time.
- Children don't know their own minds. Adults know what's best for children.

Exploration

While active listening is very helpful, and it is often all that a child needs, in many cases it is not enough, and then exploration is needed. Exploration differs from active listening in that it is not just trying to understand the feelings, but attempting to understand the *false, self-limiting beliefs that create the feelings.*

Exploration is used in the following situations:

1. When you are actively listening and your child is not responding or is getting defensive. "Is there something that I'm doing that you're responding defensively to?" "Are you feeling like I'm judging you? Criticizing? Blaming? Trying to get you to change? Making you wrong?"

2. When you think you and your child need a deeper understanding about the problem.

For example, let's say your child comes up to you and says, "How come you love Sis more than you love me?" A protective answer might be: "Don't be ridiculous. That's just not true." If you were to actively listen to your child, you might say:

"Sounds like you're feeling that we pay more attention to Sis than to you."

"Yeah, and you never blame her for stuff. I'm always the one who gets the blame."

"You feel that we're treating you unfairly, is that right?"

You could continue actively listening to your child's feelings, and that may be all he or she needs. But at some point you might want to go to a deeper level of learning by asking, "What are some of the other things I do that make you feel that I love Sis more than you?" and "What are the situations where I'm likely to do that?" Once you get the answers to these questions, you could continue to explore yourself with your child if he or she is old enough, or you can do it with yourself or with someone else.

You also might want to learn more about the child. For example, you might say, "Well, I can see where I do blame you when you and Sis get into a fight. It often seems like she's the one who gets hurt. I guess I need to understand this. There must be a good reason why this keeps happening between you. Why do you think it happens?"

"Because she bugs me a lot."
"How does she do that?"
"She follows me around all the time. She tries to listen in on my phone conversations, and she's always interfering when my friends are over. When I tell her to go away, she doesn't listen."

When actively listening and exploring with your child, you need to have eye contact and/or be holding the child, and you need to come from your *heart,* not your head. You can do everything right technically, but if your heart isn't in it, your child won't feel safe, loved, or understood.

Compelling Reasons

In the previous chapter, we talked about the concept that you need to believe that you have good reasons for your feelings and behavior in order to explore yourself. The same is true in exploring your child.

If you believe that your children have "no good reasons" for their feelings or behavior, then you will approach them from a judgmental position and they will probably not open to you. Good or compelling reasons are not superficial excuses that justify or blame—they are the fears and beliefs that underlie all behavior. When you approach behavior or feelings looking to prove right or wrong, rather than from a position of wanting to understand the fears and beliefs, you never learn anything about the underlying reasons. This is a difficult concept for most people, because we are brought up with so many concepts of what's right and what's wrong. *In order to explore, you do not have to abandon your beliefs concerning right and wrong*—that is never necessary or desirable—*but you do have to put them aside for the time being.* It's often hard to remember that your children have good reasons for their behavior when their behavior scares or hurts you, hurts themselves, or goes against what you believe to be right.

Mark's father brought 16-year-old Mark in to see Margie for therapy. Mark had recently been arrested for possession of marijuana and had already had three major automobile accidents since receiving his license eight months before. After the last accident, Mark's license was revoked for six months. Mark was devastated by this, since his car was the most important thing to him, and his parents were sure that this would "shape him up." But after returning home from an evening out, they found Mark's car gone. When he later showed up stoned, they knew they had to do something else about this problem.

Mark's parents were very perplexed. Mark had always been a top student. Getting good grades had been extremely important to him. He was a well-rounded boy with many interests. Yet recently his grades had been dropping and they suspected that he was smoking grass more than occasionally. They had yelled at him, shown their disapproval, and punished him, yet nothing seemed to be helping.

Approaching Mark with a genuine interest in discovering the important reasons for his behavior, Margie said gently, "Mark, you must have some very good reasons for your recent behavior. Do you have any idea what they are?" Mark looked surprised. No one had approached him from that perspective before.

"I don't know," he replied. "I never really thought of it in those terms."

"Well, what comes to your mind when you think of why this is happening?"

"It's fun to party. It's just a lot of fun," Mark said. "Is it hard to have fun when you're not stoned?" Margie asked. "No, it's just a different kind of fun," he answered.

Margie and Mark explored this concept for a while. As Mark relaxed, he admitted that he had been "partying" every day, starting before school, as well as during school and after school and before doing his homework. As he remembered back to when he started, he remembered that he had always had a stomachache before school and while doing his homework. He had always put a lot of pressure on himself to do well and this was creating a lot of tension within him. Smoking marijuana took away the tension. It helped him to relax, hang loose, and have fun. While he was upset that his grades were going down, the grass kept him from feeling the upset too much.

As he realized that this was one of the major reasons for smoking marijuana, he also realized that in the last year or so that he had been smoking, he had actually let go of much of his fear of not doing well. As he understood the cause, the good reasons behind his behavior became clear, and his self-judgment and rebelliousness began to dissolve. He looked at the negative consequences of smoking so much—losing his license, doing poorly in school. Margie and Mark explored some of the reasons he set such unreasonably high standards for himself in school and with his new awarenesses came some new ideas to reduce his anxiety level. He was excited about trying to find ways to relax without grass.

Mark came in for a session a couple of weeks later feeling very happy and pleased with himself. He had not smoked anything for over two weeks. While he missed it, that feeling was not overwhelming, and he found that he could stay relaxed without it. He had also decided not to drive if he had smoked, even if he felt he was okay. Mark came to these decisions himself, and he felt good about them.

By understanding the important, compelling reasons behind his behavior, Mark had cleared the way for new decisions. Had Margie judged him or attempted to get him to change by using logic and showing him how self-destructive he was being, he might have become even more locked into that destructive behavior. Her acceptance of him and of the very good reasons behind his behavior helped him feel better about himself and opened him to new choices.

Awareness of the good reasons often gives people the respect they need to clear the way for change, but change doesn't always happen as rapidly as with Mark. When the good reasons come from deeply ingrained fears and beliefs, the change process is slower since the fears have to be confronted and overcome.

Questions That Work

The questions you ask will work only when your *intent* is truly to learn. Asking questions from a protective intent is an interrogation, and your child will react defensively or will clam up. The wording of the question is not what's important. The exact same words mean two entirely different things, depending on intent. For example:

Using a hard, irritated, somewhat sarcastic tone of voice: "Why are you late? You must have some good reasons."

Using a soft, open, warm and gentle tone of voice: "Why are you late? You must have some good reasons."

The first question is not really a question at all; it's an accusation for which no answer is acceptable. It's a judgment that says, "You are wrong for being late and there are no reasons good enough to justify this behavior." Just because it is put in the form of a question does not mean the parent wants to learn anything. It is an interrogation geared to prove the child wrong. The second is a true question seeking real understanding.

Parents often say to us, "Tell us what to say Tell us what to ask." They want a formula, but formulas can't work because of the element of intent. We can suggest questions to ask, but they won't work to help your child open and share his or her feelings with you when you're not really open to learning, especially about your part of the difficulties.

Parents often think they want to understand when what they really want is to *be understood*. Telling your child your feelings—"I feel scared when you come home late and don't call me"—or explaining things to your child about the "right" way to be are examples of wanting to teach the child and be understood rather than learning about yourself and your child. This is fine and creates no problem if it works. If you tell your child your feelings about being late, and your child says, "Oh, okay. I didn't realize you'd worry. Sure, I'll call you from now on," and he or she carries through on this, then there's no problem. We're talking about conflict situations where you've told your child your feelings and explained things to him or her, tried problem-solving techniques, and the problem continues. If you continue to tell your feelings and/or explain things, then you are using this as a manipulation and are very likely starting a power struggle. Your hope may be that if your child understands you, he or she will change. This doesn't acknowledge the child's good reasons for doing whatever he or she is doing that's upsetting to you. When you're willing to learn, then you might say, "I still get scared when you come home late and don't call me. There must be a good reason why this keeps happening. Is there something I'm doing that makes it hard for you to want to call me, or is there some other reason why it doesn't happen?''

The questions we've listed below are to help you in exploring your children to find out what is upsetting them, exploring the fears and the beliefs under the upsetting feelings, or exploring why they continue doing things that upset you—the good reasons behind your children's behavior.

- Honey, you seem upset (scared, angry, hurt, etc.). There must be some good reasons why you're feeling this way. Do you want to talk about it?

Actively listen to the feelings.

If your child is upset with you:

- Can you tell me more about what I do that upsets you?
- I'd like to understand more about why this is upsetting to you.
- Can you tell me some more about it?

Continue to actively listen after each question until you fully understand.

If your child is upset with something that doesn't relate to you, such as a problem with a friend:

- When Mary said you were acting like a baby, how did that make you feel inside?
- What did you do when she said that?
- And then what happened?
- There must be a good reason why you and Mary are having this problem. Do you have any ideas about that?
- Would you like to hear any of my ideas about the problem?

Each time your child answers, actively listen to the answer. Each time you reach full understanding and need new information, gently ask a question. While you ultimately want your children to take responsibility for their part in any difficulty, you do not want to imply that they are in any way wrong or to blame. Children (and adults as well) will take personal responsibility only when they are not made wrong and blamed for their choices.

The above questions are not to be followed like a recipe in a cookbook. Wouldn't it be wonderful if parenting were like cooking? You could read the recipe, follow it exactly, and know that it would always come out right. Unfortunately, this can never happen because children are so different from each other, and each situation is unique. So in order to know "what to do when," you need to explore with the child and understand the circumstances.

For example, Nancy came in for counseling because Neil was doing poorly in school. As we explored some recent difficulties, Nancy told of this incident, wanting to know if she had handled it properly. She wanted to know "what to do when a child won't listen to you."

Neil, age ten, and his younger brother, Terry, age eight, were playing in the pool and started to splash each other. Nancy became concerned that they would hurt each other and told them both to get out. Terry got out but Neil didn't. Nancy said, "Out!" but Neil said, "No!" When she insisted, he said that if she made him get out he wouldn't go play soccer with his team later. His playing soccer was very important to Nancy so she was upset by this, but she said, "Okay, you don't have to play," and Neil came out. Later she took Neil with her when she took Terry to his soccer game, asking Neil if he had changed his mind. He said no. When they got to the soccer field, she told him that if he didn't play soccer he couldn't swim with the family for the rest of the week and he couldn't watch TV for a week. Feeling set up and betrayed, Neil capitulated and played soccer. Nancy was relieved, feeling that she had won.

Nancy had made no connection between Neil's school problems and the many incidents similar to the one above that had occurred. She did not see that Neil was angry with her for controlling him. He had capitulated in some areas, but resisted in school, an area where she truly had no control. She couldn't make him learn.

How else could Nancy have responded to the above situation?

> 1. She could have explored her fear that her boys would hurt each other—was it realistic? Did her children often hurt each other, or were they just playing and was her fear causing the problem?

> 2. If they did often hurt each other, she could explore why. Were they angry at her for something and was this their way of showing it because they knew it upset her when they hurt each other? Were they needing attention and was this their way of getting it? Was one child angry or jealous at the other because he felt the other got more attention?

By insisting that Neil get out of the pool, rather than exploring the situation, Nancy created a power struggle between her and Neil. Neil did not want to be controlled by his mother, so he tried to use his power—knowing that his playing soccer was very important to Nancy—to gain the upper hand. By insisting that her son play soccer for her rather than because he really wanted to (Nancy gained vicarious pleasure from seeing her son succeed. She didn't have very good feelings about herself and tried to get her good feelings from her son's success),

Nancy created the situation where her son could attempt to manipulate her. However, she brought out heavier artillery—withholding things that were important to Neil—so she won that round. But what did she lose? She lost her son's caring behavior and cooperation, and gained his anger and disrespect. He had been humiliated into capitulating, and he was getting back at her in an area where she had no power, an area that was very important to her—how he did in school.

As Nancy opened to exploring the many power struggles between Neil and her, she was able to take more responsibility for her own fears. As she understood how painful it was to Neil when she tried to control him, she could see why he took the position he did about school. The more she explored her own fears—for example, her fear of the children getting hurt in the pool, or her fear of her son not playing soccer—the more she was able to let go and have faith in Neil. The more faith she had in him, the better he did in school.

Becoming Aware of Your Child's Intention

It is always much easier to be aware of another's intent than it is to be aware of our own. It's easier to see and hear your child's defensiveness, anger, sullenness, resentment, or unavailability than it is to see your own. You need only look at your child and let yourself experience the quality of energy coming from his/her body, face, eyes and voice to know whether your child is open or protected. You cannot explore an issue with your child, such as homework, chores, or anything else while one or both of you are protected. If your child is protected, you must first attempt to understand the fears and beliefs behind his/her protections before exploring an issue. Helping your child move from an intent to protect into an intent to learn is essential before attempting to explore.

It will, however, be impossible for you to assist your child with his/her protections if you are in a protected state. *That's why becoming open yourself is the first step toward exploration.*

Helping Your Child Move from Protecting into Learning

Children protect themselves, just as we do, when they feel afraid of being rejected and feeling wrong, unlovable and inadequate, or when they fear domination and control. Children's protective behavior—tantrums, sullenness, forgetting, defiance, hitting or biting, etc.—is always purposeful, just as is our own. When your child behaves protectively, an essential question to ask yourself is, "What does my child need right now?" Since protective behavior *always* indicates fear or pain, the answer to what your child needs is *never* punishment. Is your child upset because of a physical problem such as hunger, fatigue, illness, or some other kind of discomfort or pain? Is your child in a power struggle with you and trying to avoid your control? Is your child feeling put down, rejected, humiliated, laughed at, ridiculed, and is his or her negative behavior trying to say, "Do you still love me?" by attempting to get your attention?

Children have the same basic fears as adults—being rejected and/or abandoned, and losing themselves, being dominated by another. When children are small they fear being left alone and not being able to survive. Our adult fear of abandonment is rooted in that childhood fear.

Without any love, survival for children is very difficult. Unloved babies have been known to wither and die, even if they are physically cared for. The most debilitating experience a child has is being rejected. Children learn to fear being wrong or failing for fear this will lead to rejection. Many children especially fear being laughed at (and many adults too), because derisive laughter says to them, "You're stupid. You're nothing. Therefore, you're not lovable."

By the time children have reached the age of two, they are faced with the dilemma that will follow them around for the rest of their lives: How much do I have to give up of me to retain mommy's and daddy's love? How much can I be me and still not lose their love? The questions that children (and most adults) ask, over and over in hundreds of nonverbal ways are: "Do you still love me?" "Am I still lovable?" "Am I doing okay?" "Am I important?" Most children's behavior, from compliance to resistance, from "good" to "bad" is an attempt to find the balance between maintaining parental love without completely losing themselves.

Because the world is, sadly, not always a loving place, all little children will have some fears—fears of monsters, burglars, being alone, being kidnapped. The less love and respect a child gets within the home, the more debilitating these fears will be, and the more protected the child will become.

Most children will release their protections fairly quickly when they receive their parents' love, acceptance, affection, and comfort. Obviously, you can't give this to your child if you are protected, but once you get yourself open, reaching out and holding your angry or withdrawn child will often melt away his or her protections.

It may be necessary to help your children release their anger at you before they will soften and open. Giving your children permission to hit the bed with a pillow and telling them to show you how angry they are will often help release their pent-up feelings of blame and open them to their fear and pain. Older children can use the Learning Letter in the Appendix to help release anger and move into love. Once they soften, holding them gently will reassure them of your love and acceptance.

This is the atmosphere necessary for an exploration. (If your child is under three, then, of course, you do not move on to an exploration.) At this point you're ready to explore why each of you got protected and then explore the issue around which the protections arose.

When Your Child Is Closed to Learning

Children, like adults, are not always open to sharing their feelings or learning about themselves. They may be afraid that you will think they're stupid for their feelings or their reasons; they may not know how they feel or why they feel as they do and they may be afraid to tell you; they may be at an age where they want to solve their own problems and they feel invaded when you want to explore with them.

How do you start with a child who seems unavailable? One way is to share your own feelings. Many children are unwilling to express and expose themselves to their parents because they feel it's always one-sided— their parents never let them in on their own difficulties with work, friends, spouse. Children often feel one down and inadequate when they think they're the only ones with problems. This is the major way that people develop the belief that it's wrong or bad to be frightened, sad, disappointed. In addition, when parents don't share their problems and take responsibility for them, children often conclude that the parents' problems are their fault. So sharing your own difficulties and concerns with your children is one way to help them begin to open up.

Another way is to ask your children directly if there is anything you are doing that makes it hard for them to open to you. You may unknowingly be doing things that leave your child feeling judged or pressured.

Pressuring children for answers will almost certainly lead to a dead end. Many people feel blocked when they feel pressured. Pressuring your children for answers often results in their becoming resistant even to considering the question. You have a much better chance of getting a response from your child when you ask a question, such as "You seem irritable. Is something upsetting you?" and are willing to wait until later for the answer. We'll often say to our children when they say "I don't know," "Well, maybe you can think about it and if you come up with anything, we can talk about it later." "Later" might be an hour or two, or a day or two, or even a week or two, or maybe never, but the point is that pressuring a child to explore generally doesn't create openness.

So, as much as you may want to know and understand what's going on, you may need to let go and wait for your child to come to you. You might occasionally say, "Have you thought at all about what I asked you?" If your child's answer is an irritated no, then you probably have to just let it go. Contrary to what many people think, children generally do know why they do what they do, but they may not always be willing to look inward to find out, or they may not be willing to share it with you.

MARGIE:

When Sheryl was eleven we were going to the market and I was in a very happy mood. I started singing (Being tone deaf, my singing has rarely been appreciated) and Sheryl got annoyed and said in an irritated voice, "Don't." "Why not?" I said. "Because it's annoying." "Why is it so annoying?" I started feeling sad and put down. I was sure she was going to say that she just couldn't stand my voice. "I don't know, " she answered with even more irritation, "I just don't like it." "Well, " I said softly. "I feel sad when you're irritated, and it would be easier if I understood why. You must have a good reason for feeling that way." "Well I don't know what it is," she barked at me.

We pulled into the parking lot and I gave her a hug and asked her to think about it and come and tell me if she came up with anything. She went off with her shopping list and I went off with mine.

About five minutes later she came up to me with tears in her eyes. "I think I know why I got irritated," she said softly. "Why?" "Well, you were feeling happy and I wasn't. I guess I felt bad that I didn't feel like singing with you so I didn't want you to feel so happy." I hugged her (feeling a wave of relief that it wasn't my lousy voice) and we explored briefly why it was hard for her when I was happy and she wasn't. On the way home we talked some more and learned a great deal about the expectations she put on herself. I learned again how sometimes I assume things that aren't true (my own erroneous beliefs). I was so stuck in believing her behavior was in reaction to my voice that the real reason never would have occurred to me. We both learned a lot.

Another way of beginning to explore is to "plant seeds." This means offering your child a concept or suggestion and then letting go of the outcome. If you offer suggestions and are attached to the outcome, then the suggestion is likely to be a manipulation. For example, let's say that you want your child to consider the possibility of taking a particular class in school, but you know that your child is generally quite resistant to your suggestions. You can plant the seed by mentioning it to your child *once* and then letting it go. "You might consider taking a computer class next year. It could prove very helpful." You've given your suggestion, you've offered your guidance, and now it's up to the child. He or she may come to you weeks later and casually say, "I've been thinking about that idea about taking a computer class. Do you really think it's a good idea?" At that point your child is open and the two of you can explore the pros and cons of this possibility.

As parents, it's often extremely difficult to let go of the outcome when you give a suggestion. But if you nag and pressure your children, a power struggle is often created with the child resisting your guidance and suggestions. Many parents do succeed in threatening and pressuring their children into complying, but this will only work until the child discovers other options. If your child does comply out of fear or guilt, there is a good possibility that he or she will, at some point, go in the opposite direction and completely resist your guidance and values.

Dealing with Your Child's Pain

Most people in our culture believe that they cannot handle feelings of fear, sadness, grief, or disappointment. When in pain, they must try to do something to make it go away rather than going into it, feeling it deeply, moving through it, and learning from it. This belief is handed down by parents who deny their children's pain as well as their own. You pass this legacy to your children when you try to take away their pain by talking them out of it, or forcing them to suppress it. Painful feelings can be masked, but bottled up pain remains like a festering wound needing to be protected from being touched. All children experience pain in the process of growing up because they must deal with separation and individuation. But when parents believe that they are bad parents if their children are in pain, or that their children can't handle pain, then they will try to protect them from it.

Children can handle *any* pain, no matter how intense, when they have a loving parent to hold and comfort them as they express their pain. (With love, adults can also handle any pain, but don't know it. Not being able to express their deep pain as children has most people convinced they can't handle pain.)

One of the most devastating experiences for a child is the loss of a parent through death. We've seen many adults in therapy whose whole lives were scarred because they lost a parent at an early age. We originally thought that it was the loss itself that caused the emotional scarring, but we later saw that it was not so much the death itself, but how it was handled that created the problems. The child was generally not allowed or encouraged to grieve. He or she was told to be strong, and the child's deep pain was denied and repressed. When pain is denied and repressed, it creates much fear within a person, and the resulting protective behavior leads to deep relationship problems as an adult.

Wendy was nine years old when her mother died after a long illness. She was fortunate in that, before her mother died, she told Wendy how much she loved her and what a wonderful child she was. After her mother died, Wendy's father was totally available to comfort her through her pain and to share his pain with her. They cried together often, holding each other and talking about how much they missed her and sharing their fondest memories of her. Wendy's father took time off from work to spend time with Wendy through her period of deepest pain, and when he did go back to work, he made sure that she could reach him any time she needed him. She remembers calling him at work and having him leave an important board meeting to be with her and comfort her.

As a result of her father's love and availability, Wendy was able to move through her pain rather than having to deny it. Within a few months she was again the happy child she had always been. As an adult, Wendy has a deeply satisfying relationship with her husband and young daughter. To a large extent, her ability to love is a result of not developing the deep fears of loss and resulting protective barriers that most adults have who lost a parent when young.

Well-meaning parents, in their attempts to protect their children, instill the false belief that they can't handle pain. When you do not allow your child to feel the deep pain associated with disappointments, rejection, fear, or death, the message that gets communicated is that pain is too overwhelming a feeling to feel, or that it's weak and bad to feel and express pain.

What messages have you given your children? When a beloved grandparent died, did you tell them to be strong, or did you comfort them while allowing them to mourn? When their boyfriends or girlfriends rejected them, did you attempt to get them to cover over their pain by telling them, "Don't worry, you'll find another one." "He/she isn't worth getting upset over." "Buck up, don't let it get you down." "Have something to eat, you'll feel better." Or did you comfort them while allowing them to express their sadness? When they are afraid do you tell them there's nothing to be afraid of or do you comfort them while allowing them to express their fear? When they fail at something, do you tell them not to feel bad, or do you allow them to feel their feelings while helping them uncover what led up to that situation? What do you do that communicates your own fear of being in pain to your children?

A word about comfort. Comfort can come from two different *intentions:* 1) To take away a child's pain; or 2) To help a child express and move through the pain. When you comfort your child with the intent to take away the pain ("There, there, don't cry. It'll be fine."), you are protecting yourself from some fear coming from a belief such as the belief that you are not being a loving parent if your child is in pain.

Pain as a Learning Experience

When we do not allow our children to experience their pain, we rob them of an opportunity to learn important lessons. Children's pain over social problems can lead them into understanding how their own behavior may be creating problems for them. Exploring their pain over school difficulties can lead to new understandings concerning what the problems are and how they can be resolved. Your child's pain indicates that a problem exists that needs exploring. If your children are afraid to come to you with their pain, then neither you nor they have any way of resolving the problems. Rather than seeing pain as something bad and something to be avoided, you can see pain as presenting you with an opportunity to learn about yourself and your child.

Megan, age eight, came to her mother complaining about being picked on and left out at school. Rita, Megan's mother, actively listened to her daughter's feelings:

> Megan (in a whiny tone): Mommy, the kids at school always pick on me and boss me around. And they won't let me play with them.
> Rita: Sounds like you're pretty upset over how the kids at school are treating you.
> Megan: Yeah. They're mean. Why do they always have to pick on me? (She starts to cry.)
> Rita (gently, putting her arms around her): So you're wondering why you're the one who gets picked on?
> Megan: Yeah. They're just mean.

Rita: You feel that the kids you want to play with are mean?

Megan: Yeah.

Rita (gently moving into some exploration): I wonder why you want to play with them if they're mean to you?

Megan (still crying): They're the popular kids and I want them to like me.

Rita (back to active listening): So it would make you feel good if the popular kids liked you?

Megan: Yeah.

Rita (sharing some of her own experiences): I think I know just how you feel. I wanted the popular kids to like me too.

Megan (tears beginning to stop): Did they?

Rita: No.

Megan: What did you do?

Rita: Well, it took me a long time to realize how unhappy I was trying to be popular. But finally I met some girls who were really nice and we became friends.

Megan (pouting and slightly defensive): But there aren't any other nice girls at my school.

Rita (again actively listening): So there aren't any other girls that you want to be friends with?

Megan: Yeah.

Rita: That's a real problem isn't it—that you just want to be friends with girls who are mean?

Megan (thoughtfully): Yeah.

Rita: What do you think you'd like to do about that?

Megan: I don't know.

Rita (giving her a hug): I'm sure you'll think of something.

A few days later Megan joyfully ran into the house.

Megan: Mommy! I met a new friend! She's really nice and she likes me too.

Rita (hugging her): How wonderful!

Megan: Yeah! Her name is Jillian. And her other friends seem nice too, and they want me to play with them.

By listening to Megan, exploring a little, and sharing some of her own experiences with her, Rita created the arena for Megan to solve her own problem. With an older child, you could go more deeply into exploration, exploring the need to be popular, fears of rejection, self-esteem and choice.

Helping your children handle their feelings about their friends is very important. If your children are not overly protected, if they have maintained their sensitivity, they will often feel deeply their friends' insults, slights and manipulations. You can be most helpful to your child by comforting them, actively listening, and then exploring with them to help them understand any part they play in the difficulty.

In addition, we've helped our children understand that when people act in negative ways, it's because they are hurting inside. The more children feel unloved and disrespected, the more they take it out on other children. When our own children were young, we helped them refrain from retaliating by understanding this concept.

Ultimately, we have always wanted our children to come from a loving place within themselves no matter how they are treated. This can happen only when they learn not to take personally others' uncaring behavior. Not taking things personally occurs as people feel more sure about their right to feel and behave as they do.

The Healing Power of Love

Love is the most powerful healing force there is. We believe that, no matter how deep the emotional pain, it can be healed with enough love. And this healing can occur at any time. If we had to deny and suppress our pain as children, opening to it as adults in the presence of someone who loves us can heal the old wound. The essence of the exploration process is ultimately to open to our deep pain with a loved one, and as our pain and fear become healed we become less protected and more loving. If we want to help our children grow up to be loving and caring human beings, then we need to be there for them when they are in pain. This means holding and comforting them—giving them our love rather than telling them not to cry or to be strong.

JORDAN and MARGIE:

We have asked ourselves whether knowing what we now know about how hard this job of parenting is would we make the same decision to become parents? Even though being a loving parent is more challenging today than it has ever been, we would certainly make the same decision. We love our children more deeply than words can describe. And their being in pain or even the possibility of their being in pain produces a deep, deep pain in us. But we know that the challenge of loving is that real love is unconditional. Only God is capable of loving that perfectly and only our Higher Selves, God within us, can help us on our journey to become better at it. Sometimes we just need to take a deep breath and pray. Our prayers are not for God to make things okay, but for guidance in how we can be more loving. This is the only path that can lead us out of misery and into peace and joy.

·14·

And They Lived Happily Ever After

Moving into the Loving Involvement of an Evolving Family

> *I have a real feeling of awe and wonder when I think of what people in the future would be like if they were brought up in nurturing families who live in nurturing contexts.*
>
> –Virginia Satir
> *Peoplemaking*

Fairy tales always end with "and they lived happily ever after," but that doesn't happen in real life. There are smooth times and rough times that come to all of us in infinitely various patterns like ripples in a stream. However, when families learn to interact with loving involvement, open and respecting each other, acting in loving ways to each other, life is satisfying, even peaceful, and often filled with good times and great pleasure.

Obviously, it's easier for everyone when parents establish loving relationships with their children from the beginning and when children are brought up with the exploration process from the time they are quite young. When children are actively listened to from the time they are born (you can actively listen to a child's cries and other sounds) and when they are involved in explorations from the time they are verbal, it becomes a natural process for them. But how do you start to do this with children who have been overly controlled and are angry and rebellious, or passive and compliant and don't know how they feel about anything? How do you start a new process with children who are so spoiled by permissiveness that they no longer care about anyone else and see themselves as the center of the universe?

Undoing the years of power struggles and/or irresponsible behavior is most challenging. It requires your willingness to allow your children to flounder and get into trouble, and yet still let them know that you love them and will be there to help them learn from their difficulties. It means you are willing to let go of them and willing to feel afraid when they mess up.

It is unrealistic to expect to read this book and immediately be able to explore with your children. Before you will be able to do this, you will first need to begin your own deep explorations.

- You will need to start the process of understanding the fears and beliefs that have resulted in your being authoritarian and/or permissive with your children.

- You will need to explore until you can be open with your children for at least a brief period of time, even if they are angry, blaming, disrespectful, defiant, or resistant.

- You will need to explore yourself until you are no longer available to giving yourself up to them all the time and until you are willing to begin to let go of controlling them.

- You will need to explore yourself until you begin to give up blaming them and begin to let go of feeling guilty when they blame you.

You may need help with this process from your spouse, a friend, or a therapist. Once you have explored your own fears and beliefs enough to reach *some* openness, you are ready to attempt to explore with them. You will have changed so much in that process that things between you and your children will already be very different.

Children often react negatively when parents either begin to let up on controls or start to respect their own needs. If you have been an authoritarian parent, keeping a tight rein on your children, you may get blasted with a lot of anger and blame if your children have previously been compliant. If they have been resistant, they may become even more so for a period of time. If you have been a permissive parent, giving in to your children's demands for your time or money, then you may experience anger from your children when they find they can no longer control you. They may even try harder for a while to make you feel guilty and responsible for them. That's why it's so important for you to begin your own explorations first—so that you won't be so available to their manipulations.

It may take a number of months before your children believe that you have really changed and that they must take responsibility for themselves. These transition months are always extremely difficult for everyone, but will be easier for you to handle when you understand what is happening. As much as children want, deep down, to have an equal relationship with you, their fears of personal responsibility may be so great that they will fight you every step of the way. It may seem paradoxical that, even though they may have wanted you to get off their backs about homework, when you finally do, they'll do everything they can to suck you back into the old system, including not doing any homework.

The transition period will be very difficult, but what are your alternatives? Is what you're doing working? What is it creating for you and for your children? Are you just going to do more of the same? Perhaps you have to believe finally that what you are doing is not loving before you will be willing to let go and allow your children to assume personal responsibility and learn from the consequences of their behavior. You aren't helping them learn responsibility when you bail them out every time, but you can help them understand why they make the choices they do, if they are available to exploring. If they get into trouble at school, they can handle it. You don't help them learn responsibility by making excuses for them. When they spend their allowances and something comes up that they'd like but can't afford, they need to feel their upsetting feelings and find a way out just as any adult would have to do.

Those parents who have been willing to stick to their new decisions have been well rewarded with happier, more personally responsible children and more loving family relationships. But it takes time.

Family Explorations

As parents become more comfortable with the process of exploration, they can then move into exploring with the whole family. Family explorations can serve a number of purposes. Each family member has an opportunity to voice whatever gripe he or she has with anyone else or with anything that is or is not happening in the family, and all the family members can help with the explorations. Exploration between two people in the family are often easier when other family members are there to help. In family explorations, one or both parents facilitate an exploration with one or more children, or with one of the parents. The other family members can observe or offer whatever information they feel will help.

Family explorations can also be a time to discuss things like vacations or other fun events that you would like to do as a family. So often the parents decide unilaterally what they will be doing for their vacation and the children feel discounted. By discussing plans as a family and giving everyone a chance to express and explore his or her feelings, you can come up with ideas that are exciting to everyone. When children are allowed to participate in these kinds of decisions, the events are generally much more successful.

Family explorations can create a sense of unity and caring within the family. It can be a time when each family member can be understood and respected by each other family member. Once the pain and difficulties are explored and understood, the gateways open to the flow of love and joy.

Parents have often asked us, "How do I know when I'm doing the right thing?" The answer has to do with intent. When you come from fear inside you and your behavior with your child is an attempt to protect yourself from your fears, then your behavior will be unhelpful and maybe even destructive to your child and to the relationship between you. The outcome of behavior motivated by fear is always negative. However, when you come from love and caring and faith, when your heart is open, your behavior will be positive.

If I Really Loved You

Most people would agree that love is a powerful force and that it is better to be loving than unloving. Almost everyone has heard that you need to love yourself and you need to love your neighbor. But although every major religion attempts to teach love, the state of the world reflects the failure to put this idea into practice.

The problem is that you can't teach love in unloving ways, and most institutions right down to the family unit have incorporated many unloving behaviors into their normal everyday routines. Unloving behavior erodes self-esteem. Truly being loving demands a level of self-esteem that few people possess. So we're stuck in a vicious cycle; waiting to be loved to feel good about ourselves, we continue to behave in the unloving ways that perpetuate our own bad feelings and create both low self-esteem in our children and the family problems that inexorably follow.

This is a book about love, but with a very different focus than we're used to. What would happen in your life if your thinking shifted from *If you really loved me* to *If I really loved you?* Love has been so misunderstood because most people get focused on getting love or being loved rather than on giving love or being loving. But what would happen if we responded to any situation with love? We're just not used to thinking in these terms.

Human interactions have never been geared to promote self-esteem, happiness, or intimacy and yet, with the rising expectations for our relationships, the results of our unloving behavior are becoming less tolerable. Treating employees as inferiors, or women as less than men will not work any more than treating children as less than adults. Everyone loses when we subjugate, control, demean, or are disrespectful to others, regardless of our relationship.

More and more people have reached the awareness that the old ways won't work. Some have had to be hit over the head to reach this conclusion. Too often tragedy or turmoil is the catalyst that wakes us up. As adults, going through a divorce, finding out our mate is having an affair, or suffering a devastating illness like a heart attack or cancer is the hit on the head we've needed to wake us up to the fact that something is wrong. In families, the shocking signal may be a child failing in school, abusing drugs, being angry, unmotivated, delinquent, disrespectful, bored, unhappy, or withdrawn

C.S. Lewis in *Mere Christianity* says that there are two fundamentals of the human condition which everyone must acknowledge: 1) people know what they should do; 2) they don't do it. We would like to add a shade of difference to his conclusion. People can know what to do if they listen to the Higher Self within, rather than to the ego's voice of fear and protection. And when people don't listen to their inner truth, it's because they haven't come to the understanding that they are choosing between being loving and unloving. It is this awareness that brings the power to choose to learn, to be open, to risk, to love.

Perhaps people won't try the path of loving behavior until they're convinced that nothing else will work. Hopefully, before it's too late, the majority of the world will see the catastrophe being created by the unloving ways we relate to each other. Meanwhile, each one of us can do our part by changing our behavior within our families.

When you realize that the old ways aren't working for you, will you be ready to give love a chance?

Appendix A

Learning Letter

Writing a Learning Letter is one of the best ways of moving from an intent to protect to an intent to learn. Each letter has two parts: 1) all the blaming feelings that come from your protections; 2) all the nonblaming feelings that are under your protections. Any of the following lead-in phrases can be used to help touch off what you are feeling and wanting. Don't worry about the language you use, grammar, or being neat. Just let it all out. No one need ever see your letter. You can rip it up when you're done if you want to. The purpose is to give yourself the opportunity to get your blaming feelings out and get to your nonblaming, vulnerable feelings. Keep writing your blaming feelings until you feel a shift from hardness to openness and softness occur within you. Then you are ready to write your nonblaming feelings in part 2.

Once you are open to your non-blaming feelings, your real learning can occur and you can use the process for exploration in chapter 12.

1. BLAMING FEELINGS—These are the feelings that make your child (or anyone else) responsible for your condition.

A) Express your anger, irritation, resentment, and criticism.

> I (hate it) (don't like it) when you . . .
> I'm (fed up with) (tired of) your . . .
> You're just a . . .
> You should/shouldn't . . .
> It's your fault that . . .
> How could you . . .
> The problem with you is . . .
> I can't stand . . .
> If it weren't for you . . .
> You make me crazy when you . . .

B) Express your hurt, disappointment, unhappiness, jealousy and pain—your "poor me" feelings.

> I feel hurt when you . . .
> You make me feel . . .
> I feel disappointed when you . . .
> I feel jealous when you . . .
> I feel rejected when you . . .
> If it weren't for you . . .
> If only you . . .
> It's devastating to me when you . . .
> I feel so unhappy when you . . .

2. NONBLAMING FEELINGS—These are the feelings that arise when you stop blaming others and take responsibility for the fear and sadness that result from your *own choices,* your part of the difficulty. When expressing nonblaming feelings the tension will be gone from your body and you'll feel soft, open and vulnerable. Write all you can about your vulnerable feelings, your fears, sadness, insecurity. Then write about your hopes and your loving feelings. Remember, there is nothing for you to fix. It's okay to feel what you feel without trying to solve a problem.

A) FEAR—Express your fear, anxiety, and insecurity.

> I feel scared when I . . .
> I feel scared when you . . .
> I feel tense and anxious when you . . .
> I feel scared that you don't care about me when you . . .
> I'm afraid to let you know how I really feel because . . .
> I feel scared that we . . .

B) SADNESS—Express your sadness over your own choices.

I'm sorry that I . . .
I feel (bad) (awful) when I . . .
I feel sad that I . . .

C) HOPES—Express what you want, your dreams and wishes, not your demands.

I often dream what we could . . .
Sometimes I fantasize that . . .
I wish I felt . . .
I wish you felt . . .
I wish that . . .
What I really want is . . .

D) LOVE—Express your love, caring, and understanding.

I love you because . . .
I love it when you . . .
What I love most about you is . . .
Thank you for . . .
I understand that . . .
I appreciate you for . . .

Once you are able to express your love, you are then open to learning. If you and your child are each writing letters, you can read each other's letter out loud, one at a time. If you do this, read the letter completely without comment.

Appendix B

ADDITIONAL BELIEFS TO QUESTION: Authoritarian

- If I gave up trying to control my children, I'd lose. I'd never get what I need and they would be totally out of control.
- There are no negative consequences when I try to control my children.
- I can have control over my children liking me, loving me, caring about me, respecting me.
- Attempting to control and being in control work to get me what I want. It makes me happy.
- Since trying to control my children is a sign of caring, they should appreciate it.
- My controlling behavior is so deeply ingrained that it's impossible for me to change it.
- I'm bad if I try to control my children.
- My anger doesn't hurt my children.
- Being controlling will protect me from being in pain.
- It feels good to dump my anger on my children.
- I have the right to hit my children.

ADDITIONAL WAYS I COMPLY

- I don't ask for what I want.
- I don't say anything.
- I don't express my own opinion.
- I agree with whatever my child says.
- I give up my own dreams and goals.
- I give away my power.
- I give up knowing what I want so I don't have to fear not getting it.

- I postpone talking about problems.
- I censor what I say about what I want and how I feel.
- I second guess or anticipate what my children want.
- I tell myself that giving in is no big deal.
- I tell myself that what I want is wrong.

ADDITIONAL BELIEFS TO QUESTION: Permissive

- Going along with what my children want, even if it's not what I want, is a loving way to be.
- Giving in will protect me from pain.
- If I do things to make myself happy, I'm selfish. To be unselfish, I have to give up myself to make my children happy.
- I can shut down my feelings and still enjoy life.
- Indifference will protect me from feeling pain.
- My indifference doesn't cause my children pain.
- I can avoid life's problems by becoming indifferent.
- Becoming indifferent is more loving than any of the other protections.
- Being indifferent doesn't lower my self-esteem.

About the Authors

Drs. Jordan and Margaret Paul, psychotherapists. have been married to each other for twenty-four years and are the parents of three children, ages 21, 19, and 16. Their unique ideas are the basis for Intention Training seminars and workshops taught throughout the United States and Canada. Authors of two best-selling books, *Do I Have To Give Up Me To Be Loved By You?* and *Free to Love,* the Pauls were awarded the California Association of Marriage and Family Therapists Educational Foundation's 1986 Clark Vincent Award for outstanding literary or research contributions to their profession.

If you would like to:

- receive more information about Intention Training and the dates of future workshops;
- arrange for the Pauls to speak to a group in your area—

call or write:

Intention Training Institute
2531 Sawtelle Blvd., Suite 42
Los Angeles, CA 90064
(213) 390-5993

Bonnie B. Hesse is a freelance writer and book editor with a master's degree in counseling psychology. Married for twenty-two years, she's the mother of three teen-age sons.

Notes

Notes

Notes

Notes

Notes